Double or Nothing

Two Lives in the Theatre

For Frieda,

a delight to meet you,

with warmest good wishes,

Thelma Ruby Frye

march 1, 2000

Double or Nothing

Two Lives in the Theatre

The Autobiography of
Thelma Ruby and Peter Frye

JANUS PUBLISHING COMPANY
London, England
in association with
The European Jewish Publication Society

First published in Great Britain 1997
by Janus Publishing Company
Edinburgh House, 19 Nassau Street,
London W1N 7RE

British Library Cataloguing-in-Publication Data.
A catalogue record for this book is available from the British Library.

ISBN 1 85756 214 3

The European Jewish Publication Society is a registered charity which makes
grants to assist in the publication and distribution of books relevant to
Jewish literature, history, religion, philosophy, politics and culture.
EJPS c/o The Joseph Levy Charitable Foundation,
37–43 Sackville Street, London W1X 2DL.

Photosetting by Keyboard Services, Luton, Beds
Printed and bound in England by
Athenaeum Press Ltd
Tyne & Wear

Contents

Acknowledgements

Many people supported and helped me with this book, and they all have my deepest gratitude, but I would like to give special thanks:

To Peter's sister Sylvia and her husband Saul Stipelman for their precious friendship, generosity and support.

To Tamar Wang and Sue Krisman for helping me to edit the huge mass of material into a reasonable length.

To Perry Bruskin, who shared with Peter the excitement of the Theatre of Action more than sixty years ago.

To Moshe Shamir, the first person in the world to read the manuscript, who gave me one of the great moments of my life when he phoned early one morning and said: 'Thelma, I love your book.' He also did the first edit, and begged me: 'Please don't call me the Editor, call me the Butcher!'

To Zmora Bitan, the publishers of the Hebrew version.

To Shimon Lev-Ari, who was in on the telling of Peter's life story from the beginning, and whose help as a friend and archivist are beyond my words to describe.

To David Zinder, Tom Lewy and the Theatre Department at Tel Aviv University for perpetuating Peter's memory with a yearly 'Peter Frye Production', and to all who gave so generously to make this possible.

To Mona Lilian, my beloved aunt, who has loved and helped me all my life.

To Yasmin Cowleard, without whose support and care I would not have survived the dark days and years since Peter died.

And to Beatrice Musgrave, whose expert advice and loving friendship have helped me immeasurably.

For our very dear
Stip and Shaindel
Geoffrey and Devorah
Dedi and Chava
Ted and Pat
and
Mona

Foreword by Oded Teomi

One of Israel's most distinguished actors

Peter yearned to taste all the sweet nectar in the world; he yearned and he tasted. Romantically. Fanatically. With love, anger, pain, loyalty, pugnacity, discovering a million ways of enjoying himself. He tasted the pleasures of the palate, the body, the pleasure of being in control, the pleasure of spirited argument, of comradeship, the pleasure of craving for eternity within the material world. He searched for every means of expression: in acting, in directing, in teaching, in cinema, radio, television, painting, stage-designing, writing, editing, in theatre, in the university, in telling a joke ... in LIFE. In searching incessantly, feeling immeasurably frustrated, for wholeness and for peace, fighting for peace. A universal peace. A Utopia of a democracy with social justice, lead by dedicated people who would know how to appreciate the individual and nurture every young bud. Peter combined a baby's naivety with a rabbi's wisdom, having a limitless ambition to undo the wrong and to love the love-of-the-right.

I loved Peter. He was my first teacher, my first director, my second father. I revered him as a boy, and later on found a soul-mate and equal, possessing unlimited honesty and an open sincerity with the masks removed. We shared every secret and experience.

Yes, a confidant. That is how I shared the secret of his wooing Thelma, a marvellous actress, full of charm, humour and sensitivity. And most of all, an angelic nature, full of optimism, and a rare capacity for love. I was best man at their wedding, a regular member of the family. My wife called Peter 'Dad' and called the young and beautiful Thelma 'Mom'. My daughters, just kids at the time, happily received an added grandmother and called Peter 'Grandpa'. They also called him Peter Pan, he who can fly. And believe me, he could fly in their presence. Because this was Peter – a magician. One does not speak of a magician in the past tense, and this tribute proves it. Peter will go on living in many people's hearts, as a creator, an artist, a revolutionary; as a man who opened for them a window to self-enrichment, as someone who fought for perfection.

More than once, while talking to Peter about the courage to know when to give up and let go, he made me swear that if he ever felt that he had become a burden then, as a soul-mate and true friend, I should understand and assist him to end his life. Some years ago – it seems as if it were yesterday – Thelma summoned me urgently to go from Israel to the hospital in London where Peter had had a stroke. Tearful, agonised, she said on the phone: 'Peter doesn't want to fight. You must come and cheer him up.'

Armed with all the positive mental powers, according to Peter's teachings, I went and saw him, half paralysed. I knew that he would ask me to fulfil my promise and help him to make an end. But out of our long years of acquaintance I believed that Peter, the life-lover, would know how to derive pleasure even from a wheelchair, because his beloved Thelma would be near him. I provided myself with a load of new jokes and was determined that laughter should be his cure. How I laughed when I succeeded in making him laugh.

All during the period when he was disabled, with many hard times of despair and near surrender, I saw how an intense and rare love and endless devotion, Thelma's love for this man, her humour, self-sacrifice and optimism, and his late ripe love for her, how healing these can be. Together they roamed the globe, with the wheelchair, having that seldom-found glue called infinite love. They continued to study and teach, appeared on TV in a cookery course for the disabled, lectured to and encouraged other disabled people, and also created this book.

These days, whenever Thelma arrives in Israel, she stays with us. Her name is on our mailbox. The girls still call her Grandma, and Peter is still among us. We feel Peter's immortality in the theatre, in the kitchen, in our soul-searching talks. And, of course, in this book. I am greatly honoured to be asked to write an introduction to it.

Peter was a superb, creative cook. Even in his disabled years, he never gave up the joy of cooking and inventing. He invented a special board so that he could cut vegetables, skin onions and garlic and perform other difficult tasks with only one hand. And with only three fingers on that hand. I also like to cook. We spent many hours, Peter and I, in the kitchen. And there among the pots and pans between the fish and the spices, Peter is hovering today, imbuing me with his spirit and encouraging me to dare. Sometimes, after the food is ready and my wife is tasting and admiring it, she says: '... but Peter would have left the kitchen clean and sparkling, without a crumb in sight.'

This book is a sparkling kitchen, full of aromas and flavours and lots of crumbs. Enjoy!

It Can't Be a Prologue Maybe It's an Epilogue

PETER

Most biographies or autobiographies begin at the beginning. 'I was born...' or 'He, she or it was born...' when and where. Now that, I agree, is eminently logical. However, I am not going to make use of this logical beginning because I choose to start at the end, or very close to the end. Everything that follows will be flashing back. I choose to begin with a brief report of my medical status.

When people come to visit someone who is ill or who has been ill, they come in and say as brightly as possible, 'How are you?' That is the conventional thing to say and conventional wisdom prescribes that you should answer this very friendly question by saying, 'Not too bad. I'm fine. Getting along. Doing my best.' Or some soppy euphemism like that.

I'm certain the truth of the matter is that when my friends and relatives – all very dear people, all very caring people, all people who I know are deeply concerned about me and want me to get better, want me to survive and want me to make the most of what is left of my life – when they ask, 'How are you?' they really mean it. They deserve an answer which is equally sincere. But for me to keep a stiff upper lip, keep my chin up and reply to them in the conventional way doesn't square with my temperament.

I have always been outspoken, always been blunt and have always been something less than diplomatic in my relations with other people. I used to have a horrible temper, always on a very short fuse. In the course of my life I have done plenty of screaming and shouting: incompetence and bloody-minded stupidity drive me up the wall! Mind you, I was always polite; I didn't use dirty words. I didn't say, 'Ohhh, you stupid cunt,' I would say – sweetly – 'Darling, how can you be so, well, feather-brained?' Which, I think, under the circumstances, was permissible. That's the way I choose to remember it.

Now when they say 'How are you?' the first reply that comes to my mind is, 'I feel like shit warmed over.' But conventional wisdom simply would not accept that as a proper mode of conversation with my guests. Often I answer in Yiddish, 'Me'schlept zich – you drag yourself along...' The implication being, you do your best. You're crippled, you've lost the use of your legs or your arms or whatever, but you drag – schlep – yourself along.

This answer does not really satisfy my visitors but, knowing me as they do, they accept it and then we go on and try to remember a joke heard recently, try to liven up the atmosphere. Most of the time they succeed and I succeed and, having overcome that difficult moment, we have a wonderful time. 'How are you?' – that really is bloody stupid. People should stop asking it.

There is another species of sickbed visitor: these don't ask 'How are you?' They *tell* you how you are. They know exactly what is wrong with you – they also know precisely what you should be doing to guarantee a speedy recovery. (Which you, obviously, aren't doing, because if you were you would, by now, be so much better already.) 'You're no worse than other similar cases who listened to us,' they say, 'they were smart enough to listen when our excellent advice was being dispensed, so now *you* listen and you'll be much better in no time at all.'

These, obviously, are my favourite visitors and sometimes, after I've managed to get rid of them before they were ready to go, sometimes I feel I would rather play dead than have to accept another visit from them ever again.

But in your case, since you asked me so nicely, 'How are you, darling?' I'm going to tell you – everything.

My case history. For the last fifteen years I have suffered from osteo-arthritis in both knees. Nothing spectacular, just one of the degenerative diseases of advancing age. The doctor, with unbearable shmalzy cheerfulness, says, 'No cure for arthritis. You can be sure only it will grow worse.'

In 1984 I started to get angina attacks which became worse and worse until, in February 1987, during a crisis, a young doctor panicked and shoved me into hospital for an angiogram. This is a relatively simple operation. It is minor, you are not anaesthetised – they inject you locally at the site of the upper thigh where they cut open the femoral artery. It is there they insert a catheter and work it up until it reaches the blocked cardiac arteries. That's what they want to see – the extent of the blockages. You are conscious and you watch the progress of the catheterisation on the TV screen. In this hospital they've done thousands of this minor operation, all successful. In my case they botched it and I had a stroke right there on the operating table. They had dislodged some fat from my artery that went to the brain.

'A medical accident. We're terribly sorry...' Not as sorry as I was.

I do not have the words to describe the pit of despair into which I sank when I realised what had happened to me. Totally helpless. To be reduced to infancy without the privilege of crying like a baby – the baby at least can shout its rage, can tell the world how miserable it is. As a grown man I am supposed to suffer and be strong and be brave. I survived only because of the love which enveloped me and the ever-patient hard work of physiotherapists. But I am severely disabled – my left arm is useless and I walk with difficulty.

During the past forty months I've been hospitalised eleven times. Don't ask for details because I'll tell you. Let's see, have I listed everything? I don't know that what follows is very important but the bitter truth is that I have an assortment of teeth clattering around in my mouth which are not the ones God gave me.

I list this here because you must appreciate that one-handed is the hard way to keep your dentures clean. So you, Thelma, have an additional daily chore.

'Thelmaaa...'

'Ye-ees,' in your sweetly ringing tones.

'My teeth, darling!'

You have scores of chores. I can get most of my clothes on by myself but not my socks, or the sleeves of certain sweaters and, on some days, I can't button my shirt...

And what about shoelaces?

I have to call – sweetly – 'Flema' or 'Thelma'leh I need some help...' And you come running. How many times a day? Three, eleven, seventeen? Will you believe thirty-three or seventy-seven?

And the hearing aids. Wherever I am the hearing aids are not...

'Thelma darling, the hearing aids...'

'Coming...' In that thrilling voice of yours.

So I *schlep* along and try to keep going. Without Thelma I couldn't survive or wouldn't want to.

And my toe. I've had to have *two* operations on my ingrowing toenail because the first one was botched. There-fore, the next time you come to visit, *don't* ask how I am. Because I'll tell you, in all the gory detail. And I promise, oh will you be sorry! From this report you might get the picture that I am a very miserable, cranky person. To be honest, I do get cranky and short-tempered periodically. My excuse is that my cup of frustration runneth over and that's when I shout at poor Thelma. I apologise immediately, assuring her that if I were she I wouldn't put up with me. But I'm not and she is and she does ... thank God for Thelma.

Apart from the above I am quite a happy person and mainly for the reason, my darling Thelma, that you are there. It is because of you that I am able to maintain some kind of equilibrium and live with my disabilities, with my new symptoms and with my uncertainties. And still have a pretty good time most of the time.

As, for example, this present moment. We are sitting in our beautiful sitting room looking out at the magnificent trees at the bottom of our garden in Wimbledon on Arthur Road, which is one of the highest points in Wimbledon, where we overlook a lake and the famous Wimbledon tennis courts. Many years ago, we could see the scoreboard from our bay window but it now is blotted out from our view by the trees that have grown up in the meantime.

I am sitting in my special chair with my special table in front of me and I am talking into a small but very efficient audio recorder onto a tape which will have to be transcribed and typed up and revised and given the first rough editing. And cut and condensed. And after we've gone through all that again and again and again, possibly we shall come out with a readable manuscript. At that point we shall have to find an agent and/or a publisher. And struggle to get somebody to read the god-damned material. And maybe, after years of effort, somebody will read it, and maybe publish it. And maybe, after another year of manufacturing, printing, distribution and transportation and getting it into the shops, maybe you, the reader, will have bought a copy of this book. If you haven't already read one that was given to you free by a friend of ours who got it free from us.

But, meantime, we're enjoying ourselves. *We are talking to each other!* Something which is not always true of many other married couples. I am talking into the tape recorder but you, Thelma, are sitting at the other end listening. Similarly we turn about and you talk into the tape recorder and I listen to you. Sometimes we even engage in little colloquies in which we are discussing certain points as one does in a drama of reason in the French mode. We are doing it because we enjoy doing it.

THELMA

The pattern of both our lives changed drastically when you had your stroke. I didn't realise it at the time. I said to myself, 'Surely, this is not going to be the pattern from now on. That Peter will be severely disabled? Surely not. Not *us*.' I am sure that everybody who has something awful happen to them says, 'Why me?'

I have lived most of my life with the feeling that it was charmed, and that nothing bad could happen to me. I was so protected and blessed. There are very few things that I can complain about or be miserable about as I look back.

But when you had your stroke it was a totally new situation. Suddenly you were hardly able to walk. You, who always walked so fast I had to run to keep up with you. Suddenly you were not able to use your left arm and hand. You, who prided yourself on the dexterity and exactness with which you could work with your hands. Gradually we made the adjustment which was made easier for us by the fact that you were in hospital for three months before we had to face the reality of daily life with such a cruel disability.

I'm an optimist by nature and I believed that you would be back to normal. I believed that you would walk normally again and that your arm would be normal again. I believed that if I believed it enough it would happen.

Here we are, four years later, and the physiotherapists tell us that there is no time limit on the possibility of improvement. But I see your face as I say this – the expression on it says to me, '*Ich zoll azoy lang leben!*' One of your favourite Yiddish sayings, 'I should live so long!'

However, a whole new life has opened up for us. When you had your stroke, the whole first week all you could talk of was euthanasia and you asked me to help you to make a dignified exit. It was a time of dreadful shock for both of us. But when I look back over this four years, I try to look back on all the good times we've had since the stroke and all the things we've achieved. We have not sat at home moping.

I know that also, during this time, there have been many stays in hospital. Times of extreme anxiety and suffering for you and for me. But there have been so many good times that I refuse to believe that our lives will not continue in this way. There'll be periods of upset and depression and misery and talk of euthanasia and then the amazing resilience of the life force will reassert itself and enjoyable things will happen. Even yesterday, unexpectedly our wonderful Yugoslav doctor, Vjera Whitehead, and her daughter Vanda, popped in to see us and stayed for lunch and in the evening our good friends Elly and Harvey Miller came round and we were laughing and we were telling stories, true stories, jokes, fascinating discussion. It turned into a delightful day.

The quality of life has changed. Yes. But I'd like to say to others who may find themselves in our situation, 'Your life changes. But there's nothing you can do about it. You cannot call back yesterday. At first you think you'll never have another happy day as long as you live. But if you carry on and try to make the best of a lousy situation, then there are compensations. Living with disability is difficult, but not impossible. There is life after a stroke.'

Book I

Childhood Memories

PETER

Which is the first street we remember? My earliest memory goes back to the winter of 1918 when I was four years old. The street on which we lived was called Cadieux Street in Montreal, now called De Boullion. After the end of the war there was a worldwide influenza epidemic – it was terrible, thousands of people died, it spread across the world like a new plague. It came to Canada and my mother caught the bug. She was very ill. The bed which she shared with my father was in the tiny front room and in the even smaller back room were two small beds. My brother Bernard, who was two, slept in one and I, then four, slept in the second. My parents were called Celia and Jack Friedman.

There was one day during my mother's illness which stands out – a day in December when it was terribly cold. There had been tremendous snowstorms like we were wont to get in Montreal in the wintertime. In our tiny flat my mother was tossing violently on the bed – she was talking out loud, screaming about terrible things she saw and, on top of everything, all the pipes froze and there was no supply of water in that miserable little flat.

My father said, 'We have to go and get water.' The two of us went out and walked along Cadieux Street – I was all muffled up in heavy clothes with a big scarf around my neck. I carried a small bucket and my father carried a couple of big buckets. We were looking for a place where they were distributing water from the fire hydrants. It was about four in the afternoon when it gets dark in wintertime Montreal. The street had a purplish colour, the snow gave off a fluorescent translucency.

We marched along the right-hand pavement in a ravine of snow, my father *schlepping* me and the buckets, and me *schlepping* my little bucket. On the right the snow was piled up, taller even than my father, against the sides of the houses. On the left the pile of snow was even higher, a snow fence between the sidewalk where we walked and the road where the snow had been impacted by traffic.

We walked many city blocks to get to a place where a hydrant was open and we could get water. Stood in a queue, got the water and walked back along the same Cadieux Street to bring water to the house so that we could put cold compresses on mother who was eaten up with a fever of 105 degrees Fahrenheit. I have never forgotten that street. Very few cars. Horse-drawn vehicles. Wagons. Carts. Carriages. Which was your first street?

THELMA

I was born in Mother's bedroom in our house on a noisy street in Leeds, Yorkshire, called Chapeltown Road. My Uncle Sam was the doctor – he lived next door – Samuel Samuel was his name. I grew up in this fine, strongly built old stone house, now a sleazy club for underworld characters. I had my own bedroom overlooking the main road with two beds in it. Compared to you, we lived very grandly. Outside our house was a tramline and the trams squeaked and shrieked and rumbled past the windows. My first street memory is the clatter of those trams rattling up and down the Chapeltown Road. I liked the noise – it was friendly and comforting. We lived opposite Margels, the Kosher chicken shop. All the women customers would pinch the chickens to make sure they were getting a really fat chicken for Shobbos – the Sabbath.

We had a maid *and* a nanny *and* a surgery nurse because Daddy – his name was Louis Wigoder – had a dental surgery in the house. In the front of our house was a little garden. As soon as I was born, I cried and I never stopped crying for the first three months. Mother – her name was Ruby – put me out in the pram in the front garden. Every patient said, 'Did you know the baby is crying?' as soon as the door was opened. I made such a racket that neighbours and even strangers came and rang the doorbell, 'Did you know the baby is crying?' So my mother put a big sign on the pram saying, 'Yes, we *know* the baby is crying.' Mother said I stopped crying after three months and from then on I was angelic.

At the back of the house was a yard where my older brother Geoffrey and I played football and cricket. Daddy's dental surgery overlooked this yard. He would see us through the surgery window playing in the yard, leave his patients sitting in the chair with their mouths clamped open and come and play with us.

PETER
At the back of our little flat was a small dining room filled with furniture including a 'lundge'. The 'lundge' was what we called our leather-covered sofa – no arms, just a raised section for the head – sort of a chaise longue, only we called it the 'lundge'. After the dining room there was a small kitchen and beyond the kitchen there was another little room. Just big enough to hold a small bed. There was a constant procession of boarders who shared this tiny flat with us and slept in that narrow bed. Refugees from Russia in the early 1920s.

There was Miss Soloway, a tiny thing, maybe five feet or less with very fine red hair, a pert little face and pert little figure. Then came Itzhak, who was the biggest thing that had happened in my life until then. I was now about six years old. He was enormous. He must have weighed two hundred and fifty pounds and had an appetite to match. Since the deal was that he had the room and ate with us, we had a problem with Itzhak. He was an expense. He also had a pair of yellow shoes. Now where in the world they treated leather so that it finished up so yellow, I don't know. Maybe he brought them from Russia, maybe he picked them up en route. But everybody in the family remembers Itzhak and his yellow shoes. Then came Motl Garril, a childhood friend of my father's – they had grown up in the same village near Odessa. Garril was a little, thin fellow who quickly became known by the diminutive Gerreleh. We also used to call him Gergeleh which, in Yiddish, means the long thin neck of the chicken which you put into soup. Why? Because he was so thin, as thin as the neck of a small chicken.

When I was eight years old, my mother secretly saved up a small amount of money to put a down-payment on a Victrola, which was the name of a record-player in those days, and brought it home. It was one of those that you wound up by hand on the side and it had come with a bonus, a couple of records. One of them was part of Beethoven's Eighth Symphony – we played that over and over again. The other was a popular song – 'Five Foot Two, Eyes of Blue'.

Papa came home that evening and saw the Victrola and was amazed – where the hell did this come from? He hadn't bought it! My mother told him that it would take a certain number of months to pay it off and he was *furious*. He raved – and he had a violent temper. Papa could, in the middle of an argument, if he was sitting at the table with a bread-knife in his hand, slice the entire loaf, bang, bang, bang, bang, bang, bang, just like that to take out his anger. This was one of his famous rages but then he quietened down and listened to the records and shame-facedly accepted the fact that it was very important for the children to hear some music. He didn't say to Mother, 'You did well,' or 'I'm glad you did it.' He said, 'OK.'

Very often on Saturdays we used to go to visit my mother's parents who lived in their miserable, two-room, dingy little flat behind their miserable, dingy grocery shop. There was a bedroom and a combination kitchen-dining-sitting room in which there was a lundge, like the one we

had at home. That's where we used to sit when we came to
.visit and inhale all the smells from the grocery which wafted
through the entire flat. In those days most of the food was
delivered to the shop and sold in barrels. Flour came loose
in a barrel, generally filthy after all the people handled it.
Herring, of course, came in a barrel and smelled up the
entire place. Olives came in a smaller barrel. Various grains:
rice came in a barrel, also *kasha* (buckwheat groats) and each
of these had its own individual smell and altogether they
spelled out the very complex and very potent stink of the
grandparents' grocery shop.

One Sabbath morning my mother decided to surprise my
father. She bought a record with the great Caruso singing an
operatic aria from a French opera called *La Juive* by Halévy.
We went to my grandparents and my mother put the record
in its sleeve in a bag on the lundge. Father came to join us
and sat down on the lundge – on the record! Those were the
old 78s which were very fragile and the record was smashed
to smithereens. I remember the agony we all felt and my
father's agony when he realised that he had sat on the
precious record.

Our house used to fill up once or twice a week with
friends of my parents – all arrived from Russia, all having a
terrible struggle to stay alive because there were no jobs.
Right after the First World War there was a period of
economic depression – serious depression came in 1922.
They all spoke Russian or Yiddish. I never learned to speak
Russian but I learned to hear Russian. My mother-tongue
was Yiddish, the first language I spoke – that's what my
parents spoke at home. To my great surprise, the first day
they took me to a regular school, where I was one of only a
few Jewish kids in a classroom full of French-Canadian kids,
Scots-Irish kids and English kids, they all spoke English. I
wondered, why are they speaking English? Why shouldn't
they all speak Yiddish, then we'd understand each other – a
major theme which runs through my life.

THELMA

My father spoke Yiddish. But my mother's family had been in Britain for several generations so Mom knew no Yiddish. Neither did her parents.

In the house where I grew up we didn't have a lundge, we had a lounge which my mother decorated with black lacquer Chinese furniture and a huge black grand piano – the colour scheme of the room was wine and black. On the piano was a very colourful, hand-embroidered Spanish shawl. The lounge and dining room were rarely used – only when we had visitors. Can you imagine in your childhood having two good-sized rooms that were hardly ever used? At the back, facing the yard, was the morning room which is where we lived. That was where we ate, sat round the fire – the cosy room. Down underground was a big two-room cellar – one room was for storing the coal and the other for keeping food cool – this was before the days of the fridge. Just inside the door to the cellar at the top of the steps was a shelf where we kept milk, butter, eggs, known as the 'cellar head': 'Go and fetch the milk from the cellar head!'

Across the yard was a wash-house, a dark, cold, stone-floored room with a huge copper in which to boil the clothes, a scrubbing board and a mangle. Next to it was a workroom where Daddy's mechanics used to make the false teeth. Mr Pearce, a quiet, dedicated Yorkshireman, worked for Dad as his mechanic for more than forty years. He was very sweet to me and I enjoyed the hiss of the Bunsen burners and the smell of plaster of Paris, used for making impressions. On the small upright piano in the morning room there was frequently a row of dentures grinning at us while we were eating.

When I was very small I had a nanny called Nanny Beadle. How I loved her – Nanny looked after me while Mother was busy as a singer and actress and with a full social life. Which is a very different story from yours, isn't it? When I was told that Nanny Beadle was leaving, I was devastated. Truly heartbroken. I cried and cried and cried. I was inconsolable. Then Nurse Peet came to us. She was a buxom Yorkshire woman – big bosoms, big thighs, tremendously efficient. She did the cooking, she looked after us, she took care of the house. She was very, very patriotic, and every time 'God Save the King' was played, she would stand to attention. Even if it was in the background of a play we were listening to on radio. Geoffrey and I once got an idea. We waited until Nurse Peet was sitting in the bath and we stood outside the door of the bathroom and sang 'God Save the King'! She became Daddy's surgery nurse. Mother was jealous of her because she virtually took over Mother's job. It was she who gave us tea when we came home from school. My favourite day was Monday because we had tea in the kitchen with the smell of the clean washing which would be hanging on the rack near the ceiling and we ate *tinned cherries*. It was many years before Mom got up the courage to ask her to leave.

My childhood was very much tied up with my Grandma and Grandpa who lived just up the road. We lived at 134 Chapeltown Road and they lived at 307 Chapeltown Road, about eight minutes' walk. My Aunt Mona lived there too. Grandma was often compared to Queen Mary – a large, handsome, stately lady, always dressed immaculately. White hair down to her waist which she washed herself with a dry shampoo and set in a classical, elegant style – never went to a hairdresser, continued to do it herself until her death at the age of ninety. Grandpa was a tall, good-looking Yorkshire-man with a bristly moustache. Mona is my mother's youngest sister – ten years younger than Mom and fourteen years older than I – never been married, an actress, generous and fun to be with, we have always been very close. She held me in her arms when she was a schoolgirl and I was one hour old.

Geoffrey, who is two years older than I, was a big influence in my early life: not only was he maddeningly older and bigger and cleverer, he was also my friend and ally. We used to wrestle. He always won, of course, and I would lie there while he pressed both my shoulders down into the ground for a count of ten. He also took me to recitals and concerts – Piatagorsky, Mischa Elman and Sir Thomas Beecham. We had a set of theatrical curtains – they could stand anywhere in the room and you could open and close them. Mother had a big trunk full of old clothes which was our dressing-up box. We were always putting on theatrical productions. The manager, the boss, the author and the director was Geoffrey. I was his devoted assistant. We would bring in the neighbours and family and charge a penny entrance (which we gave to charity). At school there was very little opportunity to participate in drama so our homemade productions were an important part of my increasing longing to be an actress.

The only sexy story from my early childhood is that one day Geoffrey ran out of the bathroom waving his little dick around and shouting, 'I've got a banana, you haven't.' That was my first introduction to a man's anatomy.

PETER
I hope it hasn't left you confused in your maturity. It's not a banana, you know! Tell me about your mother and father.

THELMA
Although they were both Jewish, my parents were an ill-assorted couple because they came from such different backgrounds. But it was a very successful marriage. Married in 1920, they adored each other and stayed happily married for fifty-eight years until my mother died. They were always having little squabbles! 'Oh, Louis!' Mother would say, exasperated, going up an entire octave with that musical voice of hers. Dad, with his Irish brogue, would burst out with, 'Don't get funny!' But at every family gathering, Dad got up to make a speech of fulsome praise for 'My darling

Ruby – we've never had a single cross word since the day we were married.'

My mother was born in Leeds in 1901 in a snowstorm. Her parents were a middle-class Jewish family named Lubelski and Mother was the eldest of four children – she was adored and pampered. My grandfather Sim inherited from his father a small clothing factory called the Utilus Coat Company that manufactured raincoats. Mother's name was Paula Ruby, but she was always called Ruby and later she used the name Paula Ruby as a stage name. From a very early age she showed that she was a very gifted child – she had a beautiful singing voice, was lovely to look at and loved to perform. At the age of four she appeared in a seaside concert party called Carlton's Cosy Corner in Southport, where she danced wearing a frilly dress with an accordion-pleated skirt. Her parents recognised her talent. There was a direct line of artistic talent through the family of her mother, my grandmother Gertie whose family name was Hollander. The Lubelskis weren't artists, they were north-country businessmen. There were no artists among the Wigoders, my father's family, either. But the Hollanders painted, wrote, sang, danced, acted. Grandma Gertie played the piano very well. She had a trick that we children used to love. She put a scarf over the keys of the piano and then we would blindfold her and she would say, 'What would you like me to play?' Then she played anything we asked for. Gertie and her sister Florrie played the mandolin in a mandolin and guitar band in Derby in 1896 – I still have the poster. Grandma also painted – we have a charming picture on the wall which she did before she was married, roses painted on china.

Grandpa Sim Lubelski adored his wife, the strong-minded, talented, witty, bossy Gertie. He never dared not to agree with Gertie so they both encouraged my mother to perform. When Mom was eight she had an offer to play Fairy Queen in pantomime at the Grand Theatre in Leeds. She started to rehearse but the authorities stepped in and said she had to wait until she was ten to appear professionally. Finally, at ten she became a professional performer and was the Good Fairy in *Jack and the Beanstalk*.

She then travelled around the country on the music-hall stage doing impersonations of music-hall stars – often she had never seen or heard them, but she was dressed in a small version of their costumes and sang their songs. In 1911, when she was ten, she appeared in the entire summer season in Morecambe. The bill changed every week, but she was permanent and appeared with the big stars of the variety theatre. She was billed as 'Dainty Little Paula Ruby – a real juvenile star' and during that one season she appeared with Hetty King, Vesta Tilley, Nellie Wallace, George Formby, R G Knowles, Ernie Lotinga, George Robey and many other top stars.

When Mother had a booking away from Leeds, my grandmother left her other children with a nanny and went off with Mom to make sure she was cared for. Grandma would stand at the side of the stage with a shawl and as soon as Mom stepped off the stage, Grandma would whip the shawl round Mom's shoulders, take her straight back to the dressing room, straight back to the digs, and straight back to Leeds when the week was over. She didn't let her talk to anybody in the theatre.

As she got older my mother developed a lovely lyric soprano voice, studied singing for a year and grew into a beautiful, charming, bright, vivacious girl. Her uncle, my great uncle Sol Levy, was a pioneer in the film business and knew a lot of theatre people. He helped to get Mother started professionally – in theatre, in musicals, in concert, and even one film, *The Man Who Won* directed by Maurice Elvey in 1917. Once the entire unit sat around all day doing nothing, waiting for the five o'clock sun to shine on Isobel Elsom's hair – she was the star and the wife of the director.

Mother also sang standing in front of the screen before

they showed silent films. For one film called *Romance*, shown at the Palace Theatre in London in 1921, she wore the identical dress as the star of the film – a black velvet crinoline with an ermine cape and a *very* long string of pearls. She sang '*Connais-tu le pays*' from *Mignon*. Geoffrey remembers when he was very small being taken to hear her sing before the film *All Quiet on the Western Front* but to his disappointment he was whisked away before the film was shown.

My father, Louis Ely Wigoder's background was entirely different: born in Lithuania in the Kovno district – 'Kovno Gobernia' is how he described it. He was born after his father had left Lithuania and had gone to Dublin to try to make a new life for the family. When my father was three months old, Grandpa sent for the family and Dad left Lithuania for ever. He was brought up in Dublin in great poverty. Grandpa Meir Joel Wigoder was a very learned man, a writer of scholarly books. He loved to study. He was a Talmudic scholar, wrote commentaries on the Talmud and Rabbinic literature, poems, books which were sources for sermons, and he was a pioneer among orthodox Jews as a dedicated Zionist. He also published Jewish jokes – *bon mots* of the rabbis and other examples of Jewish humour. He wrote mostly in Hebrew, though his autobiography was written in Yiddish. He was a simple, sweet, religious man.

First of all he eked out a living, to keep his wife and nine children, as a door-to-door salesman and then he opened a wallpaper shop. The custom in Dublin was that a shop that sold wallpaper also framed and sold pictures to hang on the wallpaper. Mother told us how she was taken over to Dublin when she got engaged, to meet her future father-in-law. She walked into the shop and there sat this beautiful, bearded, venerable man – a true Jewish patriarch – with the skullcap on his head. The story of Jesus is totally outside the strict parameters of Orthodox Jewish beliefs, yet although in front of him was a large book in Hebrew which he was studying, incongruously all around him were pictures of Jesus on the cross and the Virgin Mary with the baby Jesus.

When Dad was young he slept with his older brother Harry on the kitchen table. There weren't enough beds. They were hungry. When the youngest child was just a few months old, my poor grandmother died of exhaustion at the age of forty-two. Tamara. I am called after her. Tamara is my Hebrew name and they anglicised it to Thelma.

The older sisters brought up the younger children. As soon as the oldest brother, Harry, was old enough he realised that his father would never make an adequate living and was determined that the rest of the family should have a better start in life, which meant a chance to learn a profession. He opened his own wallpaper shop and made a success of it. Thus he was able to put all his brothers and one of his sisters through university, where they qualified as doctors and dentists. Daddy went to Trinity College and became a dentist. Although our family has had no connection with them for many years, you will still find wallpaper shops in Dublin called Wigoder.

As soon as Dad was qualified in 1914 he came over to England and became the first qualified Jewish dentist in Leeds. He lived in one room, sharing a bed with Uncle Sam, the same Uncle Sam who brought me into the world. My grandmother Gertie was very hospitable. She always had open house, especially for young people who didn't have any friends or family to go to on Shobbos. She heard about this young Jewish dentist just arrived from Dublin and she invited him to Friday-night dinner. He fell in love with my mother, who was then a thirteen-year-old schoolgirl. He encouraged her to take good care of her teeth and visit her dentist very often! When Mom was sixteen, Mona was six. Mona clearly remembers being given sixpence by Dad because she had caught Mom and Dad cuddling in the surgery behind a screen – a bribe not to tell her parents.

Dad was ten years older than Mom. As soon as Mom was seventeen he proposed to her. Mother said, 'No. I want to go on with my singing and with my career.' Dad said, 'You can. As far as I am concerned, you can do whatever you like. I love your singing and I want to make you happy. If you want to carry on with your career, then carry on. But let's get married.' Mother's parents were delighted. They thought Mom was getting much too tied up in theatre work, and wanted her to get married and 'settle down'. They had always been fond of Dad, who was by then building up his dental practice.

My parents were married in 1920 when Mom was nineteen. Grandpa bought them a house on Chapeltown Road. That's when Geoffrey and I come onto the scene. Now tell me about your parents.

PETER

Curiously enough I know a great deal more about my father than I do about my mother. It's curious because I spent a lot more time with my mother than I did with my father. I rarely saw my father. He was always working, always away on business. He was never at home in the evening because of his manifold activities in the Union, then later as a Union Organiser. He was, although uneducated, a very gifted individual, very colourful, a rich personality.

My mother, who came out of a similar background, was a rather simple person who was dominated by my father and didn't come into her own until after his death. He died at fifty-seven. She was the same age, fifty-seven. It's a curious thing to say, but my mother flourished after his death and that's when we suddenly felt the strong outlines of her personality and character.

My father told us very little about himself. Nothing that gave me a clue to what the real story of his life was. All I knew was that he was a socialist, a violently anti-traditionalist Jew. It was only later in life that I learned the full story from

Motl Garril – Gergele – the thin little lodger who lived with us when I was a child and who came from the same village as my father. He came to visit me in Israel in 1960, ten years after my father's death, and told me:

'Yankl, your father, grew up in a very religious home in a small town in Russia. The name of the town was Talna, in the southern Ukraine not far from Odessa. It was a famous town because it was the home of the very famous Reb Dovidl of Talna. Dovidl is the diminutive of David in Yiddish, and this Rabbi David was already a distinguished rabbi in another town, Vasilkov, before he came to Talna and in the course of time became the famous Talna Rebbe.

'Reb Dovidl was the most celebrated of the eight sons of Menahem Twersky, founder of the Chernobyl Hassidic dynasty. Thousands of people came to Reb Dovidl's court, which he maintained in luxurious style, even retaining a court jester! His house contained a silver chair bearing the inscription in gold, "David, king of Israel, lives and is in existence". This gave his opponents a means of denouncing him to the Russian authorities as a rebel against the government. He was thrown into prison and freed only after numerous appeals.

'In spite of his aristocratic way of life, he was a man of the people; his speech was flavoured with popular proverbs so that it would be more readily understood by the common people. He was fond of music and brought to his court the most famous folk singers and musicians in the region. The Talna melodies became popular among both Hassidim and Jews in general. He exists in all the anthologies, in all the encyclopedias. Everybody knew about Reb Dovidl, "der Talner Rebbe".

'Yankl, your father, was the youngest son of Ben-Zion Pribluda who was the right-hand man of Reb Dovidl and he lived in the courtyard of the Rebbe's house. Your grandfather, Ben-Zion, was a devout Hasid, a perspicacious man of business, and in charge of all the Rebbe's affairs. Your father was brought up as a good Hasidic child – in the Heder and in the synagogue.'

So that was the mystery my father had never revealed to us – not only am I a Jew, I'm the descendant of Hasidic Jews.

Garril also told me that when he was starving – literally starving as a child – my father Yankl kept him alive by stealing food from his mother's kitchen and smuggling it to him! 'I would have starved to death without the help of Yankl Pribluda.'

My father was twelve years old at the time of the Russian Revolution of 1905. Comes the revolution and there is a need for clever youngsters who can be used as couriers. The revolutionaries could not use the mails, they were heavily censored by the Tsarist police. They certainly couldn't send telegrams to each other, because those were certainly censored. So they took youngsters and trained them to memorise messages by heart, and then would send them out by road, walking, or in wagons, carriages. Or on the train. They would give them a list of places they had to arrive at and a list of addresses of revolutionary centres where they came and rattled off the message which they had memorised. My father was one of these children.

When he would get through with the list of places where he had to deliver his message, at the last place they would say to him, 'Forget it. Forget what you've learned.' Like wiping off a tape. And they said, 'Learn this message and take it back to your centre.'

Then came the great disaster. The revolution was put down very brutally, very fiercely, and in a relatively short time by the Tsarist police, the mounted Cossacks with the murderous sabres and the big whips. Those revolutionaries who hadn't been killed or hadn't been taken prisoner to be sent to Siberia were hiding out. Amongst them, my father – who was approaching his thirteenth birthday!

His parents saw what was happening, they saw that

prisoners were being caught, those that were in hiding were being found out and sent off to die in Siberia. They thought, 'Oh my God, this child will be found and sent off to Siberia.' They decided to send him quickly to America, to which he had been preceded by an older sister, who was in Canada and an older brother, who was in the United States.

The family name in Russia was Pribluda. The meaning of this name was, 'One who arrives after wandering'. The little boy, now aged thirteen, arrives at Ellis Island and he has to be passed by the immigration. He stands in front of an inspector who says, 'What's your name, Jack?' There was an interpreter there who translated into Russian and Yiddish. My father said, 'Yankl Pribluda.' His given name was Yaakov (Jacob) but the diminutive in Yiddish is Yankl. Yankl Pribluda. So the inspector says, 'Listen, Jack, you can't come into America with a name like that. Pick an easier name.' This is duly translated; my father stands there and he starts to weep. 'What do you mean, pick another name? That's my name. I'm Yankl Pribluda. I don't want to change my name.' And the little boy stands there weeping.

An older man, who was standing behind my father, tried to quiet the boy. He says, 'Don't be so upset, tell him your name is Friedemann.' That was a very popular name during that period. We are now into 1906 and many Jews took this name. They'd had Russian, Polish, Estonian, Latvian, Romanian names – all of them too difficult for the immigration officers to write down – and they took this German name 'Friede-mann', which means Man of Peace. My father says, 'Yankl Friedemann', so the inspector writes down F-R-I-E-D-M-A-N, which is the way Americans spell 'Friedemann'.

That's how Yankl Friedman arrived in America and our family name became Friedman. Papa's older brother, Uncle Dave, got him a job working in a factory in New York where he worked eighty hours a week and his pay was $4 a week. Five cents an hour.

My father told us how he struggled with the English

language. No night school, no day school, no organised learning of any kind – only what he picked up in the street. The first phrase he picked up when he was looking for a job in the street – before Uncle Dave got him the job in the clothing factory – the first phrase which stayed in his memory was G-E-H-R-A-R-R-E-H-E-R-E! If you repeat it often enough it will come clear to you as it became clear to him: gehrarrehere settles down to 'get out of here', which he heard everywhere he tried to get a job as an errand boy or shop assistant – gehrarrehere. Welcome to America!

This little boy of just over thirteen started to work in a factory under conditions of slavery. No chance for education, no chance for schooling, no time to read. My father's education began later, when he grew older and went to Canada. He became a self-educated man.

My mother came from a town called Balta, also near Odessa, not far from Talna, but she never met my father when they were children. She came with her family to Canada. They were terribly poor but her parents had enough money to open the little grocer's shop in the Jewish ghetto of Montreal.

I know very little about my mother's childhood except that she had finished two classes of Gymnasia in Russia so that she had more education than my father because she was a little older when she left. But once she arrived in Canada, no more education. No schooling to learn English – for the rest of her life, she spoke English with a heavy Russian-Jewish accent.

For a while my parents were living on a street called Van Horne. And my mother always said, 'Wan Horne'. Peevishly my sister Shaindl said to her one day, 'Mother, can't you say *Van* Horne?' My mother replied, 'Vat do you vant from me? I can't say Wee.'

How did my parents meet? My father had a cousin whom my mother knew and they had been going together. Then this cousin decided to go to Palestine, which in those days was a very daring thing to do. He was among the first pioneers who came to Palestine to carry out the ideals of the freshly minted Zionist movement. They were going to purify Jewish life through labour. No more little merchants, no more saloon keepers, but labourers. Farm labourers. This cousin of my father's wanted my mother to go with him but her parents wouldn't agree. When he left, he sent my father with a message to my mother to say that if she could get to Palestine, he still wanted her to come. Dad delivered the message and Mother chose him instead! They were both twenty when they got married and before my mother's twenty-first birthday, I was born.

*   *   *

THELMA
I went to the Leeds Girls' High School on the other side of the city from the age of five until the age of fourteen. We wore a green and silver uniform and underneath my mother made me wear combinations – an all-in-one garment that goes down the legs, buttons up the front and has short sleeves. On top of that a garment called 'stays' – a small corset with bones in it. I *hated* my underwear! At school there were prayers every morning, Christian prayers, but we Jewish children went to a separate room where we had Jewish prayers. I never felt any anti-semitism, I never felt at all awkward being a Jewish child, although there were very few of us. My greatest chum was Shirley Silverton. She lived just one block away from me and we used to go to school together. I got a shilling a week pocket money, from which I had to pay my tram fares and could do what I liked with the change. Usually I bought sweets but Shirley and I also loved to go to Smucklers – the Jewish delicatessen across the road – to buy Dutch dill-pickled cucumbers, instead of sweets, and then go and sit on her back gate and sing songs. She used to pretend to be Judy Garland and I was Deanna

Durbin. The feeling that floods back when I think of my childhood is the security of being nurtured, encouraged and loved.

PETER

You say that, although you were only a handful of Jewish children at the Leeds Girls' High School, as far as you can remember there was never any overt anti-semitism. Unfortunately, my story is different. From the time I was a small child, we were distinctly aware that we were Jews and that we were a separate community which did not belong to the majority. At different periods of my childhood there were overt acts of anti-semitism against which I had to defend myself.

As my father had been forced by the immigration official to change his name from Pribluda to Friedman, so my name was Peter Friedman. When I was at Mount Royal school, I came home to my mother one day, aged seven, and in a very troubled, weepy voice, complained to her, 'Why do the kids in my class make fun of my name? Why do they call me Fried Man?' They also took great delight in calling me 'Friday' or 'Fried Potatoes' and their special favourite, 'Fried Ham'. I said to my mother, 'They have funny names, like MacGillicuddy and LeFevre and Jambonier or McGonagle. But the only one they make fun of is mine.' She said to me, '*Azoy is dos*,' which means, 'That's the way it is!' and didn't explain anything more.

On our table every morning we drank cocoa and there was a tin of Fry's cocoa. So Friedman, Fried Man, Friday, Fry's Cocoa and day after day, month after month, year after year, I kept turning this over in my mind until, at the age of thirteen, I decided to call myself Peter Frye – I added an E at the end to distinguish me from the cocoa. It was only then that the other kids stopped making fun of me.

Choosing a new name was also important for me for another reason. I had worked in a show in Yiddish at the Young Men's Hebrew Association in which, for the first time, I actually got paid. We were a semi-commercial troupe. Our director was a wonderful young man by the name of Joe Gordon whom I remember with great love. I was only thirteen when I appeared in a play he directed, a play by Yacob Gordin, *Vemmen Die Getter Lieben*, which translates as, 'Whom the Gods Love.' At the end of the week we would divvy up the profits and I got paid a couple of dollars – I was so proud! I had acted already before that and appeared in public before that, but this was the first time I got paid for acting. Now that I was a professional actor I needed a *nom du théâtre*. So, Peter Frye!

Also at the age of thirteen I went to the Baron Byng High School which had mostly Jewish children but not a single Jewish teacher. They were all English or Irish or Scots or Welsh and they were wonderful people. It was a marvellous school. On the way to school we Jewish children would very often be beset by gangs of French-Canadian kids who used to arm themselves with sticks or barrel staves. They'd ambush us and beat the hell out of us. So we got together! 'There's one way to prevent this and that is to go to school in greater numbers and be better armed and beat the hell out of *them!*' Which we did. Going to school in the morning was like crossing a battlefield.

Whether you like it or not, when you're born Jewish, there is a worldwide conspiracy to keep you Jewish no matter how hard you try to get away from it. My father was anti-religious. He didn't allow my mother to keep Kosher, he didn't make a fuss about the Jewish holidays. But if I had no religious education, I did have Jewish education because, at a very early age, in addition to going to the regular English school, starting at age seven, I also went to a Yiddish school. We would be released from the English-speaking school at three o'clock, I'd come home and get something to eat very quickly, and then walk a good fifteen-minute walk to the Peretz Shulle. This was a school named after the great Yiddish writer Yitzhak Leib Peretz. We had all our classes in

Yiddish. There was a certain amount of repetition, we learnt
many things in Yiddish that we had already learnt in English
but what that did was to fortify the learning process and I
knew I was a Jew. I had no religion but I had a strong
love of the Yiddish language, love of Jewish history as
told by these wonderful Yiddish writers. I knew the writer
Shalom Aleichem from a very young age. On Friday evenings, the Sabbath, my mother prepared the one good
meal of the week. She didn't bless the candles, as in orthodox
Jewish homes, but she prepared a traditional meal with
the *gefilte* fish and the chicken soup and the *lockshen* –
hand-made noodles – and the roast chicken or the boiled
chicken and, of course, the *tzimess* – carrots with honey.
At the end of the meal, father would sit us down and
read to us from Shalom Aleichem.

From the age of six, I sat on my father's lap on a
Saturday morning when he wasn't working. My Daddy
read to me in Yiddish from a Marxist pamphlet – a very
famous piece of Marxist theoretical material called 'Value,
Price and Profit' – an analysis of how the capitalist system
works. I understood the words he was saying but I didn't
know what they meant when put together. He would try
to explain it to me. The way he told it, capitalism was a
very bad thing. 'The capitalist expropriates the value of
the product produced by his workers,' he explained. 'He
pays his workers as cheaply as the market will allow. He
sells at the highest price he can get. The workers do not
receive an equitable share of the profits – they receive a
shvartze choleriya (a black cholera) plus the constant threat
of unemployment,' he elucidated.

'Sometimes the capitalist goes bust, bankrupt. The working men and women are unemployed again. The children
are hungry, their shoes are worn out. The mothers are dis-
traught. They are full of complaints. The men are depressed.
The next job that comes along – *when* and *if* it comes –
offers a lower scale of pay than before – take it or leave it...

'Then there's a shake-out, a recession or a depression and unemployment followed by a war, by prosperity, by recession, by depression etcetera. The workers get *drek mit layber* (chopped shit and liver) at any stage of the cycle.'

'*Farshtayst?*' he would ask, 'you understand?'

I didn't dare admit that I didn't understand. (I still don't!) But Poppa, I believed you then and, Poppa, I believe you now.

Marxism in one easy lesson.

THELMA

I also had a Jewish upbringing but it was totally different from yours. Here we both are talking about our Jewish upbringing – I think it's a strong bond between us. But our Jewishness comes from two entirely different directions.

I was brought up in a home where we observed all the orthodox rituals. Mother would light and bless the candles on Friday night, Daddy would bless the wine and the bread. We kept a strictly Kosher kitchen – separate dishes for meat meals and milk meals, separate washing-up bowls and drying-up cloths. Friday night and Saturday we observed the Sabbath – Friday night was absolutely sacred. We all stayed home and after the special meal, we sat around the fireplace reading. Dad would leaf through the *Jewish Chronicle* and be asleep within minutes. We were not allowed to ride on the Sabbath, in a car or on public transport, not allowed to play the piano, tear paper or poke the fire. However, Daddy and Geoffrey would sometimes walk to the football match on Saturday as long as they didn't have to carry money to get in.

On Saturday mornings we went to synagogue and I sat upstairs with the women. We girls always sat in the front row so that we could look down at the boys – they were privileged. They could sit near the holy ark, hold the holy scroll, go up onto the holy raised platform, the Bimah. This contributed to my lifelong feeling that men are superior beings and to my problem of feeling inferior.

My friends (outside school) were all Jewish, my parents' friends were all Jewish. Although I went to a non-Jewish school, we lived a sort of ghetto life. Many of Dad's patients were non-Jewish but they never visited us socially. If I'd wanted to bring one of my gentile schoolfriends back to the house it would have been frowned upon. My parents were terrified it might lead eventually to inter-marriage or we might be swayed away from the strict path of the Jewish religion.

But, unlike you, I had no Jewish education. For a short while, a Palestinian boy tried to teach me Hebrew as a language. I remember the boy but I forgot the Hebrew. Geoffrey went to Cheder, Jewish classes, after regular school but it was not for a Yiddish education, it was only concerned with teaching religion. I went there once and only once. There was a stale, unwashed smell in that classroom and when a child did anything he disapproved of, Mr Walters, the teacher, caned him on the hand or pulled his ear. I was so upset I wouldn't go back.

PETER
We moved from Cadieux Street to St Urbain, and I changed my English school from Mount Royal to Belmont, and my Yiddish school from the Peretz Schule to the Folk Schule. The years at the Folk Schule, which went on from the age of nine to the age of twelve, were very, very important years in my life and it may be correct to say that I wound up working in the theatre, in the Arts, because I went to the Yiddishe Folk Schule. One of the things I was asked to do was to memorise Yiddish poems. Once there was a competition and we were asked to choose something to memorise and to declaim. Whoever was chosen for the best declamation would get a prize – well, I wasn't to be kept out of that! I was currently studying Jewish history in a Yiddish book *The History of the Jews* by Dubnov. In that book was the very sad story of King Saul, the young David and his friend Jonathan,

King Saul's son. David's lament for Jonathan. It's a beautiful passage, very beautiful in the St James version of the Bible, very beautiful in the Hebrew and very, very beautiful in Yiddish.

I set to work to learn this passage – this was going to be my declamation. I came to the competition and there were other little boys and girls reciting different selections. Harmless little things, pleasant little poems. Then comes Pinye – my Yiddish name that my parents always called me – with his heavyweight material from the Bible, translated by Dubnov and it's beautiful. I gave a great performance! I fell down on my knees and I threw my arms up to heaven and I covered my head with my arms – David weeping for Jonathan – I was serious about it – and I won the prize.

The following morning I was called in to see the principal, a man by the name of Schloyme Weissman. But he was not a 'wise man'. He said to me, 'Who helped you with that declamation?' I said, 'Nobody.' He said, 'Your father helped you? Your mother helped you?' I said, 'No.' He said, 'Who picked it for you?' I said, 'I picked it.' He said, 'Who told you to fall down on your knees and weep and put your arms over your head?' 'I did it!'

'You're lying!'

I broke into tears – I was then nine years old. I had the prize, I had won in public, but here was this man reprimanding me because I had shown initiative. Nevertheless, very shortly after that, there was a concert given by the Yiddishe Folk Schule. On the programme there was some instrumental music, there was some choral music and there was Pinye Friedman reciting David's lament for Jonathan. It was in a French theatre in the lower part of town called Le Monument National, an old Victorian building with a huge stage. I'm standing alone on the stage reciting my thing. There was a hush in the theatre as these beautiful words came tripping off my tongue.

At the end there was a silence and then, enormous applause. I went offstage in a sort of a delirium, a sort of intoxication of happiness from that applause. It was my first experience of feeding a public and holding a public. I had held them. Just to gild the lily, as I stood there alone backstage, nine years old, with a lot of movement going around, people coming and going, the concert just over – they had put me on near the end – a lot of commotion – a man comes on the stage, a grey-haired man, balding, like Ben-Gurion, with tufts of hair sticking out at the sides and at the back ... he's weeping and he's saying to all and sundry, '*Voh ist dos yingele?* Where is that little boy?' He found me. He fell to his knees, put his hands on my shoulders looked me straight in the face and he said, '*Du bist doch a wunder-kind!* You are a wonder child. *Ich dank dir, mein kind.* I thank you, my child.'

Well, when that kind of thing happens to you, you *have* to become an actor. How can you avoid it? I was not going to give up that applause, the tears of that man, his embrace as he said, 'a *wunderkind.*'

Starting about the age of eight I became enamoured of movies. They started to fill my life. There was a new cinema house which had been built not far from where we were living and every Saturday morning I would get ten cents – the cost of a ticket to the cinema – and off I would go. It was not only that I saw the movie but I remembered what I saw and I would come home and I would re-tell it and I would embellish it ... with voice and gestures and acting. My enthusiasm became terribly exciting – my parents would also get excited and they used to be so impressed by what I had told them about the movie that they would go to see it. Then they would come back disappointed. 'It wasn't the way you told it. You told it much better.'

THELMA
I too always had a feeling that I'd be an actress. I was only a

few months old when I was carried to the theatre to watch my mother on the stage. Daddy kept his promise to Mother, when they became engaged, that she could continue with her career as a singer and actress. When I was three years old, in 1928, she went away to London for a year, coming home only on Sundays, to be in a revue written by Noël Coward, *This Year of Grace*. It was presented by C B Cochran whose lavish productions were legendary. This was her only West End appearance – she was twenty-seven and at the full blossoming of her talent and beauty. Leeds to London in those days was a long, arduous journey and it must have been very tiring for her to travel all the way from London to Leeds each week just to have a glimpse of us. If she had been free to stay in London and follow up her success, who knows where her talents might have led her.

The effort was too much. She decided to give up her aspirations to stardom and to appear only locally and each year she was in a musical comedy either at the Leeds Grand Theatre or at the Bradford Alhambra in the leading role. These were productions mounted by local amateur groups but in those days they used to engage and pay professionals to play the leading parts. Throughout my school years I saw Mother many times: in *Bitter Sweet* – she was beautiful as Sarah – *The Vagabond King*, *Rose Marie*, *No No Nanette* and many more popular musicals of the late twenties and thirties. I would watch her, half loving it and half terrified that she was going to forget her lines or that something would go wrong on the stage. It was *my mummy* up there! She was absolutely enchanting on the stage. I was a very shy, quiet child but I had an inner longing to follow in her footsteps and to be an actress.

Aunt Mona was an actress but different from Mother. She was a straight actress (whereas Mom was in musicals, revues and variety) and worked in several Yorkshire repertory companies – professional, not amateur. I used to help her to

learn her lines. I loved to go backstage to visit her: the smell
of the greasepaint and the lights around the mirrors and
going through a stage door ... I was thrilled, absolutely
thrilled. In my school, unlike yours, there was no programme
of drama, even as an extra-curricular activity. Only twice was
I in a play. The first time was when I was six, and the play
was *The Old Woman Who Lived in a Shoe*, the one who had so
many children she didn't know what to do. I played the star
part, the Old Woman. At the performance, at the end of the
first half when the curtain was supposed to close, nothing
happened. The curtain was stuck. I stepped forward and
pulled the curtain across with my hand and said to the
audience, 'You thought you were going to see me put my
children to bed, didn't you, but you're wrong' and with that
I closed the curtain. Mona can vouch for the story – she was
in the audience and she says she knew from that moment
that I would become a professional actress.

The one other play that I had the chance to be in was
called *A Kiss For Cinderella* by J M Barrie. I played a man!
Because of my shyness, because of lack of opportunity or
stimulus at school, my acting ambitions were completely
secret. I had two mirrors in my bedroom. In one I pretended to be acting on the screen and the other was me on
the stage.

PETER
Starting from approximately the age of seven my parents
used to take me with them when they went to the Yiddish
theatre. We're talking about the decade of the twenties. The
Yiddish theatre was thought to be the best theatre in New
York and we used to get New York companies which came
up to Montreal. I saw plays in Yiddish by Dostoyevsky, Ibsen,
Chekhov. My parents were barely literate but they loved the
Yiddish theatre and rarely missed a New York show and they
took me, which I think was very wonderful of them. There
weren't many things that my parents did that I can praise so

whole-heartedly because, generally speaking, they were quite primitive in their understanding of what a growing child needed. But on this one score they were very good. I heard the Yiddish language spoken beautifully by very good actors. They had come out of Eastern Europe or from the Vilna Truppe – a company of professional actors in Vilna (the centre of Jewish learning) which came to America. They were the first to translate Ibsen into Yiddish, Shakespeare into Yiddish, Gorky into Yiddish. They made a great contribution to Yiddish culture. All of this of course was wiped out by the Nazis, all of this went up in the furnaces.

Among the top Yiddish actors I saw was a very great actor and beloved matinée idol by the name of Jacob Ben Ami, a beautiful man with a beautiful voice which he used brilliantly. Quiet, soft, velvety, sensitive, delicate with strength when it was required, like a fine cello, strong enough to come over the footlights and be heard in the entire theatre. I saw him in Dostoevsky's *The Idiot*. I was tremendously impressed.

I once saw something that was to remain a treasured memory – a great actor by the name of Rudolf Shildkraut who was essentially a German actor. He'd had a great career on the German stage and he played in a Yiddish which was quite different from the Yiddish of the others, more Germanic, but you understood what was happening from his body language and from the expressions on his face, from the way he used his voice. It was marvellous! He had a gritty, deep bass voice and what an excitement when that man was on the stage!

Although I'd been active in the Yiddish theatre, as an actor, as a stagehand, as a carpenter, as a stage electrician, and as a spectator, I did not see a play in the English language until I was about fifteen years old when I saw *The Merchant of Venice* at His Majesty's Theatre in downtown Montreal. Shylock was played by the great English actor, George Arliss – a stunning performance – I was in a swoon.

THELMA

In Leeds we had three main theatres: the Theatre Royal was where the repertory company performed – the Arthur Brough Players – that is where Mona appeared. The fine old Empire Theatre, where we saw the great music-hall artists. The glory of Leeds was, and is, the Grand Theatre, a magnificent Edwardian theatre, where we saw tours of West End shows, opera and ballet.

The first professional productions I saw were *The Mikado* – my grandparents took me – and a musical called *Wild Violets* with Vera Pearce, both at the Grand Theatre. When I walked into that temple of red plush and gold, I was smitten. At the age you were hypnotised by Yiddish drama, I was in love with the colour, the charm, the gaiety of musicals, ballet, pantomime, Ivor Novello at the Grand, Arthur Askey at the Empire, *The Ghost Train* at the Theatre Royal. And that magical night once or twice a year when my beautiful mother was the star.

Mom and Dad had a permanent booking on a Saturday night at the Grand Theatre – the same seats in the stalls. One or other of them would often give up their seat to us but, if they both wanted to go, Geoffrey and I used to queue up and get tickets either at the back of the stalls (which was called the pit) for sixpence or to the gods just under the roof of the theatre, which was all wooden benches and wooden floors. Or we would stand. *Judgement Day* by Elmer Rice, with Glynis Johns as a child giving a memorable performance, *Idiot's Delight* with Vic Oliver, an Ivor Novello musical in which a ship sank on the stage – I was certainly standing when that ship went down!

*   *   *

PETER

As a child I excelled in everything I did – compositions, drawings, reciting and dealing with the problems of the

world because I was reading – Voltaire, Alexandre Dumas
Père or Knut Hamsun. My father used to go to the second-
hand bookstalls that they had outdoors and come home with
books.

One year I had the misfortune to become ill with a
children's disease – acute nephritis, a disease of the kidneys.
I was eleven, and I missed a year of school, stayed home and
learned to cook from my mother. The period of my
childhood illness was not easy for me and certainly not easy
for my mother who gave me great care.

When I was in my last year of Elementary School,
approaching thirteen, I was studying very hard to try to
win a scholarship to High School. Now comes a shattering
change. Suddenly my father is out of work. He loves
good clothes, he has a closet full of beautiful suits and
he's a wonderful looking man – and he's out of work. My
father was a Socialist and a Union organiser. He was a
founding member of the Canadian Labour Party but in
his Union there were a lot of workers in the factories
who by now had taken up the Communist philosophy.
There is great prosperity in America and Canada. The
stock market is booming but there is also great poverty.
The Russian Revolution is flaming all across Eastern Europe
and there are ancillary revolutions – one in Germany,
one in Hungary. Many of the workers in the shops, Jewish
but also Italian and French-Canadian, became Communists.
There was an election and the Communists out-voted the
Socialists in the Union. It was decided to throw out all
the 'right-wing Socialist Union organisers'. So my father
got the sack.

He came home, and you never saw such a bewildered
man. He was absolutely shocked because he'd been riding
high on a wave of optimism and self-confidence. He was
coming into his own – making speeches, meetings with the
bosses, with the arbitration boards, had given him a confidence which he had never had before. He found he had

abilities that he didn't know he had. Suddenly the salary stopped, suddenly everything changed, suddenly my father disappears. I say to Momma, 'Where's Poppa?' She whispers, 'He went to New York.' 'Why?' She says, 'Because he can't get work here.' 'So what's he doing in New York?' 'He got work there. He's gone back to working in a factory and he's making much more money than he ever made here as a factory worker. And he's sending us money and that's what we're living on.' All this is whispered because Poppa is in New York illegally.

We had to leave our lovely house on St Urbain Street where I had a little room all to myself where I could play with meccano and construct whole towns from empty cotton spools. Sometimes I would work for weeks on the same construction. All of a sudden, all of that is over. We have to move – we can't afford to pay the rent – the money that Poppa sends from New York is insufficient. We move in with a family with seven children and they rent us one room with two beds. Bernard and I slept in one bed, and my mother slept in the second bed. The name of the family was Champagne. You can imagine how tight everything was in that house – the queues lined up to get into the only toilet.

Suddenly we went on a trip by train which we hoped would take us to New York to join Father. The plot was as follows: A certain Mr Markovitch was an official in the Union of which my father had been a part. He was working in Montreal, although his home was in the United States and he had an American passport. When my father was kicked out, Mr Markovitch remained a friend because politically he was on the same side as my father. So Mr Markovitch took my mother and Bernard and me on a train which crossed the American border at a town called Plattsburg, New York. Plattsburg had a big station of border police because that whole area was famous for people 'stealing the border' from both sides. Into Canada or into the United States. Mr Markovitch told us that if anybody asked us, he was our

father, we were his family because he had an American
passport.

We cross the border and we're into Plattsburg. We've
been inspected by an immigration inspector and it looks all
right. But it isn't all right. Because Mr Markovitch did a
rather stupid thing – he got off the train in Plattsburg and
went back to Montreal. Our train was standing there in the
station – it was a long stop – some huge American policemen came to where we were sitting and asked to see our
papers. We, of course, had no American papers, we had no
visas, no entry permits. So they took us off the train, my
mother and Bernard and me, and into a big touring auto-
mobile – everything seemed very big to me – huge policemen, they were monsters! Good looking, but monsters.
My mother and the two small boys were put at the back
with a policeman, and two more very large policemen at the
front. I remember the rifles in the car, I remember the
pistols in the holsters on their waists, and I remember the
terror of being stopped, arrested, questioned. They drove us
to their station somewhere near the border, then took each
of us into a separate room and questioned us. I was ten,
Bernard was eight and my mother was pregnant with
Shaindel. They didn't really need such fancy tactics to get
the truth out of us, because we had no experience with
police, we had no experience with the kind of lie that was
necessary to cover our situation. My mother spoke English
very badly. I still spoke English with a strong Yiddish
intonation.

I tried to lie, saying, 'Yes, Mr Markovitch is our father and
we're going home to New York. We live in New York.' It
didn't help but they were very nice to us and they put us on a
train and sent us back home to Montreal. I'll never forget
how terrified I was and I'll never forget how grateful I was
when they let us go, wished us good luck and sent us home.

There was a second attempt and this time my mother was
carrying a babe in arms. Without much explanation my

mother tells us we are going on a trip. A man comes in a taxi, we get into the taxi. I am sitting behind the driver and I am terrified by his neck. He was a man in his forties and he had a very fat fold of flesh at the bottom of his skull. I kept looking at this big, greasy fold in the back of his neck. Altogether he was a tough guy, this driver, and his name was Venetzky.

We drove out of Montreal in the late afternoon – frightened, because my mother said we are going to my father in New York. We have to be good children, we have to behave, we mustn't make any noise, we mustn't make any trouble. In the gloaming we arrive at the mountains on the Canadian side of the Province of Quebec lying across the border from Vermont. The driver brings us to a huge farmhouse, parks his taxi inside a barn and takes us into the house and jokingly says, 'When you stand here, this foot is in Canada and this foot is in the United States.' He says, 'We've got to wait until it gets dark.' We get back into the car.

Night comes. Around midnight the driver says, 'Look, you stay here in the car for a while, I got to go fix something. I'll be back, don't worry.' He goes off and he leaves us. Midnight. Dark. No light from anywhere. It was terrifying. We were too frightened to eat the sandwiches Mother had brought. We sat there until three o'clock in the morning when Mr Venetzky with the fat neck came back and said, 'Look, it didn't work out. I'm taking you back to Montreal.' This came as a terrible shock to my mother because she had paid him $400, in those days an enormous amount of money, to take us across the border. My mother starts to argue with him and he said, 'Listen missis, shut up. Don't ask any questions, I'll bring you back to Montreal and that's all there is to it.'

We get back to Montreal at six o'clock in the morning and my mother says to the driver, 'Please tell me what happened.' 'I won't tell you nothing, missis, don't ask any questions. Be satisfied that you're back home.' Mother got the money back because he wasn't a bad guy, Venetzky, but later we found out that he had a deal with the American border police. He would take money from different people who wanted to get into the United States, deliver them to the US border straight into the hands of the American police, and got money from the police for delivering them. He wasn't altogether a *good* guy but he didn't have the heart to deliver my mother with her three small children, so he took us back to Montreal.

While we lived in the Champagne's house there arose the question of my barmitzvah. My father had given my mother strict orders, 'No barmitzvah! We don't want any of that superstitious nonsense.' But my mother had parents who were still alive and my grandfather insisted that I would be barmitzvah, he would kill himself if I weren't! Mother gave in and, in my father's absence, she hired a *melamed*, that's the Hebrew word for teacher, to teach me my portion of the Bible which I would have to read in the synagogue. I gave that *melamed* a tough time – like Poppa I was pretty certain that I too was an agnostic.

In that house, while I was studying with the *melamed* for my barmitzvah, there was an unforgettable incident. I wasn't going to the Yiddish school any more, but I was going to English school. Until now I had always been dressed extremely well. My mother used to sew clothes for us when we were small but now I was growing up to be a big boy and I was waiting for my first pair of long pants – I was still wearing knickers which buckled and folded over at the knee. I had developed a tear in the right knee and my mother tried to sew it up. It wasn't very successful and I was very ashamed of it, so I used to sit in school all day long with my hand covering my right knee so that nobody would see that I was wearing torn knickers.

My mother decided to wash my pants – in those days you didn't send clothes to the cleaners because it was expensive, so you washed things. If you were my mother, you certainly

washed things. My mother washed everything in sight. She
washed the pants and she hung them out on the line to dry,
and that was the only pair of pants I had because there was
no money and there were no new clothes and I was growing
so fast that she couldn't keep up with me. I wake up in the
morning and say, 'Ma, are the pants dry?' She said, 'I'll go
out and get them from the line.' She went out and they
weren't there! She looked up and down that back yard, she
nearly went crazy trying to find the pants, but they had
disappeared.

Finally she came and said, 'They must have been stolen.'
I have a very strong image of my crouching in a very
peculiar corner of that room – it wasn't a square room,
one corner of the room had been cut away diagonally
and there was a very narrow triangular space. I pushed
myself into this space and shouted at my mother, 'There
is no God! There is no God! There is no God!' This was
rebellion against the rabbi and the painful flicking finger
of the *melamed* teaching me my portion of the law and all
the business about the barmitzvah, which I knew my
father didn't want. Mother found a pair of pants for me
to go to school, borrowed from the Champagnes. I got
my first pair of long pants in time for my barmitzvah.

THELMA
At that age I was very religious, and when I was fourteen my
parents found out about a Jewish boarding school for girls
called La Râmée in Lausanne, Switzerland, and they decided
to send me there for the summer holidays. There were girls
there from many different countries but the language of
conversation and studies was French, so this was a great
opportunity for me to improve my French. It was what was
called a 'finishing school' – girls went there for a year after
they had finished school, so I was at least three years
younger than the rest of the girls. I was sent with my great
friend Sheila Nathan, who was older than I was.

No air travel in those days. Sheila's mother, Mrs Nathan, took us to Switzerland by boat and train. We stayed overnight in a hotel in Paris and Sheila and I shared a room, high up in the building and with a tiny balcony. We decided to be really wicked, two girls in Paris, so we took off all our clothes and ran out naked on the balcony for all of five seconds!

La Râmée was a dream come true for a girl of fourteen. Beautifully situated in La Rosiaz, on the outskirts of Lausanne up the mountainside, it was run by a woman with a vibrant personality – Madame. She was very feminine, attractive and amusing, elegantly dressed, with blue hair and best of all she had a gorgeous son called Pierre, aged twenty-six. He was the only man in this all-girls school and we were all mad about him. In the dining room we sat round tables for eight, and we took it in turn to wait on table. I learned to stack a pile of plates on one arm. I sat at the head of a table and because of that Madame used to call me her *institutrice*, or teacher. End of August, 1939. One day the twelve English girls were called into Madame's room. We had not been following the news, so we were completely astonished when she told us (in French, of course) that there were certain rumblings in Europe and some people feared that war was about to break out. She believed that if there were a war, Switzerland would not be involved so she had phoned all our parents to ask if they wanted us to be sent home, or to stay in the safety of Switzerland.

She went around the room and spoke to the girls one by one, telling them what their parents had decided, 'You're going home. You're going home...' All of them were going home, until she came to me. 'Your parents think it would be better if you stay here! My little *institutrice!*' I managed to fight back the tears until I fled to my room, threw myself on the bed in an agony of weeping. I was devastated. Through the fuzz of my heartbreak came one sentence from a friend that gave me comfort, 'Think how much French you'll learn.' About an hour later a call came through from England from my parents. I howled in agony down the phone, 'Please, let me come home!' Naturally they said yes.

Next day we twelve girls set off with one of the teachers, Mlle Tauxe, an Eton-cropped, masculine woman. Exactly a week before the Germans marched into Poland. We set off on the train to Paris in the evening, already the trains were blacked out. There was only a dim blue light in the compartment. All through the night we travelled in the darkened train, no chance of being able to sleep. The only refreshment Mlle Tauxe had brought was our usual mid-morning snack, dry bread and chocolate.

We arrived in Paris at six in the morning, just as the sun was rising. We had to change trains there. The station was chaotic. Thousands and thousands of people all trying to get home. In Calais the chaos and confusion was even worse than Paris but we pushed our way onto a boat. Among the crowds on the platform in London meeting the train I was overwhelmed with relief to see Mummy and Daddy. Mother said to me, 'You have three choices: you can stay in a hotel in London overnight, you can go straight to Dublin – that's where we think you will be safest – or we can just catch the last train to Leeds.' There was no hesitation, 'I want to go home!'

Four days later, my parents insisted that I go to Dublin. On the Friday, two days after I arrived, I took my baby cousin Leonora out for a walk in her pram and a man stopped me and said, 'Hitler has just marched into Poland.' The following Sunday we listened with shocked incomprehension as Chamberlain announced that we were at war.

PETER
Don't you find it interesting that there is a strong parallelism between your stories and mine. I just got through telling you about how we 'stole the border' twice, in trains, in cars,

movement, travelling, fright, uncertainty. You tell exactly the same story.

THELMA
Yes. Soon afterwards Grandma and Grandpa arrived in Dublin from Leeds because Grandpa's raincoat factory had been gutted in a fire, Geoffrey arrived too, and we all lived together. Geoffrey and I adored Grandma and Grandpa. Grandma with her sharp wit, intelligence, her all-embracing love, even her never-known-to-be-wrong bossiness, and Grandpa with his Yorkshire bluntness and carefulness (I hesitate to call it meanness) over money but a dear, sweet man. The nine months in Dublin were full of laughter.

Geoffrey started Trinity College, Daddy's old university, where he stayed for a few years and received his BA degree. I went to Alexandra School which was for girls only. I never went to a co-ed school. I regret this and I'm sure it was another reason for my shyness and awkwardness with boys. We didn't even have male teachers. But Alexandra was a nice school, despite my father having to pay the school £12 for me *not* to learn Gaelic.

I went back to England in June 1940. The phoney war had just finished and the air raids were starting. Leeds was relatively lucky, though I was very frightened on the occasions I heard enemy planes flying overhead. We knew when we were being raided by the enemy because we could distinguish the sound of the German planes, a sound which went up and down, different from the British planes which sounded a steady engine roar as they passed overhead. My parents were worried, not only because of the possible dangers of the war, but they wanted me to have an uninterrupted education. It was decided that I should be evacuated to America. I didn't want to go. I thought people would think I was running away and that I was a coward. Dad said, 'You *must* go and Mother will go with you.'

PETER

At about the same age, shortly after my barmitzvah, I became a member of a left-wing Labour Zionist organisation, Poale Zion. I was bored to death. What they told me was not interesting to me because they believed that once we captured and reconquered Israel we would solve all the problems of the world. That didn't check with what my father had told me about 'value, price and profit'. Then I was picked up by the Yipsels (YPSLs, which stands for Young People's Socialist League). This was Socialism *without* Zionism. This was closer to my father's beliefs. I listened and participated in the meetings which were mostly dull and boring. I was restless.

By now my father was home, back from New York. He was making a living by buying sacks of rags from the various clothing shops he'd known as a Union organiser. The bosses let him pick up all the little bits of material that were cut off and were too small to be used. He used to pick up these rags and sell them to cap-makers.

We moved to a new flat which was small and crowded on Clark Street. At Baron Byng High School I had a wonderful master, a big, tall Swede. I think he was six foot six, a mountain of a man but the sweetest man you could wish for and he was our drawing teacher. Mr Jackalin soon discovered, after a lesson or two, that I was way ahead of all the other students. He said, 'OK Friedie, we'll give you something else to do.' 'Friedie' he called me. 'This stuff that the other kids are doing, you're way beyond it. How would you like to learn mechanical drawing?' I said, 'Oh, yes sir.' I didn't know what it was, but I said 'Yes, sir' and he taught me how you prepare drawings for the manufacture of metal parts for machinery. You have to learn how to draw a pipe showing the diameter of the pipe, showing the length of the pipe and, if one end is threaded, you have to learn how to draw the threads, the screw threads. During my four years with this teacher, he took me through an entire course of architectural draftsmanship and the beginnings of architectural drawing. When I got through high school I had done all the preparatory work that students have to do when they choose architecture as a profession.

After high school there was a question of going to university. My parents said, 'If you want to go to university you'll have to earn the money to pay for it. We can't afford it – we just haven't got the money.' I said, 'Yes, OK.' I had worked through all the years I went to high school, I worked in the afternoons and evenings – sometimes at two jobs – and all through the holidays, so that didn't scare me. One summer job I had when I was twelve years old reinforced the convictions I had learned from my father's Marxist teachings. I felt on my own skin the inequalities and evils of the capitalist system. I worked in a shop in the Rachel Street Market for a cousin, Joe Weinrauch. He had two shops, and he left me in complete charge of this shop, including the financial side. It was a chicken shop – there was a wall of cages holding live chickens, one to a cage. The women would go over to the cages and blow on the bums of the chicken ... when the feathers were blown aside they could judge if they were getting a good fat chicken. There was a *shochet*, a ritual slaughterer, at the back to kill the chicken, I would wrap it and sell it. Joe was a capitalist, a red-necked Conservative, and he made me work long hours. Especially on a Saturday, when I would be there from seven in the morning until eleven at night, doing the accounts after the shop had closed. I came home exhausted and weeping to my mother, 'It isn't *fair*. I do all that work and at the end of the week Joe gets $180 and I get $4.'

So when I left school, I enrolled at the Ecole des Beaux Arts to study architecture. I was the only Jewish boy in a classroom full of Roman Catholic French-Canadians and a sprinkling of English-speaking Protestants, and they said to me, 'Hey Friedman (Frye was just for theatrical use!), you think you are going to be an architect in Montreal – never,

never! There will be no Jewish architects in Montreal.' This continued every time I came to class and I have to confess I couldn't take it. I hated their guts. So I quit and that was the end of my formal study of architecture but I never lost my interest in the subject. The only outlet that I had for this kind of ability was the work that I did all through the years – whenever I directed a play – I would design the scenery. It was also the end of my higher education.

When I was fifteen, I joined the Young Communists League (YCL). In the Young Communists League it was very lively. There we talked about the revolution and how we had to organise the working class into one strong party and become the majority so that we could take over. We went on demonstrations and we got pushed around by the police. I even got hit lightly on the head by a police club but that was exciting. We were doing something. That was real. Not like the other youth movements where they talked and talked and talked – this was action.

There's something I've touched on before, but I'd like to go into it more deeply. My relationship with my father. I was still living at home, paying rent of $4 a week and I find I have no contact with my father. We don't talk. We can't talk. One of the reasons was that I was devilishly arrogant and when I did have two minutes to talk to him, I would say, 'You Socialists don't understand. You're old fashioned. You really don't know what's going on in the world. There's only one way and that's a Communist revolution.' Why he didn't kill me on the spot, I don't know. He never slapped me. Never beat me, never. Just sat there and listened to my fatuous arguments, gritted his teeth and didn't say a word. Because here I was making common cause with the people who had thrown him out of the Union. Can you imagine what that was for him? When I think of it now, I think of how terribly cruel I was – the cruelty of youth – where out of ignorance you behave like a murderer. How much I regret that now. How much I would have loved to have had a talk with my father when I was a little older and discerned things a little better, to apologise to him for my terrible behaviour when I was young.

In the YCL they had agit-prop groups. Agit-prop is short for agitation-propaganda. It was an idea that had developed in Germany in the twenties where they had what they called 'blue-blouse troupes', groups of young performers who all wore blue blouses so that they could be recognised and they went around agitating and propagandising through entertainment. There were songs written by people like Berthold Brecht and Kurt Weill. We learned some of those songs and sang them there in Canada, and we were fed material from all over the world. In my group of the YCL there were some young Canadian lads who were sailors. They had been to different countries and been in contact with the revolutionary youth, and they came back with songs. This was terribly exciting, meeting these young sailors, learning songs from all over the world – Italian songs, Russian songs, French songs, about the working class, about the working-class movement.

When it was discovered in the YCL that I was an actor, they said, 'Can't you do some agit-prop for us?' So I became a one-man agit-prop group. I found a poem by Michael Gold, a left-wing writer. In his book *120 Million* (the total population of the USA in 1930), he had written a dramatic monologue called 'Vanzetti in the Death House'. The celebrated Sacco Vanzetti case happened around 1926. Two men, who were obviously innocent, had been railroaded in a court which was completely prejudiced and sentenced to death in the electric chair. They sat in jail in the death house for a long time because there was agitation all over the world for these men to be freed. There was Sacco, who was a cobbler, and Vanzetti, who was a fisherman, he caught fish and sold it in the market. They were anarchists and for that reason they were accused of a holdup in which some men were killed – a factory payroll was held up. A policeman was

killed and, in cases like that, the law becomes very, very
vengeful and must find somebody to punish. They found
these two simple Italian workmen, Sacco and Vanzetti, and
they were sitting in the death house while the whole world
agitated and tried to get them free. In 1926 they were finally
put to death.

I grew up with this. Michael Gold's poem was based on
the letters that Vanzetti had written to Sacco while they were
in the death house. In the dramatic monologue which I
wrote, Vanzetti is pacing up and down his tiny cell and
trying to find words of encouragement for Sacco who was
not quite as developed as Vanzetti. Vanzetti was a thinker.
Sacco was a very simple man and Vanzetti tried to explain to
him why he was sitting in jail, though he was innocent. Why
the courts didn't believe him. Why the whole world was
agitating to free them. It's an absolutely marvellous poem
and has the strength of historic validity, these were Vanzetti's
own words.

Wherever there was a strike meeting, at some point in the
proceedings I would recite 'Vanzetti in the Death House'.
The most memorable time was one night when we were giving a farewell party for five young men who had been Union
organisers trying to organise a textile plant where the girls
were working for $6 and $7 a week when the minimum wage
law, which was pretty miserable anyhow, was $12. Employers
were cheating them, so these young members of the YCL
organised a strike and it became a celebrated event. The
police arrested them and charged them under an old 1867
law of subversive behaviour, conspiracy against the welfare
of the state ... they railroaded them and they were sentenced to five years' jail with hard labour. After sentencing
they were immediately taken off to the prison. On this
special night there was a party in the factory where they had
been Union organisers in honour of the young victims.

Naturally, I was expected to recite 'Vanzetti in the Death
House'. It was in a hall which was tremendously crowded.

There were six hundred girls working in that factory and they came with boyfriends or with fathers or with mothers – a mass of people in that hall. There was no stage, there was no place to perform, so we took six dining tables and we put them together, and that was my stage. Approximately the size of Vanzetti's cell. I put a chair on it and I climbed up and sat for a minute. Then I got up and paced the length of the tables in one direction, then in the other direction, then sat down on the chair and started the poem. I recited the whole thing, I didn't lose my place, I didn't get thrown. When I finished there was no applause – there was this shocking quiet in the whole hall. What I had told them about was the whole terrible history of the oppression of the working class all over the world and the injustice of the law.

At seventeen, I left high school and met and went to live with my first girlfriend, an American girl seven years older than me, called Basya. For a while we ran a theatre together, the Montreal Art Theatre, the following year we decided to try our luck in New York.

THELMA
When you were eighteen in 1932 and eight years later in 1940, when I was fifteen, we both headed for New York.

Book II

New York, New York

Montreal to
New York

PETER

The prime reason for my departure for New York was
Basya. She had decided to return to her family in New
York. She was my first woman. It was a great discovery
... sex ... better than anything I had ever imagined and I
wasn't going to let go of it so easily. But there were other
factors as well. The economic pressures in my life at
home did not make for warm family ties. Everything was
reduced to an economic proposition. Are you paying
your fair share of family expenses? I don't think I had
bad parents, I had poor parents, primitive parents, uneducated parents. So Basya and I decided to go to New York.
We set off to cross the border illegally, to 'steal the
border', me carrying a portfolio of drawings and paintings.
We were caught. Basya was an American so she was
allowed through and I was sent back to Montreal and I
started to walk back on the road with my portfolio of
drawings and then hitchhiked back to Montreal, a distance
of some fifty miles.

THELMA

How did you get to New York in the end?

PETER

Quite simply – on a bus. I just went through the border as a
visitor. Basya was at the bus station to meet me. I had no job,
no money. The next question was where do we live? Basya

said, 'Come and stay with me in my parents' house.' Her parents were living in Coney Island in a tiny flat and there was very little room. I slept in a room with Basya which we shared with her younger brother, just a kid. One day with our last nickels we took the subway out to the Bronx where Basya had been recommended for a job as a Hebrew teacher. We got to the address but she didn't get the job. We had no money to get back to Coney Island. From the Bronx to Coney Island must be a distance of twenty miles. How the hell were we going to get home? We passed a jeweller's shop. I had a ring which had been given to me by my school chums from Bancroft Elementary School – a barmitzvah gift inscribed by friends. Basya said, 'We could pawn this and when we get some money we'll get it back.' The jeweller looked at the ring, weighed it and gave us three dollars. I imagine it was worth at least fifteen because it was gold. The only ring I have ever worn all my life and I never got it back.

So we had three dollars. We went to eat something and got back to Coney Island. I said to Basya, 'This can't go on. We'll have to do something.' We volunteered for and became members of an organisation then called The Workers' Laboratory Theatre, later called the Theatre of Action. It was a Communist front. In those days the Communist Party used to organise and give support to all kinds of groups which were dominated by Communists inside but on the face of it were independent, liberal, progressive organisations. The Workers' Laboratory Theatre was an agitation-propaganda group which serviced trade unions.

We performed on the back of a truck in the street.

But also we would be asked to come out to a picnic of, say, the Needleworkers' Union, or get a call saying there was a very important mass picket line at Orbachs, a big department store on 14th Street, and we would come running over. Earl Robinson and the rest of us would get up on a little platform or right down on the street level and we would sing to the picketers, do sketches, join them on the picket line. There was a sense of celebration. The strikers on the picket line responded enthusiastically. They didn't know who the hell we were but there we were supporting them, encouraging them and being part of them.

We also did our shows down on the waterfront in the streets down in the docks area of New York. Many times we had to get away quickly when we were chased by the police. As happened during a Merchant Marine strike when we set up our little platform in the middle of the street and attracted hundreds of people. We would do little sketches on those platforms. Peter Martin, one of the writers, created a whole series of sketches which were a satire to show how the workers were really being fooled rather than being helped and how they should stay together and in the trade union movement there is strength.

We were at May Day celebrations as well as other left-wing gatherings. We also were concerned for ourselves as actors, as people trying to do things better. We took singing classes with Earl Robinson and speech classes given by people within the group who had enough experience to lead us in these areas. We had friends from the famous Group Theatre coming down to teach us acting techniques. This was the introduction of Stanislavsky into America and we were one of the first groups who were infected by it. The Group Theatre looked on us as their little brothers. We had memorable dance classes with Anna Sokolow who was strict and rough on our bodies.

It wasn't a *job*. It was a task, it was a mission! I was an idealist. Nobody got paid, we got our keep. We shared an old slum of an apartment up rickety stairs on the fifth floor way over on the east side of New York, on 12th Street. The building must have been easily a hundred years old. There were four mattresses on the floor in each room. Basya and I had one corner of a large square room, the three other corners were inhabited or populated or domiciled by three other guys, with or without girlfriends.

I got put on to the kitchen crew because I knew something about cooking, and the food was donated by different unions. Our studio nearby, sometimes used for a theatre, was part of a warehouse not far from the editorial offices of *The Daily Worker*, which was the Communist newspaper. One of the editors of *The Daily Worker* was the advisor of our theatre – V J Jerome whom none of us liked because we felt that he was the extremist kind of bureaucrat. We weren't concerned with the conditions of our surroundings, we were concerned with our work, with each other and with the excitement of being together. We were representing the political left and we quite deliberately used theatre as a weapon. At that time there were right-wing Republican newspapers and radio stations but this was the left-wing cultural arm making its statement and those statements were damned important.

The jewel in our crown was a short play called *Newsboy*, a collage which had started life as a revolutionary-type poem written, I must confess, by V J Jerome. We changed headlines with the events of the day which were shouted out by a newsboy. The issue was to show that the capitalist world was in decay and falling apart and that the only future for mankind was Communism. The thing is we believed that the capitalist system was in decay. We had much evidence to prove it. We had no jobs, most of us hadn't had enough education. We couldn't afford to go to university – we all came from poor families. There was hopeless unemployment all around us – sixteen million unemployed men in the United States. Including their dependents, two-thirds of the nation was affected by unemployment – ill-housed, ill-fed and ill-clothed. 'One-third of the nation' was one of Roosevelt's famous phrases. I think he had it wrong, it was two-thirds of the nation.

That whole period was a revolution from the old-fashioned kind of robber baron capitalism to the beginnings of social responsibility. We were part of a revolution that has never been called a revolution but America was never the same after that period. Just a year or so later Works Progress Administration came around – that was the key to the revolution. The NRA, the National Recovery Act, the Federal Theatre, the artists programme, the writing programmes – the golden age of culture in America. We had theatres all over the country. We had artists working in every post office painting murals, we had books published ... it was an incredibly active cultural period in the life of America. Nothing ever matched it since. As part of the Theatre of Action, we saw how effective we were being in our theatrical presentations and *we were helping working people*.

Al Saxe, our director, was not great but he was not uninteresting. A very frightened man, worried about his leadership position, suspicious that any of us might want to take over from him. His greatest weapon against any possible conspiracy to seize power from him was the weekly meeting of self-criticism. Anybody who has been through the Communist mill will recognise what I'm talking about. It is one of their great weapons for controlling everybody in an organisation. This is the standard procedure in Communist Party cells, employed to destroy the personalities of everyone in the group except the leader, who is conducting this self-criticism. He finds nothing critical to say about himself. And nobody dares to say anything critical about him, because he is the leader and infallible. After close to sixty years, I'm still angry. I couldn't take those weekly meetings any longer. By now I was also somewhat disenchanted with Basya. I had a little affair with a young dancer as a way of freeing myself and we parted. That was over, and my membership in The Workers' Laboratory Theatre was over too.

Leeds to New York

THELMA

I hesitate to tell the story of my arrival in New York after that
– no 'stealing the border', no wild sex, not penniless in the
Bronx nor leaping onto a truck to avoid the police during a
sailors' strike ... ah well, we've promised each other not to
fabricate so I must tell it as it was.

Before sailing for New York there had been a farewell
party and everybody had given us parting gifts. If it weren't
for those gifts my life would have been totally different.
After the party, two days before our departure date, news
came through that a ship bound for New York full of British
evacuees, the *City of Benares*, had been sunk by a U-boat
resulting in a huge loss of life. I had often said I didn't want
to go and after this shocking news my parents, frightened of
the risk of the journey, gave me the choice ... if I *really*
didn't want to go they would cancel. It was those gifts – I
couldn't face the notion of giving them all back. I said, 'OK.
Let's go!'

Mother and I took the train to Manchester lugging
eighteen cases. Dad's brother, Uncle Philip was on the
platform and gave us a large box of chocolates so that we
then had nineteen packages. In Liverpool we had to wait
in a long queue before getting on the boat and I was so
tired I kicked Uncle Philip's chocolates along like a football. Liverpool, 6th October 1940, we boarded a very shaky-
looking boat, the *Northern Prince* – it wasn't even a steam boat,
it was a motor vessel with two motors to drive it. When
we boarded, we learned that, because of Jewish New Year,
they hadn't been able to get Kosher food for us. On top of
that, it was a small boat of only ten thousand tons with only
a hundred and one passengers, including children and babies.
Mom was so upset she wanted to get off and go home but
I persuaded her to stay. At that moment the sirens went

for an air raid, so we couldn't have disembarked if we'd wanted to.

We sailed from Liverpool in a big convoy of ships including naval escort vessels which gave us a feeling of security. Eighteen hours out of Liverpool, the two motors of our ship broke down – both together. We watched the convoy sail off, never to be seen again, while we floated around, helpless. The silence was terrifying. If there had been a submarine in the area, we would have been a sitting target. Eventually they got the motors started and off we chugged – ten days to cross the Atlantic in crowded, uncomfortable conditions. While at sea it was Yom Kippur, the Jewish fast day. They gave us a good meal at 5.30, then eleven of us crowded into a cabin where a family of German refugees, father, mother and daughter, the father with his prayer-shawl and skull-cap, sang the entire service by heart, the daughter singing in harmony. I was fifteen, I made friends, it was exciting – I had my first alcoholic drink sitting on a stairway. Somebody had given me a Tom Collins. It tasted like lemonade, only afterwards was I told it contained gin. I even gambled and lost a shilling playing dice. Mother strongly disapproved but I started to grow up on that journey. The thrill of sailing past the Statue of Liberty and into New York. Images from newsreels, from films, had prepared me for this moment but I wasn't prepared, I was overwhelmed – the excitement of arriving in this great, important, huge country, the gigantic impact of the city of New York – and what was my future going to be like? On the very next sailing, our boat, the *Northern Prince*, was torpedoed and sunk.

Much of my shyness as a child was caused, unwittingly, by brother Geoffrey. I felt inadequate that I could never be as old as he and never as clever. I was in the United States from the age of fifteen to nineteen, and during that time I became – me. I always longed to go on the stage, like Mother and like Mona, but if I hadn't gone to America, I would never have had the courage.

To be evacuated to the USA it was necessary either to go with a large group of other children on a government scheme or to be sponsored by an American citizen. The sponsor had to agree to be financially responsible for you, as no money was allowed out of England. Daddy wanted to be sure that we would never be penniless so he used his dental drill from the surgery and put a valuable diamond into the handle of my tennis racket. I knew nothing about it at the time (I still have the diamond in a safe deposit box in the bank).

As Mother was coming with me, we needed a sponsor. My grandfather had a friend in Leeds called Maurice Stross who was in the rag trade. That term is used for anybody in the clothes business but I mean literally the rag trade – the recycling of rags, leftover pieces of material. Maurice Stross had a friend in the same business in Albany, New York, by the name of Henry Barnet. Grandpa asked Maurice Stross and Maurice Stross asked Henry Barnet if he would sponsor us. Without hesitation he agreed. We had never met him, we did not know him, but he offered at once to finance our stay in America for as long as it should be necessary.

I still have the letter from Henry B Barnet to Dad written 3rd September 1940: 'We will try very hard to make your wife and Thelma's visit as happy as possible. I am putting myself in your frame of mind and can readily understand your temporary parting is a difficult one. We are all hoping that the time will not be too distant when you will all be reunited. Please understand that I do not want any thanks for my willingness to sponsor your wife and daughter. I consider it a privilege.'

A few days after our arrival we went up to Albany to visit our sponsor. The journey from New York through the autumn colours was breathtaking but we were nervous. We were dependent on the generosity of this stranger, Henry Barnet. We were greeted in their lovely home at 123 South Lake Avenue by Henry and Selma Barnet as if we were the dearest and closest members of their family. Uncle Henry, as I called him, had a warm smile, a soft American drawl, a twinkling eye. Aunt Selma was tall, slim, well-dressed and always called her over-seventy friends 'the girls'. 'I'm just going out to do some shopping with the girls.' We stayed with them. They had a black servant, Ollie, who had been with them for many years. Not only was it the first time I had seen a black servant, she was the first black person I had ever met. Manners were precise and meals were formal. Cut your food, put down your knife, then eat with your fork in the right hand. A side dish of cooked fruit to be eaten with the meat. All these customs new to me. The Barnets were Reform Jews. Another first – I had been brought up Orthodox and knew nothing of Reform Jewry. They were Jews so I assumed that all the food would be Kosher. The first hint that it might not be was when they served a cream dessert after a meat meal. It was at their table I ate my first non-Kosher food. When I found it delicious and I hadn't been struck by lightning, I started the first step of my walk away from Orthodox Judaism. We went to their Reform Temple – they didn't even call it a synagogue – in a car. I had never ridden in a car on the Sabbath. Men and women sat together, the men did not cover their heads, the whole service was in English instead of Hebrew – it was all so strange. We met their newly married son Bill and his wife Mary and all the rest of the family. Very soon we learned to love them.

Mother thought that life in Albany would be too provincial – and she'd had enough of that in Leeds – she wanted the thrill of living in New York and so it was decided that we would not live in Albany, but that we would settle in New York and visit them whenever we could. Over the next four years Mom would say to Uncle Henry, 'I'm so sorry we are such a financial burden on you – if only they would allow money to be sent from England. I promise that I am keeping careful accounts and every penny will be repaid as soon as it is possible.' Henry would stop her very firmly. 'I don't want to hear about that. If I never see the money again it doesn't worry me in the slightest, you have brought nothing but pleasure into our family.'

We always kept in touch with this beautiful family. After the death of Henry and Selma, their children Bill and Mary and their children became our special friends. I did not return to the US for twenty-eight years, until I went to Canada in 1972 to meet your family for the first time and then we went to New York via Albany. We stayed in Albany with Bill and Mary, and when Mary opened the door, after twenty-eight years, she said to me, 'Welcome home, Thelma.'

I enjoy thinking that during the four years that I was in New York you were there at the same time. We may have walked the same streets, we may have been at the same theatres. We may have been at the same concerts. We may have actually seen each other. I went to see a production at The New School for Social Research, *Nathan the Wise* and you were teaching there at the same time. Although it was many, many years before we met, I like to think that our lives just brushed each other's.

We found a room in the apartment of a nice lady, Mrs Wilkinson on 1 West 68th Street. We made a great effort to spend as little money as possible, as we didn't want to take a penny more than was necessary from Uncle Henry. It was the first time that I had gone short because I had been brought up with everything I needed. I started at once at Julia Richman High School. The following is an extract from an article I wrote when I was fifteen for the *Yorkshire Post*:

The American school, which is free, admitted me at once. I needed no entrance examination, but every girl takes an Intelligence Test, known as the IQ. There are special teachers in charge of the European girls – they admitted

about one hundred evacuees and refugees from Europe
during the autumn (which is called the 'Fall' in America).

Standing in the entrance of the classroom I see a mixed
crowd of girls – forty-six of them talking at the top of their
voices in a dozen different languages. As well as the
Europeans, there are Chinese, Japanese, Puerto Ricans
and crowds of black girls – I specially enjoy the experience
of making friends with black girls, the first I have ever
met. All the girls are dressed to suit their tastes as there is
no school uniform. Many of the girls wear jumpers and
skirts and flat-heeled, rubber-soled shoes called Saddle
Shoes. Some girls go to the other extreme and wear
beautiful but most unsuitable dresses from Fifth Avenue
shops and expensive high-heeled shoes. On the other
hand, brightly coloured socks are very popular and girls
of seventeen and eighteen walk around school with bare
legs – no stockings.

There are no restrictions on the wearing of jewellery, so
that rings, jangling bracelets, brooches and even ear-rings
are in evidence. Hair styles are worn high this season with
elaborate curls on top. Every girl, from the age of thirteen
upwards, is plastered with lipstick, rouge, coloured nail
polish and powder and throughout the day can be seen
doing her hair and improving her face. The teachers, too,
wear bright red lipstick and most of them have husbands
and children at home, unlike our teachers in England who
are not allowed to be married.

Julia Richman has between seven and eight thousand
girls and is the largest girls' high school in the world.
There are two buildings joined by covered bridges – six
floors and two elevators in each building which you get to
use only if you are very lucky. The fifth floor of one
building is entirely taken up by a cafeteria. Each girl picks
up a tray and slides it along a rail in front of counters of
food. She can have the choice of one of the special hot
dinners or some of the exciting cold dishes and sweets

displayed before her for the equivalent of ninepence. When she comes to the end of the rail she helps herself to cutlery, paper serviette and straws, pays and takes the tray back to one of the tables. This system works very well.

Being in the heart of New York City, the school has no playing grounds. There is no break to go outside, so we are in the building from 8.30 to 3.00. There is a beautiful auditorium with a full-size stage with electrically drawn curtains, microphones and all the equipment necessary for a successful presentation. The auditorium holds four thousand people...'

The other day I found an old exercise book in which I rhapsodise over a journey to school at 7.30 in the morning during a spectacular sunrise. Dated 5th February 1941, it ends: 'Returning at 3.30 p.m. I saw a few buildings on Central Park West lit up by the evening sun, but it shares not the fresh glories of its rising brother...' I know, I know, darling, but I was a dreamy fifteen year old.

I stayed at Julia Richman for a full academic year and graduated the following June 1941. Dad had said the main reason he wanted me to go to America was for me to have an uninterrupted education and here I was – nine months at school in Dublin, nine months at school in New York – and now a High School graduate aged sixteen.

Mother and I got to know each other for the first time. We were living in such close proximity that there developed a deep, deep friendship which we hadn't had before. But there was one subject she had never had the courage to discuss with me – sex. Once, when I was around twelve she had locked the bathroom door and sat beside me as I was sitting in the bath. She wanted to prepare me for menstruation so, in a delicate and ladylike fashion, she started to explain to me about hens laying eggs. She was obviously in difficulty and I took pity on her and said, 'You mean that business of a woman bleeding every month!' Her relief was evident. And that was the full extent of my parental sex education. However, one night in New York when I was about fifteen, I took advantage of our both lying in bed in the dark and asked her, 'Mom, when you get older and you stop having periods, can you still enjoy having sex?' There was a pause, and she whispered, 'I really don't know.' I never asked or discussed with her anything intimate again.

Mother was at the acme of her beauty and her talents and the Americans went crazy about her. They made a great fuss of me, too – they loved my English accent. They said, 'I don't care what you say, just talk!'

Left-wing Theatre in the Thirties

PETER
I was jobless. One day I stood on a breadline to get a bowl of soup. To stand in a queue on the street in a line to move up slowly until it came your turn to get a bowl of soup is not per se a humiliating thing but it was not like the cafeteria in your school. The whole idea that here in the middle of the day in one of the biggest cities in the world – this was one of many breadlines where thousands of men stood patiently in line waiting to get a bowl of soup and possibly a crust of bread – adds up to a terrible sense of humiliation. You are being made to feel worthless. Nobody's doing it on purpose – nobody you know wants you to feel that way – but the net result is that you feel worthless. You feel, 'I'm not even good enough to get a little job to earn fifty cents to go and buy myself a couple of meals in a restaurant,' which in those days you could get for twenty-five cents. I stood on a breadline only once. It was too much for me to take.

One night when I had no place to sleep, I went to a flop-house. Again I stood in a queue with a long line of men outside this building which was a warehouse which they had fixed up as a barracks. Finally the line arrived at the entrance but before we could go in we had to go through a turnstile where we were sprayed from head to foot with some de-lousing powder – there was no escaping it. Of course there was also no escaping the thought that you were being treated like a herd of cattle. I survived the de-lousing experience and was ushered into this huge place where there were thousands of army cots. There was a thin mattress on each. There were no sheets, there was a blanket and there was a pillow. Nobody took off his clothes because there was no place to put them. You took off your shoes and hoped they wouldn't be stolen; some of the men put their shoes under their pillow. You covered yourself and slept through the night. I never went back.

One of the members of The Workers' Laboratory Theatre was a Canadian lad of Irish origin by the name of Curt Conway. He was just a lad of my age, nineteen, maybe twenty. Already a drunk, a good actor, he was sharing an apartment with his girlfriend, Bea, and another couple – a good-looking girl with a very good figure with a Japanese boyfriend who was a sculptor. There was room on a cot for me.

This apartment they had gotten from the government because they were all on Welfare. As I was a Canadian, illegally in the United States, I couldn't apply for Welfare. All of us in the apartment had to be fed but when the Relief cheque used to arrive, Bea bought a new blouse and there was never any money for food. She was a wacky little girl, very pretty and she had blouses! Somebody had to get a job, somebody had to earn some money. The Japanese sculptor wasn't making any money and his girlfriend wasn't working, and Curt was still getting no pay with The Workers' Laboratory Theatre.

I got a job conducting a drama group in the Bronx with an organisation called The Workmen's Circle, which was a working-class liberal progressive organisation. I earned six dollars a week for two sessions which was used to feed my little commune with Curt and Bea and the others. Even in those days, six dollars a week couldn't feed five people so I scouted around in our neighbourhood and found that if I waited, bananas which were selling for ten cents a dozen when fresh I could buy for four cents a dozen two days later. I bought ripe bananas by the dozen. I also found a bakery shop where the fresh bread, which cost six cents a loaf, I could buy for two cents two days later when it wasn't so fresh any more. I bought bread and I bought bananas and I had fierce arguments with Bea who said, 'Why don't you buy coffee sometimes?' I said, 'Bea dear, because you buy blouses. I'm the only one who is earning anything here and for six dollars, all you get from me is bananas and stale bread.' I didn't stay very long.

In the summer of 1935, I got a job as social director of a summer camp run by Followers of the Trail, a small organisation of working-class people. One weekend I had Zero Mostel up there for the entertainment programme. Zero was really a madman. He was funny because he was outrageous. After breakfast the Saturday of the weekend – I had him up to entertain on Saturday night – we got into a slanging match where we were insulting each other across the width of the dining room and throwing rolls at each other, and pieces of vegetable and the whole camp was rolling about on the floor in laughter because it was so funny, because Zero *made* it funny. I never felt that I was a comic. As I grew older I learned how to tell funny stories quite well but when I was young I didn't see myself as a comic actor. But with Zero anybody became a comedian.

Girls used to come to this camp who were not members of Followers of the Trail but they were friends of members. One of these visitors was a girl by the name of May Garelik. May was a very charming girl – not particularly good-looking. She had a nose that looked as though it had been broken – it hadn't been broken, but it looked like that. She was very short-sighted and when she didn't wear her glasses she squinted. But she had an attractive personality and a wonderful sense of humour. She worked in the publishing business. I didn't know it at the time, but again, like Basya, May was older than me. How much older? She said that she had been brought into America from Russia as a babe in arms and when her older brother had to go and register the family as new immigrants, they didn't register her. May said she did not know the date of her birth. For the second time in my life I got attached to an older woman. I went back to New York and started living with May. At first I didn't have a job which meant I was also living off May.

I was active in all the progressive, liberal, radical theatre life of New York. I had got to know many of the members of The Group Theatre, and my friends and I flocked to their productions. The Group Theatre did its first production in 1932 and around 1934 Clifford Odets, who was a member of The Group Theatre as one of the actors in the company, appeared with a script and they mounted the first performance of *Waiting For Lefty*, his first play. Elia Kazan had a leading role and he was a *fantastic* actor. Volcanic. Everything that Marlon Brando later had, Kazan had only more and better. That was one of the most exciting and exhilarating nights of my life.

I was a terrific admirer of The Group Theatre and became one of a bunch of young people who were called The Group Theatre Apprentices. This gave me the privilege of attending classes conducted by Harold Clurman, Lee Strasberg, Morris Carnovsky, Elia Kazan and by an actor by the name of Roman Bohnen – a wonderful teacher and a wonderful director. We were allowed to watch but not participate in them – so I watched and learned. We were also allowed to attend rehearsals.

When The Group Theatre produced a play, a musical, called *Johnny Johnson*, I got a part in it as an extra. This was my first paid professional job as an actor in New York. As well as being in the crowd, I had one little part where I sang. It was a war scene and on either side of the stage stood two priests. The other one was Paul Mann (a well-known Canadian actor, who later gave a brilliant performance as Lazar Wolf in the film of *Fiddler on the Roof*). He was an American preacher and I was a German preacher and we sang a duet, in which each side asks God to bring victory to the troops of his nation. The whole point was the stupidity of war. Both priests interceding with God for victory for their side.

The play unfortunately ran for only six weeks although it was a fascinating production. Lee Strasberg started to direct the play, but then Harold Clurman took over because Lee Strasberg was incapable of finishing a production. He would get so involved with the psychological intricacies, with the cabalistic interpretations of the meaning of each word that he could never get beyond the second act. And in those days, plays had three acts.

Harold Clurman finished the production. Harold used to splutter, Harold was full of words, he had a marvellous flow of language. He was very emotional and uncontrolled, shouting at the top of his voice and explaining things with an unending torrent of suggestions and images. He was very funny. He was very, very good.

Then I was offered a job as the drama teacher at Commonwealth College, a Labour university backed by trade unions and various middle-of-the-road and left-of-centre radical groupings. It was an attempt to create a university for working people based on – it's a strange phrase – a 'working-class ethos'. Commonwealth College was a place where young working people got scholarships from their trade unions to study the history of the Labour Movement, social studies and a certain amount of Marxist study.

I didn't get much pay – I got some pocket money – but I got my food and my housing, and what did I have to give in return? First of all, my labour – teachers, students, all belonged to various work teams. I was on the wood-cutting team. I was a big fellow, broad shoulders, and I was learning how to use an axe, how to cut down small trees. This was in a place called Mena, Arkansas, where we were surrounded by hard-bitten, tough, Southern American farmers for whom we were the Communist devils who had infiltrated from the North and they gave us a lot of trouble. Wood-cutting was very important, because that was the only source of heating that we had, but not more important than any of the other work. It was a quite marvellous place.

I didn't study myself but I kept my ears open. I was too busy teaching and directing plays. I did a production of *Waiting For Lefty* up against a mural of paintings with working-class themes. To put on *Waiting For Lefty* against that background was terribly exciting. I loved the production and the people involved were all very happy. However, I made up my mind that I was going to leave Commonwealth College because I had a letter of recommendation to the Workers' Theatre of Chicago.

I'm on the way to Chicago by bus in my lightweight clothes. Arkansas is in the South and has a very easy winter. Therefore I had come with only lightweight clothes, and now it's January, and as the bus is going further north, I am growing colder and colder. I have an address in Chicago of some Swedish people, Einar and Arvid Jakobsson, an elderly couple with no children of their own who were going to put me up. I arrive in Chicago and I am told which bus to take to my address. I'm on the bus, frozen – moving along in a strange, frozen city – the driver says to me, 'Hey, bud! This is where you get off.' I get off and cross in front of the bus, and ... bang! I'm knocked down by a car.

I wake up from the anaesthetic and the doctor tells me, 'You're lucky you haven't got a concussion. I just had to sew up your scalp.'

'Where am I?' I said.

'You're in Chicago.'

'Chicago? What am I doing in Chicago? Where in Chicago?'

'You're in a hospital.'

I left the hospital, found the piece of paper with the name of the family. I arrive at their home with a bandaged head. They're terrified when they see me but they take me in, feed me, try to warm me up and put me to bed.

Two days later, I went down to the Chicago Workers' Theatre. They were working on a play called *The Young Go First*, which was an anti-militaristic play, about the way that armies enlist young, unemployed, working-class boys. This was the winter of 1935–6, a period of massive unemployment. The man in charge of the theatre, who was also directing *The Young Go First*, was called Charles De Sheim. I designed the scenery – my first professional scenery-designing job.

I didn't have a room. The Swedish couple were very kind to me but it was too far, so I slept in the rehearsal room in the theatre. There were no beds, I slept on a big table which was left over from some production. I used to spread some curtains to make a mattress and stretch out on the table. I don't remember getting paid. I do remember going hungry.

Then a trade union organisation decided that they wanted a pageant to celebrate May Day, the great working-class holiday, and I became the director of this pageant. I started to have an affair with a tall girl, five foot ten inches in flat shoes, Polly Weill, when she participated as an actress in the pageant. I even went to a party in her huge apartment overlooking the shores of the lake. But it didn't last long. She was rich and I was poor. Her brother broke up the romance by taking us out to dinner in a very fancy place. I wore a vivid yellow shirt, didn't know how to order or how to behave. Polly was embarrassed. I went back to New York.

Adolescence in America

THELMA

New York. A high-school graduate, I worked as a counsellor in a summer camp for children. I did this for three summers. They were Jewish camps, a collection of small wooden buildings in a beautiful, wooded area in the Catskills in upstate New York; the activities were sporting, arts and crafts. Each camp was near a lake for swimming and boating. It was my first experience of teaching, of caring for children, of earning money. Once I had had some drama training, I was a Drama Counsellor. I slept in a bunk with six young children for whom I was responsible and I also directed and was in charge of the drama programme. Although yours was a summer camp for adults and mine was a summer camp for children, you'll know what I mean when I say it wasn't easy.

By the summer of 1941 my problem remained – how to get an uninterrupted education. I wanted to go to university, but I would not dream of asking Uncle Henry to pay the high fees and I was not eligible for any of the free colleges because I was not an American citizen. Luckily I got a scholarship to a small Junior College in New York called Finch. In return for the scholarship, I worked for a few hours a week, in the main office and in the library. Sounds incredible today, but the full fee for tuition at this very prestigious and upper-class girls college was $700 a year. My scholarship was for $500. Dad applied to the Bank of England and was given special permission to send the extra $200. We moved to 106 West 76 Street, the house of Mrs Heck, a German lady, and instead of a room in an apartment we had our own apartment in a typical New York brownstone house. One big bed-sitting room and our own kitchen and bathroom. Central heating was included in the rent but we weren't used to central heating and found it unbearably hot. We opened the window, and Mrs Heck would come storming in saying, 'You are trying to heat up Manhattan? You are vasting my central heating!'

I cannot remember any period of my life in which I felt such unalloyed happiness and achievement as my two years in Finch. It was *the* turning point in my life. In Finch I found my career, I found my self-confidence, I found encouragement, praise and love. When I took you there thirty years later you said how lucky I was to have been to a small college and you were right, a feeling that everybody knew everybody else, and everybody cared. Recently Finch, like many small colleges, had to close and when it closed something very precious was lost.

The principal of the college was Mrs Cosgrave; she had founded Finch in the early years of the century. In a Junior College you studied for only two years, and specialised from the beginning, unlike a four-year college where you did general studies for the first two years. So I had to choose a Major subject. When asked by Dean Kincannon what my special interests were, I replied, 'My father thinks that I have talent to be a writer, but I would very much (and I practically whispered it) like to be an actress.' She said, 'You can do both here. We have a writing course – fiction writing – and you can major in Theatre Arts.' That was the moment when my fate was sealed. I had no aptitude for fiction writing, which was just a once-a-week lesson, but Theatre Arts – ten hours a week – became my passion. What a chance for a provincial Leeds girl of sixteen. There was a fully equipped theatre where I learned to build scenery, do sound effects, run the lighting board (after this I had the dubious honour of being the only member of my immediate family who could change a plug or mend a fuse). We put on excellent productions. The men's parts would be played by professional actors and the New York critics came to see us.

Finch had the reputation of being a finishing school for rich girls. That was only partly true. It was a serious

academic institution and ahead of its time. The head of the
Theatre Arts department was a petite, blonde bundle of
energy called Frances Pole. One of those gifted teachers
who send you out of classes flying – there was an aura about
her, and a wisdom that went far beyond the boundaries of
theatre studies. I adored her. She is still a magnificent
future-oriented, vibrant lady in her mid-eighties. And because
I was an English evacuee, all the teachers made a special
fuss of me, many inviting me to their homes. As a scholarship girl, the college gave me money for my books, a loan
which I could pay back whenever I liked in the fullness of
time.

I scrupulously refused to spend anything on luxuries, only
on necessities. It was part of the Theatre Arts course to go as
a group to Broadway shows. The first play we were to see
was a preview of *Candle in the Wind* by Maxwell Anderson,
starring Helen Hayes. But I considered buying theatre seats
a luxury so the day of the performance I told Miss Pole, as
offhandedly as I could, that I wouldn't be able to join them.
'You're coming tonight,' she said. 'If you feel embarrassed
about taking a gift of a ticket, you can do some extra work in
the department to pay for it.' I went that night to see *Candle
in the Wind*. In the first interval Miss Pole took me on one
side. 'Thelma,' she said, 'there's somebody at the college
who has known great kindness in England and wants to
repay it. She has put aside a sum of money to pay for all your
theatre seats for the two years you will be at the college.' I
gasped at such generosity. 'Who?' I asked. 'She wishes to
remain anonymous.' I *never* found out who it was.

Each spring there was a big social occasion called the
Finch Ball, held at Sherrys on Park Avenue. I was working in
the office one day when the director of the office, Tanya
Lehtinen, said to me, 'You are going to the Finch Ball, aren't
you?' A luxury, I wouldn't dream of spending money on a
ticket for a ball. Again I mumbled in embarrassment, 'No,
no I can't go,' 'Oh yes, you can! Come with me.' She took me

upstairs to the fashion design department, run by Christine Block. 'Please would you design and make a dress for Thelma to go to the ball,' said Tanya. 'With pleasure.' Tanya turned to me, 'There will be two tickets for you to go to the ball, all you have to do is to find yourself an escort.' Now I know how Cinderella must have felt! Mother, by this time, was working as the receptionist at the British Consulate in New York. She sat at the entrance and said, in her most English and musical voice, 'Can I help you?' She found me an English naval officer in uniform to take me to the ball. I was far too busy and far too young to have any boyfriends.

For two years, from 1941 to 1943, I grew as an actress and as a person. For the first production I did sound effects for *Ladies in Retirement*. This was before the days of recorded effects and for the rain storm I took handfuls of uncooked rice with the right hand and dropped them on to a sloping dress box held in the left hand – that was the rain beating down. Later I played leading parts, like Olivia in *Night Must Fall*; I was learning my craft from wonderful teachers and in ideal circumstances. It was not surprising that, along with another girl, I was the first girl to graduate from Finch 'With Distinction' as a result of my having been on every Dean's List. For graduation I had a white cap and gown and walked down the aisle of a church to the music of 'Land of Hope and Glory' with the feeling that I could achieve anything.

I was a prudish teenager. I wanted to save kissing and cuddling and all that goes with it until I got married. It didn't work out that way, far from it. But in those days that was my ambition. I wanted to have one man for life. I lived a lot in the fantasy world. I used to have daydreams as to what would happen to me in the future. There were two major ones – that I would become a famous actress and take a bow at the end of the show with the audience applauding and cheering. In the other, I would marry a handsome Jewish boy – intelligent, kind, witty, tall and of course wealthy – and he would be the one man for me all my life. I fantasised the wedding and having the first baby, then I got bored with the fantasy and had to start again with somebody else. But I lived a lot in that fantasy world until maybe into my twenties.

After I graduated from Finch in June 1943 I stayed another year and a half in America doing many jobs. The last year Mother and I managed to support ourselves without help from Uncle Henry. One night I went to babysit at the house of a rabbi, Rabbi Granison. I used to walk home at night without any fear but the rabbi insisted on accompanying me, and he took me to a café and bought me an ice-cream. I told him about my Orthodox Jewish family – he was a Reform rabbi and had a congregation in Great Neck, Long Island. Next day he phoned me, 'I'm looking for a teacher for my Sunday School. After our conversation last night it struck me that you would be ideal. Would you like to teach nine year olds Jewish history?' I bravely said, 'Yes, I'd love to.' Little did he know that I knew *nothing* of Jewish history. I hurried to the library to learn what I could for the first lesson but I was full of doubt about my abilities as a teacher and very frightened. The following Sunday I caught a train to Great Neck and met the other teachers among whom was a very big, corpulent Rabbinical student called Bill Kramer. I confessed my fears to Bill, 'I really don't know what I'm going to teach today.' He said, 'It's very easy. Walk into the classroom, take a chalk and write on the blackboard W I G O D E R. For the first half-hour you teach them how to pronounce your name. Then get them to read a chapter of the text book. If they ask you a question and you don't know the answer, you say to them, "That was a very interesting question, I'm glad you asked that. I want you to go home, look it up and bring me the answer next week."'

I enjoyed teaching Sunday school and I learned with the children. I taught there for two years. Bill Kramer and I became close friends. He wanted to be my boyfriend but I wasn't going to start all that nonsense! But I was very happy for him to take me out. We used to go every week to a different synagogue and that opened my eyes. Not only Orthodox but Conservative and Reform, Ashkenazi and Sephardi – the small synagogues of immigrant communities from Bukhara, from Morocco. I'd no idea there were so many Jewish ways of praying. Bill, for all his huge bulk, was delicate and kind, he danced well, he was intelligent and inventive, and he made me laugh a lot.

Five years after my return to England I received a telephone call from Bill. We had completely lost touch with each other. He had come to London to search for me. He'd never forgotten me and he was determined that I was the one he was going to marry. When he arrived he looked in the phone book and found the name, Wigoder – Lionel Wigoder. Lionel was a cousin of my father's who was a dentist in Sloane Street. Lionel gave him my phone number. I was living in London at the time. 1949.

Bill had qualified as a Reform Rabbi and was by this time living and working in San Pedro, which is the port of Los Angeles in California. We met. He was an impressive figure – he was still bulky and tall, and the years had added authority and self-confidence. He had a sharp non-conformist brain, a lively irreverence and still retained a quick and delightful sense of humour. And he wanted to marry me. I refused. Although by this time I was twenty-four and no longer living in a fantasy world as far as men were concerned, I was still hoping that the man I married would be a man I was in love with. (I had to wait twenty-one more years for that to happen – but it happened!) I liked Bill, I enjoyed Bill, I respected Bill – but I wasn't in love with him. But Bill had come a long way to press his suit and he wouldn't take 'no' for an answer.

That summer, wherever I went – there was Bill. I went to a Theatre Exhibition in Birmingham – Bill was there. I went to visit my parents in Leeds – Bill was there.

PETER
What did your parents think of him?

THELMA
They were firmly opposed to the notion of my marrying
him. He was too unconventional for them – he was unlike
any rabbi they had known. He believed in enjoying life to
the full – he called himself a hedonist – and he had no time
for orthodox rules of religion and unthinking cant. He was
big and blustery and they felt he was not right for me.
Added to which, they did not want me to go off and live in
California.

I went with my parents and Geoffrey for a holiday in
Dinard, a seaside resort on the Brittany coast in France.
When we went down onto the beach on the first day – there
was Bill. He left before we did, and when I went on my own
for a short stay in Paris, there was Bill at six o'clock in the
morning on the platform to meet me off the train. He had
booked in at the same hotel. Paris is beautiful, Paris is
romantic and I started to wonder: Nobody, nobody has ever
loved me this much, nobody has ever paid me this much
attention. Perhaps nobody else ever will ... maybe I will
grow to love him, maybe I shouldn't throw away this
opportunity that may never come again. Under the spell of
Paris and the influence of his all-embracing love, on our last
day instead of saying, 'No' I said, 'Yes. I will marry you.'

Bill went back to San Pedro and I stayed in England. As
soon as he'd gone my doubts returned. I thought, I've made
a mistake, I mustn't marry this man, I don't love him. But his
long, loving letters came every day, and parcels, and phone
calls. I wrote to him of my doubts. He assured me he had
enough love for the two of us and that all would be well after
we were wed. He left me in September 1949 and in a kind of
stupor and unable to stop the ball rolling, I made preparations for our wedding on 12th June 1950. I had ten young
cousins to be my bridesmaids and around two hundred

people were invited to the reception. Then my grandfather
– Grandpa Sim – took very ill with cancer of the liver.

Bill arrived exactly two weeks before the wedding. I went
to the airport to meet him and when I caught my first
glimpse of him I was shattered. Going round and round in
my brain was: I can't go through with this, what am I going
to do? The hall for the wedding reception was booked, the
presents had arrived and all of us, including the ten bridesmaids, had our dresses made and paid for.

At that time Mona and I were sharing a flat in East Sheen.
The evening Bill arrived, Mona got a call that Grandpa was
dying and would we go at once to Leeds. Mona was acting in
the West End in *A Streetcar Named Desire* with Vivien Leigh,
but the management agreed to let her go to her dying father
and we hired a car and driver to take us from London to
Leeds. Mona sat in the front with the driver and I sat in the
back with Bill. This was long before the days of the M1
motorway and it was a long drive in the dark. At a time of
crisis and distress I should have felt close to the man I was
about to marry – but I didn't. I wanted to get away from
him. I wanted to scream and make a scene but this wasn't
the place and that isn't in my nature. It was a nightmare.

When we arrived in Leeds, we dropped Bill off at a hotel
and I said to Mona, 'I can't go through with the marriage.'
Poor Mona! Driving through the night, not knowing if she
would be in time to see her father still alive and suddenly
confronted with this. There was nothing she could do, there
was nothing I could do because two days later Grandpa
died. Poor Bill! He had come flying over from California full
of happiness and hope to get married, to be confronted by a
cool bride and a family in mourning. There is a Jewish
tradition that you must not cancel a wedding because of a
death. It was expected that ten days after Grandpa's funeral,
the wedding would go ahead with the two hundred guests
and the ten bridesmaids.

I was in despair. The house was full of wedding presents,

and I was answering each one with a thank you letter. Mother was fussing over all the final details. Friends and family were planning to come long distances to be with us. At the same time that we were 'sitting shiva' – in accordance with Jewish tradition, for a week after the funeral, friends come to pay condolence calls while the family sit on low stools (symbolic of sitting on the bare earth).

I was very fond of my Auntie Lily, Grandma's sister – a wise and humorous elderly lady with whom I had a special relationship. She had already arrived from her home in Birmingham to stay with her daughter Fay in Sheffield in order to be present at the wedding. I phoned her up and said, 'Can I come and talk to you?' She said, 'Of course.' I spent a day with her in Sheffield and poured out my heart. 'What should I do?' She advised, 'Tell him you want to postpone the wedding – maybe you feel this way because of the sadness of the death of Sim. Whatever you do, don't go ahead with the marriage just because everything is arranged and it is expected of you. Listen to your heart.'

I returned to Leeds and, in the sitting room of our house, told Bill that I wanted to postpone the wedding. He said, 'No, no postponement – it's either now or never.' I said, 'I'm so sorry, Bill. I'm afraid it's never.' Bill stayed in our house that night, ostensibly to sleep on the couch in the lounge. I lay awake in my bed listening as, melodramatic as it sounds, he howled like a wounded animal. He was heartbroken. I had made my decision only six days before the wedding.

There are not many things I've done in my life that I am ashamed of, but the next part of the story is hard to tell. About two years later I was in a touring show and I was in Cardiff. I was driving through the centre of the city one day with friends and through the window of the car I spotted Bill Kramer. He had come all the way to England again to find me and to try to persuade me once more to change my mind. I did a dreadful thing. After the performance that evening I worked out that he would be waiting for me at the stage door, so I went out of the theatre via the front of house to avoid speaking to him. There was no reason why I shouldn't have seen him – it was cowardly and hurtful and something I'm going to have to answer for when I reach the pearly gates.

I heard about him through mutual friends in Los Angeles. He became an eminent rabbi and a leading personality, for a while he dressed in hippy clothes with a circlet of flowers on his head. He appeared on radio and television, and it was he who performed the Jewish marriages of Elizabeth Taylor and Sammy Davis Jnr. Later he also qualified as a lawyer. My very first visit to Los Angeles was in 1980 with you. I had a great urge to see him and to apologise. I phoned him and he seemed pleased to hear from me – his wife had just died, he told me, and he had two grown-up boys. He invited us over to visit him. By this time he was around sixty, with a big beard and fiery eyes, like one imagines the prophets to have looked. He greeted us with great warmth and friendship and it was evident that he liked you very much. While you were out of the room he said, 'I do like your Peter – he's my kind of guy.' He gave me a beautiful shawl which had belonged to his wife. At last I had the opportunity to say what I had wanted to say for thirty years: 'I'm sorry.'

Trials of a Stage Manager

PETER
One of the assistant leaders at The Workers' Laboratory Theatre was Steve Karnot, the tallest man in the group – he was six foot four, had a big, black, full Stalin moustache – a very impressive figure. He was invited to stage a pageant for a Communist-front organisation. He took me to work as his

assistant director – this was years before the Chicago pageant – and stage manager. It was a big affair, to be staged at Madison Square Garden, employing a workers' volunteer orchestra, some workers' choruses, workers' dance groups and some volunteer actors. It was done on the cheap.

Two days before the performance, Steve Karnot decamped with one of the girls from a dance group, leaving behind his wife Greta – a beautiful red-haired girl in the Collective – and me, landed with running this pageant and getting it on the stage as promised.

The next two nights I hardly slept. I was still the stage manager – now I was also the de facto director. I didn't try to change Steve's direction but I had to pull it all together – you know what goes on two nights before a big show – confusion, uncertainty, indecision – and earthquake tremors of impending disaster. We had rented an empty warehouse for rehearsals, set construction, costume storage. Rehearsals went on literally morning, noon and night: actors, dancers choral groups, orchestra ... during seventy-two hours I didn't go home, I'd lie down for a couple of hours on piles of stage curtains. I was all of twenty years old. The day of our show hundreds of our people connected with the pageant are straggling in. We were not allowed into Madison Square until late as they had another performance in the afternoon. All our people have to be assigned to dressing rooms, they have to be grouped, organised, orientated. There was time for a brief dress rehearsal, entrances and exits. We had no time to do the numbers. I couldn't work out the lighting – it would have to be improvised during the running of the show.

For running the show I had a high stool at the side of the stage hidden by a screen from the audience who filled Madison Square Garden. I had on a headphone and microphone which put me in contact with eight booths, points of lighting under the roof of the Garden. There was a commentary read from another booth. I was connected to the reader. The conductor of the orchestra had headphones, so I could talk to him during the run of the show. I could talk to the lights, I could talk to the music and I could talk to assistant stage managers. We started to run the show in front of an audience of twenty-two thousand five hundred people.

We get to a cue and the orchestra is supposed to play: 'A-hunting we will go, a-hunting we will go. Hi-ho the merry-oh, a-hunting we will go.' No, the conductor doesn't come in on cue. Silence. He doesn't hear me screaming at him. Something has to happen. If the people on the stage don't hear the music cue they won't do the choreography that goes with that music. What does Pinye do? I switched on the microphone which can be heard in the auditorium and I sang it! It was heard in all the lighting booths, it was heard through the entire Madison Square Garden and the people onstage did their choreography.

At the very end of the show the orchestra struck up 'The Internationale'. As they finished singing it, I give the last cue – 'House lights on,' and I fainted! Slid off my stool and disappeared under the stage. People came looking for me and shouted, 'Pete, where are you, where are you?' After a few moments I came back to consciousness: 'I'm down here!'

After the Chicago pageant, I got a job on The Federal Theatre Project which was part of the Works Progress Administration, one of the inventions of the first Roosevelt regime to pull the country out of the doldrums of unemployment. My friend Nicholas Ray, who had been a member of The Workers' Laboratory Theatre at the same time that I was, hired me as a 'special aide'. Nick was a big six-foot-three American. We shared an interest in architecture, in theatre, in movies and he was the stage manager of something called The Living Newspaper. They hired a staff of newspaper writers, an editor, an editorial board and leg-men who went out and did research, then they brought all the material together and created a documentary play out of factual data collected as though for a newspaper. Instead of being printed as a newspaper it was acted out on the stage.

The one that Nick was stage manager of was called *Injunction Granted*, a history of labour in the courts. It tried to show how prejudiced, how unfair, how evil were the machinations of the courts and the justices any time there was a case involving labour. When there was a legal argument between a trade union and employers, the employers won hands down. They had only to apply to the judge for an injunction to stop the strike, or any other action, and they had labour bound hand and foot, helpless, in the face of court judgments.

To direct this play, they brought in a young director who hadn't proved himself yet on Broadway. He'd been abroad and studied in Russia and Germany, and he knew what was going on in world theatre. His name was Joseph Losey. Nicholas Ray was the stage manager, and both these men later became famous and important film directors in Hollywood – great directors.

Losey asked for, and was given, a cast of about a hundred and twenty-five – there were mass scenes, demonstrations and fights – you name it, it was in that show. He also had dozens of technicians, because he used rear projection, and a Linnebach projector – a special projector for transparent slides that allows scenes to be projected on a backdrop – it has a wide angle enabling large scenes to be projected. He used slide projectors, newsreel films, and there was a huge constructivist set, with stairways and ramps. In one of my bits as an extra I had to do a flying vault over the side of the construction and land on my feet about nine or ten feet below. I was scared shitless every night but I did it. When you are young you do it and you think about it later.

There were one hundred and sixty-nine light and mechanical cues. I know because later I took over from Nick. My job when I was hired was to be an extra and one of five assistant stage managers. Each of us was assigned a group of people whom we were responsible for. There was one old man in the show whose name was Fuller Mellish senior who was then eighty-four years old. His job in the show was to walk across the stage between all of these great events – coming and going, exits and entrances – and when he got to the centre he said, 'Injunction not granted,' and walked off. He was playing a historical judge who, for the first time, did not grant an injunction to an employer and he found for the employees. That's all he had to do, but he was eighty-four years old, so it was quite a responsibility, mine, to get him downstairs on time, then shove him on stage to start him across. You would hear the audience taking a long breath as he hobbled across the stage, got to the centre, spoke his line and went off to a huge round of applause. Unfortunately, he died during the run of the show.

Nick announces that he has been offered a very good job in Washington under the auspices of Mrs Roosevelt and I took over. Then the government decided to cut the budget, and they decided to cut me. Thus started a period where every Friday afternoon, when the pay cheques were handed out, I got my pay cheque plus a pink slip. A pink slip was a note of dismissal. Every Friday I was fired. Nick had trained me and Nick had given me his cue book and taught me how to run those cues – I was the only one who could run that show. So every Monday I was re-hired. This went on for a couple of months – and it was tough. Joe Losey was very sympathetic, he said, 'I'm sorry kid, I can't help you. All I can do is re-hire you after they fire you.'

Into the Real World

THELMA
As soon as I graduated from Finch I went to Yale Drama

School. Yale, one of the most famous universities in the world with a renowned drama school. My friends were very impressed, especially as Yale was an all-male university. But the drama school was a post-graduate course and women were allowed. After a lifetime of all-girl schools, to be on a campus with all those gorgeous young men...

Yale University was beautiful – much of the architecture pseudo-Gothic. Trees and green lawns with beautiful young people lolling around. The library was just like a cathedral and Walter Pritchard Eaton, one of the distinguished lecturers in our department, told how he once entered the library, walked the entire length of the nave to reach the desk under the stained-glass window at which the librarian sat, solemnly crossed himself and walked out again. The theatre department had two fine theatres – a large auditorium which served the whole town of New Haven, Connecticut, where Yale is situated, plus a small experimental theatre. Unlike our little theatre at Finch, the Yale theatres were professionally equipped with up-to-date lighting and sound.

I was influenced by advice from my parents: 'Qualify for a fall-back career in case you don't succeed as an actress.' My experience in summer camps had made me interested in directing and teaching. I had visions of starting the Children's Theatre movement in England. So I majored in directing and also took courses in acting. The chance to study, to work in the theatre, to be part of the main regional theatre, *and* to be part of university life was an ideal combination. When I go for an interview with an American director, I enjoy throwing in the fact that I studied at Yale Drama School and they are always impressed. What I don't mention is that I stayed only for a summer semester.

The last year in America was full of activity. I tried to get a job as an actress, but without success. So I pursued my second choice – working with children. I taught speech and drama at the Dwight High School in Englewood, New Jersey. This was a large and excellent school for girls and I was treated as a real teacher, as if I'd had a teaching degree or certificate. I continued teaching Sunday School in Long Island and I cared for three year olds at the nursery school at the Young Mens Hebrew Association, the YMHA, on 92nd Street.

As well as teaching, I ushered at concerts at the YMHA and worked as an extra in the ballet at the Metropolitan Opera House – one of the crowd. I earned a dollar a night. The pay may not have been great but it was the nearest I came to performing. I appeared in two ballets, *Petrouchka* with Leonid Massine, once conducted by Stravinsky himself, and *Fair at Sorochinsk*, in which Anton Dolin danced on point, a skill otherwise exclusively reserved for the ladies.

One night our conductor was Sir Thomas Beecham, and one night another item on the programme, which I watched from the wings, was a new ballet by a new composer, Leonard Bernstein, and a new choreographer, Jerome Robbins. The ballet was *Fancy Free* on which they based the film *On the Town*. I didn't actually speak to any of these glittering names, of course. Just stood there in my Victorian costume and gazed agog.

In the summer of 1944, Mother said, 'We must go back to England. It isn't fair to leave Daddy on his own any longer.' She had loved the American years as much as I had and was as reluctant to return. But she was right – there was no choice, we had to return.

My teenage years were golden. It sounds as if I spent all my time in New York studying and working, but that's not true. Intense though I was, priggish though I tended to be, I had a lot of fun – dances when the boy brought a corsage, girlfriends, free concerts, window-shopping. A trip to Washington, two trips to Montreal, the second time so that we could immigrate officially into the US and be allowed to work. Parties. Trips to Albany. The spectacular Worlds Fair, hot pastrami and Howard Johnson's ice-cream. The Frick museum and blossoms in Central Park. Bright lights and food and laughter. Getting to know my lovely mother. Growing up. Oh yes, I had a very happy war.

On exactly the same date we had sailed from England four years previously, 6th October, we sailed from New York to return to England. This was 1944, some seven months before the end of the war in Europe. The boat was a small cruise ship converted into a troop carrier. Again there were no facilities – no comforts, we slept in hammocks on converted decks and there was one big washroom shared by all the passengers, with a row of metal basins. The voyage took ten days, the same exactly as four years earlier. I was put in charge of two young, unaccompanied children, and I also took it upon myself to organise some sort of entertainment for the passengers. I did plays with the children and concerts with the adults – this wasn't like a cruise with deck games and swimming pools – there was nothing, not even a library.

On 16th October 1944, I arrived back in England and a most important and formative period of my life was over. Although I am not combative by nature, I have spent the rest of my life leaping to the defence if ever I hear Americans criticised. I was there from the age of fifteen to nineteen, never did a young girl receive more kindness, generosity, encouragement and friendship than did I during those four unforgettable years.

Book III

Volunteer for Liberty

PETER

I was in my apartment. 1936. Either late October or November. The *New York Times* was delivered at the door and I always read it as I had my breakfast. There, on the front page of the *New York Times* was a photograph six columns wide and eight inches high. It was a photograph of a street in Madrid, on the sidewalk they had laid out the corpses of eight young children, victims of the first civilian bombing of Madrid.

I looked at this. I gulped. I was not merely moved, I was torn apart. It's a cliché to say my heart was bleeding, but I really think my heart was bleeding as I looked at that photograph. I said to myself, 'Oh my God, I can't live in a world where things like this are allowed to happen. I have to fight it.' At that moment I made up my mind to volunteer to fight in Spain. Spain had been in the news since 18th July 1936.

Later in my life, after years of self-analysis, I came to have a much clearer understanding of what drove me to this momentous decision, to risk my life in Spain, but at that particular moment it was an intense emotional reaction. I hated Hitlerism. I hated what it stood for and I hated his carrying out in Spain what, until then, had been a theory of the German General Staff, the theory of *Schrecklichkeit*, which means the use of horror as a weapon of war. To horrify the citizenry. To destroy their will to resist, their will to fight.

I went to the telephone and called a friend. 'How do I join the International Brigades to get to Spain?' He said, 'The only way that I know of is through the Communist Party.' I

said, 'OK.' They had organised a mobilisation apparatus.
There were doctors, secretaries, recording officials. You
had to be examined very carefully and classified A1 TOP
HEALTHY because, ironically, they didn't want to send some
weakling to Spain to be killed. They wanted only the
strongest, the healthiest, the best. I passed the test and was
accepted. 'Now you wait until we let you know where, when
you go, what you do.'

I waited a couple of months until I got my marching
orders. I was to sail to Europe on the first leg of the journey
to Paris, France, on a little Dutch motor ship called the SS
Volendam. I informed my family. My father understood so
well my need to go to Spain, because if he were a young man
possibly he would have gone too, that was consistent with his
character and with his modus operandi. He came down to
meet me in New York, and we met at a railway station. We
walked out of the station and we stood in the street where a
lot of cars were parked. We stood between two cars and my
father opened his little suitcase and he pulled out a pint
bottle of whisky. I remember the name on the label. The Isle
of Mull. It was a Scotch Malt whisky. The first time in my life
I tasted it. But of course it meant much more to me than a
bottle of whisky. It meant to me that my father finally
accepted my manhood.

It was the end of January 1937 when I packed my bags and
got on the SS *Volendam* to sail for Europe. Then I was
in Paris at a Communist centre in a working-class area
with a large crowd of boys from all over the world, fellow
volunteers. By now it was early February 1937. They stripped
us of any of our belongings that had any real worth. To prepare myself for this trip I had bought myself a new raincoat.
I figured a good raincoat would come in useful. I had seen a
lot of films where the young heroes always had wonderful
trench coats and that's how I saw myself. I also had a pretty
good wristwatch and some good clothes. They said to us,
'You won't need any of these clothes where you are going

and we don't want you to be recognised as foreigners, we want you to look as French as possible. We're going to take your clothes and we're going to give you some of ours.' We got some *shmatte* clothes, real rags – French trousers, sweaters, berets and coats, pea-jackets, a naval cut jacket. It was a cold February. I never saw my watch or my trench coat again.

Then we were bundled off. The first part of the trip was on buses. We stopped to eat at Lyons – it took a day to get there. Back on the bus we were surprised to see French gendarmes in the street, the men who were running the traffic, giving us the left-wing salute, which is the right arm lifted half-way up with the clenched fist near the head. Our French disguise couldn't have been very convincing. We disembarked from the bus at Carcassonne, in the south of France at the foothills of the Pyrenees, where we were put up in farmers' houses.

I slept that night in an attic which was open to the birds – the entire floor was covered with bird shit. I hadn't been brought up in a wealthy home but I was still a little too refined for this. It was very hard for me to put down my coat on the bird shit, thinking that tomorrow I'll have to get up and put it on and how the hell do I brush off this crap? Surprisingly enough we slept. Very early in the morning we were called down and given breakfast.

We waited at the farm until evening to meet the mountain guides who were going to lead us across the Pyrenees into Spain. The guide we drew was a Catalan who spoke Catalan, Spanish and French. The officials who were in charge, party workers, asked, 'Who speaks French around here?' I said, '*Moi. Je suis Canadien.*' 'OK. You'll do. You walk behind the guide and if he gives any instructions, you translate it into English, and if you know any other languages...' We started to walk and at first it wasn't too difficult. The hills were low. It was up and down the hills. Then it grew difficult: the mountains of the Pyrenees are not high, but they're high enough. The guide set a pretty tough pace; the way I kept up with him was that my eyes were on his feet and every step he took, I took exactly the same step. Every stone he trod on, I trod on as well. It was tough to keep up with him, but I did. Periodically he would stop and say, '*Pas de fumer.*' The lights would give us away to the border guards. I said, 'No smoking, guys. *Nicht rauchen.*' I knew enough German from my Yiddish. And, of course, I translated into Yiddish. All along the line there were people who spoke different languages, so there were Germans who could translate into Czech. There were Czechs who could translate into Yugoslav. There were Yugoslavs who couldn't translate for anybody!

Overnight. At dawn we reached the peak of the hills. There was snow on the ground. It was chilly, but there was sunshine so we didn't feel the cold. The guide said, '*Maintenant vous êtes en Espagne* ... You are in Spain.' I translated, there was a little shout went up, a little hurrah. In the group there was a big, burly American boy who had served in the National Guard. He had been a sergeant. He was a natural-born sergeant. He was big, he was deep-chested. He had no neck and a funny little head squatting right on his shoulders. 'OK,' he said. 'Form up!' What the hell is 'Form up'? I'd never heard the expression. He said, 'Get into line. I'm going to organise you.' He organised us. Somebody had a red handkerchief and somebody got a twig and tied the red handkerchief to the twig, and he said, 'We'll go in singing.' We started to sing 'The Internationale' which was the only song we all shared. We had all come out of the left-wing working-class background and that was the great revolutionary hymn. We started to sing 'The Internationale' and marched across the border into Spain.

We who went to Spain were a real *mélange*. The Canadians and the Americans came out of different backgrounds, they were the children of Hungarian immigrants or Yugoslav or Czechoslovak or Ukrainian. Already a great variety of people. When we came to Paris we were mixed with other groups –

there were German anti-Fascists who had managed to
escape from Germany; some had been in concentration
camps and escaped. There were men from Poland. There
were men from most of the European countries, men from
Romania, from Bulgaria, from Palestine, South America and
the Antipodes ... this truly was an International Brigade.
Here, for the first time in history, you had men of the same
political belief coming together from different parts of the
world, ready to march under the same flag and to the same
tune. It wasn't so clear to me then. I was excited when we
crossed the border with that pathetic little flag and that
pathetic chorus, but I didn't then realise the tremendous
significance of what was happening. Most of the world
hasn't yet realised the significance of the formation of the
International Brigade. We stopped Hitler and Mussolini at
the gates of Madrid. General Franco had announced to the
world that he would complete his insurrection in three
weeks. With our help the people of Spain held out against
enormous odds for thirty-two months. History will record
that we delayed Hitler's timetable for the conquest and
destruction of Europe, *und morgen die gantze velt*, and
tomorrow the world. It was a period of tremendous events
on the stage of world history. To this day the majority of
people alive in the world do not realise what a debt they owe
to the people of Spain for their foolhardy, valorous decision
to oppose the Fascist rebellion of Francisco Franco and his
fellow generals, those myrmidons of the great, worldwide
Fascist conspiracy led by Germany, Italy and Japan.

The trip down the mountainside leading towards our first
village stop inside Spain – it was a beautiful spring morning,
the light was clear and brilliant and, as we came lower down,
we saw the cultivated mountainsides, all terraced with vines
and other kinds of agriculture growing. We were captivated
by what we saw. Our first stop was the village of Set Casas,
which means seven houses. Here the war started for us.
They gave us food and drink, because we'd had very little

since we'd started out from that attic in Carcassonne – there hadn't been time to stop and eat. There wasn't much to eat; all the time we were in Spain we were hungry. We ate mostly mouldy chickpeas, *garabanzos*, and olive oil. I didn't think that olive oil could get spoiled, but it seems it can or maybe it was inferior to begin with, but we had these mouldy gara-banzos cooked in unpleasant-tasting olive oil. Fortunately, later on, we were in places where there were oranges so we used to pick them off the trees and that's what saved us.

A man in blue coveralls, looking like Winston Churchill, came in to the house where we were gathered and he said, 'Could you all give me your passports.' We didn't know who this was and he didn't speak English, he spoke Spanish and French. With our system of translation we got it across to all the others that this man was asking for our passports. We were so young and so naive that some of us were ready to give up our passports. We thought this was part of the procedure, like the way we had given up our good clothes in France to some comrades who said we didn't need them. I've always wondered who got that beautiful raincoat of mine.

I was in the centre of things because of my so-called language ability. I said, 'I'm willing to give him my passport – what about you guys?' A lot of naive guys – just as stupid as I was – start to pull out their passports. Until some of the older German comrades said, 'Idioten! Idiots! *Vos machen sie?* What are you doing? You don't give up your passport. Who is this guy? Let's find out who he is.' This in German. Which I roughly translate. There's this big to-do about the passports and the Germans are holding on to this guy, saying, 'Wait a minute, we're not through with you.' It turns out that he's a member of the POUM, the Trotskyite wing of the Communist Party. They wanted the passports so that they could infiltrate spies into the Soviet Union for their purposes on our passports. When the German comrades questioned him and finally found out who he was, they said,

'Hang on to your passports and don't be such assholes in the future!'

That was our first taste of what it meant to be involved in a civil war. Later we were to learn that in the course of the three years of resistance to the Franco rebellion the people of Spain went into the fight with pitchforks because they had no other weapons – the armaments from Russia were piled up at the French border. The Socialist French prime minister, Leon Blum, was part of the agreement with America and England to observe 'Non-intervention'. To be neutral. So the arms, which came from Czechoslovakia and from the Soviet Union, didn't get across into Spain.

Later, when we started to add it all up, it was calculated there were over a million people killed in that war. Spain at that time had a population of twenty-four million, so one million is more than four per cent of the population – executed, tortured – both sides, the Republicans were just as fierce as the Fascists. The Fascists led by Francisco Franco introduced the technique of wholesale executions. They walk up to somebody's door, knock on the door, they say, 'Come outside,' and they shoot him down in the street before the eyes of the wife and children. We didn't know this at the time. We were involved in our immediate problems, like learning to hang on to our passports. We did give up our passports later when we arrived in Albacete, the administrative centre for the International Brigades. From Set Casas we were moved by truck to a place called Figueras. In Figueras there was an old fifteenth-century fortress – tremendous walls, tremendously thick. Dirty, ancient, *vast*, occupied by Napoleon when he invaded Spain. Here we found others who had preceded us and others would join us. We were kept here for three days.

It was a pretty tough crew that I was with: there were a lot of little, young shmucks like me, but there were some older men who were sailors and marine workers. And they are tough guys. Their idea of fun was to pick me up and throw me in the air from one group of men to another, just for fun! If the victim falls and cracks his head, that's too bad. I was terrified of these tough guys, huge, tough men – even when they were little they were tough!

The food was of such an evil taste that it is difficult to describe. We all had diarrhoea. There were no toilets, just some holes in the wall in this ancient fortress. There was no way you could get out of this structure and walk in a field. There we were, stuck in this place with these wild sailors. How they managed to get something to drink I don't know, but they were drinking and most of them were drunk.

Finally it was announced, 'OK. Tonight you're moving out.' We were moved from the fortress by trucks and brought to the railroad station late in the evening when it was dark. There were a few blue lights but it was very dim because the railway station was one of the popular targets for the Fascist air force. The Republicans didn't have an air force. They had a few planes which were flown by men like André Malraux; he piloted one of the junky planes the Republicans had. They used to throw bombs made inside bottles wherever they thought they could be effective. The other side had advanced aircraft. Hitler had been developing his Stuka planes which were to do such incredible damage in the Second World War a few years later. They were being tried out in Spain and the best way to try them out was on the civilian population.

We were still in the clothes they gave us in France. I looked at the other guys: unshaven, dirty – and figured I must look like that too, so what the hell. We're loaded into the train, jam-packed, there's no room to move – if you're lucky you get a seat. The whole train was filled with International Brigaders. This was the period of the highest density of volunteers. Forty thousand men is a lot of men.

I didn't get a seat, I sat on a pile of knapsacks. The train starts its journey down to Valencia. We were headed for Albecete via Valencia. The train moves very slowly because you never know when a piece of track has been torn up by saboteurs. The train is moving slowly down the line, so slowly that some of the guys, looking for some excitement, jump off the train, run alongside it and jump on again. Just to see if they can do it. The last time we had food was God knows when, the last time we had water was God knows when, which is just as well as there were no toilets on the train. Remember that all of us have upset stomachs.

Suddenly we hear the sound of music. 'Where the hell could music come from? What is there – a band on the train in one of the cars ahead of us? It sounds like it's coming from ahead of us,' we ask each other. Slowly the sound becomes distinguishable, it's very tinny and very brassy and it's 'The Internationale'. We say, 'Where the hell is that coming from?' The sound is closer and stronger as the train slows down as it goes through a station. Standing on the platform are old men, women, children and in their hands are pieces of bread, sometimes a few olives, sometimes a few grapes. They are offering these up to the soldiers in the train, crying '*Hermanos! Hermanos!* Brothers!' They had brought out the firefighters' band to play 'The Internationale' as the train slowed down in the middle of the night.

The train pulled away from that station and continued its lugubrious journey. We had all been deeply touched. The bits of bread that had been handed in through the windows were broken up and shared out amongst the fellows. 'That was something, wasn't it?' we said. '*Hermanos*, what does that mean, *hermanos*?' Brothers. Brothers. The train goes along for another half-hour, and again we hear music and now we know what it is. Sure enough in another few minutes the train pulls in to another station and slows down and the same story is repeated. Toothless old men; old women, creased, beautiful faces; little children with their hands outstretched, sharing their bread, of which they didn't have very much. Sharing the last few olives and telling us that they knew that we were brothers who had come to help them.

During that night, the train slowed down at ten stations along the way – always the same reception. How did they know a train was coming? It was the middle of the night. Had somebody organised it? Probably, yes. It was then we realised the people of Spain had a tremendous regard for the International Brigade.

The train brought us to Valencia, from Valencia we were moved again in trucks to Albecete. It was close to the border of the siege lines which the Fascists had established around Madrid. I was somewhat overwhelmed by the size of the barracks. Albecete had been a garrison town for the Spanish army. Many of the soldiers and officers of the Spanish army stayed with the Republic, they weren't all on the Fascist side. In Albecete we start being processed. The first day I got my uniform and my identity book. I still have a little photograph which went into the identity book. Albecete was big, it was overrun with troops and we were all getting outfitted with our first military uniforms. That photograph of me, like a passport photograph only smaller, is nice – I look like a brave young soldier.

Movement. Activity. Next place we arrive at is a town called Tarazona. We got from Albecete to Tarazona in lorries again, open to the air. It was slightly romantic ... reminded me of scenes from Soviet films – the revolutionaries going into battle, the red flag flying, with us standing there and the wind blowing our hair back, feeling so young, so potent, so daring. It wasn't true. It wasn't like that at all. But if the imagination was glossing up the real reality so much the better. Long live imagination!

Tarazona was the training centre of the American battalion which at this time was already called the Lincoln-Washington battalion. There had been two battalions, there had been a Lincoln Battalion and a Washington. So many men were killed in the defence of Madrid that the remnants of the two battalions were put together and were now in one battalion. So it was my honour to become a member of the Lincoln-Washington battalion.

There was one incident of my training which is terribly important – I think later when I was in battle it saved my life. We were being taught how to advance up a hillside. We would get an order to advance, we would run a certain number of steps and then the order was, 'Hit the dirt!' You had to throw yourself down in such a way that you protected your rifle – remember we didn't have rifles yet, we had sticks – and turn over in a zigzag pattern. Then get up and run ten steps forward again, hit the dirt, turn over in another direction. This is so that the enemy hasn't got time to get a bead on you. The enemy is looking at you, trying to get a shot at you, but if you are running and falling and turning and zigzagging, it makes it that much more difficult for him to hit you. So I hit the dirt once, I hit the dirt twice and I'm getting very dirty. I say to myself, 'Look, I'm an actor – I've done it, I've rehearsed it, and when the time comes I'll know how to do it.' The next time the order comes to 'Hit the dirt', I go down on one knee and contemplate the scene around me, which is very interesting, all these guys hitting the dirt and zigzagging. The order comes, 'Forward!' and I get up from my knee and run forward. Then the order comes, 'Hit the dirt!' I go down on one knee. The order comes, 'Zigzag!' so I hop along into a new position. Until suddenly there is someone behind me and I get a very strong blow on the back of my neck and I really hit the dirt! I am down flat and the drill sergeant is standing over me. He says, 'You stupid son-of-a-bitch! When I say "Hit the dirt" I mean *hit the dirt!* And don't give me any of your tricks. Now get up and run and *hit the dirt*!' And by God I hit the dirt. We kept practising this for quite a long time that morning and each time I hit the dirt very seriously. I was afraid I was going to get another whack on the back of my neck, which still hurt.

There was one more training session that we had where, for the first time, we were given real rifles and we were each given five bullets. We were taught the different firing positions. The basic position is the prone position where you lie on the ground on your stomach and then you have to use your elbow in a certain way and you have to hold the rifle a certain way. They teach you that. It's not hard to learn. We never got to the other firing positions because all we had was five bullets.

They say, 'All right, there's the target over there. Fire your five bullets. Breathe properly, don't pull the trigger, squeeze it.' I squeeze off my five bullets and then the target is brought back, and we were shown what we did. My five shots were in a cluster, which is good, it means my aim didn't change much. But the cluster was a good three or four inches off centre to the right. The young officer who was in charge of this exercise looks at it and says, 'You've got some kind of astigmatism in your right eye. You'll have to learn to compensate and move your rifle slightly to the left when you fire.' 'Very interesting,' says I to myself, 'I'll have to remember to move my rifle to the left.' That was it. There wasn't another bullet – no. More training – no. That was it, that was my training with the rifle.

The seat of the pants of the uniform that I had been given didn't fit terribly well and had a tendency to split from the front round to the back, which means the pants were in two separate pieces. You put on each leg of the pants, button them up and put a belt through the loops and that held them in place, but the seams never held. Because of the fact that our posteriors were open to the air, we called ourselves 'The Balls-Ass Naked Brigade.' So when you had to keep running to the latrine, there you were all ready to go.

We were awakened at five o'clock in the morning to stand outside on parade, balls-ass naked, unshaven because there were no razor-blades and no hot water. It's 5.30 in the morning and you never saw a more miserable-looking, raggedy bunch of young men. Out comes our commissar – the political officer who made sure we followed the correct

political line, and whom we called our comic star – Dave
Doran. Dave Doran is wearing a silk shirt freshly washed and
pressed, he is wearing a beautiful pair of cavalry breeches
which fit him magnificently and are not open at the seams
front and back. He is wearing a pair of hand-made Cordovan
leather riding boots – he was beautiful! He was a picture!
This was the speech he made to us every morning at 5.30:

'Comrades, we all know that we are here to fight Fascism.
Comrades, we are going to suffer in the struggle against
Fascism. But, Comrades, we have to maintain our discipline
and we have to do our best in order to be victorious in the
glorious fight against fascism. Any questions?'

I stick my hand up.

'Yes, Comrade.'

'Comrade,' says I, 'how is it that some of us fight fascism
under conditions that are more easy than the conditions of
the others?'

'What do you mean, Comrade?'

I said, 'Comrade, my shirt hasn't been laundered for two
weeks. Comrade, my pants are open all the way around.
Comrade, I don't have a pair of shoes because they don't
have any my size so I am wearing Spanish alpargatas with
rags to bind them around my feet. And comrade, I look like
a *muzhik*.'

'What is your name, Comrade?'

'Frye, Comrade.'

He takes out from the breast pocket of his beautifully
pressed silk shirt a little black book, literally, and a pencil,
and he writes down FRYE. I was in the little black book. So
this was Communism in action.

I went to a barber to get shaved because of the lack of
water and blades – the barber must have used an unclean
razor and I broke out in some pimples on my chin so I grew
a little chin beard and a moustache. Up comes comic star.
'Shave off that beard!'

I said, 'Why?'

'Because I'm telling you to!'

I refused. Out comes the little black book and into it goes a notation. Next thing, I'm in jail. I didn't have a trial or a court martial, nobody sentenced me. I was conducted, in a friendly manner, and locked up in the *calaboose* which was one of the town buildings doing service as a jail.

In this jail I met some marvellous people. One of them was Roman Kendzierski, an American lad of Polish descent. He was not a Communist, he didn't even know what the party line was. He had come to Spain to see his brother. Roman had been in jail in Chicago. When he came out he went home to see his family and asked for his young brother. They said, 'He went to Spain. There's a war going on there and he's a young Communist and so he volunteered to go and fight.' Roman said: 'I'm going to Spain to find him!' He found out how you get to Spain. They told him the only way to get to Spain was through the Communist Party. He said, 'What the fuck do I care?' And he went to Spain.

Roman was not very tall, a middle-sized lad, extremely handsome, Slavic blue eyes, blond curly hair, a thick neck, wide shoulders – truculent, combative and absolutely charming because if he was your pal *he was your pal*! And there was no mistake about it.

Released from jail after two or three days, I am loaded on to a truck and we are being sent to the front. We are being sent as replacements to the newly reorganised Lincoln-Washington Battalion and right now they were at rest, they were not in the front lines. They had been taken out after the terrible losses in the battles of Brunete and Jarama.

*   *   *

We joined the remnants of the Lincoln and Washington battalions in a village called Albares some distance from Madrid. We slept in the fields, some in tents, some on blankets on the ground. There was a stream and in that

stream we could bathe, we could wash our socks. Roman
Kendzierski found his younger brother here in Albares but
was bitterly disappointed to learn the boy was unpopular –
he had been marked down as a coward. The town of Albares
was on a steep hill. We had to climb up every day because
the place where we had our meals was up inside the village.
The one church in the village had been taken over and
turned into a military installation and a mess for the army
and for hungry citizens of the town. There was a place where
we could buy a bottle of wine and a bar where you could
have a few shots of Spanish brandy which isn't all that bad.
There wasn't much else in the town – a municipal office and
a mayor. Meanwhile the Catholic press worldwide was
shrieking that the Reds were killing priests and violating
nuns.

The village was full of children. There was one little girl
who attached herself to me. Her name was Juanita and I
would guess she was about nine years old. Juanita became
my Spanish teacher. I would give her whatever ration I got
of chocolate which was very rare. Whatever food I could get,
I would share with Juanita and she took it home for her
mother. I loved that child. I used to make myself clean for
Juanita, I used to make sure that I was shaved for Juanita.
She was a gorgeous Spanish child with that typical Spanish
thin long face with the gorgeous, gorgeous dark brown eyes
and a haircut with a fringe.

She was a clean little girl, her mother took good care of
her. Every day we would meet and Juanita would give me a
lesson in Spanish. She would show me with gestures the
meaning of the Spanish words. One day I said to Juanita, 'I
would like to come and visit you at home. I would like to
meet your mother.' The following day she came back and
said, 'My mother says you are welcome. Please come. Come
tomorrow.'

The following day I had a bath in the stream and I put on
a pair of clean socks and cleaned myself as well as I could,

combed my hair and went to meet Juanita in order to go to
her home. I had bought two bottles of wine for a gift. When
I got to the village square up on top of the hill it was
announced that certain of us were going on a three-day
leave to Madrid. I hadn't had any leave since I had arrived in
Spain. I explained to Juanita that I couldn't come. I gave her
the wine for her mother and said to her, '*Me voy a Madrid*',
which is probably incorrect grammatically but that's as
much as I knew. 'I am going to Madrid. *Que quieres de
Madrid*? I want to bring you some presents, what do you
want?' She said, '*Cosas* – things!' We got onto the lorries and
set off to Madrid.

Madrid. Soldiers on leave in any army anywhere in the
world do the same thing. They look for a whorehouse. I
was taken along with some other boys – we went in a
gang. I sat around for a while but I was not attracted to
the scene, I was certainly not attracted to the girls and I
slipped out and walked around the streets of Madrid. I
went back to where I was sleeping which was in a barracks
they had arranged for us. Tomorrow, I said, I am going
to buy the *cosas* for Juanita.

We got up early in the morning and it was announced to
us that we were being taken to the Front. We were not being
returned to the village. Again we are in lorries and again the
wind is blowing and again I feel like a central character in a
Russian film. Our commanders tell us we're going to
advance in a big Loyalist offensive in the Aragon, a province
north of Madrid. They say, 'Don't worry. Our planes will be
in the air to protect us.' Ha! That was an outright lie. We got
down from the lorries and I advanced with the troops. We
lay in the fields and there were bombers overhead. Enemy
bombers. We were told to keep our helmets on and to put
our faces into the ground so that if we got hit we would get
hit in the back. This was the battle of Quinto, but I wasn't to
know that until later. They don't tell you where you're
going, they don't tell you what you're going to do, they

move you around like pawns on a chess board.

We finally moved into position near the town of Quinto. Lots of confusion, lots of groups of men moving in different directions. We are moving into action. Our entire brigade, which was several battalions – a Canadian battalion, the Lincoln-Washington battalion and a British battalion. It was the fifteenth brigade. The enemy is shelling us and I'm walking along across fields, up and down little hills and I see the shells exploding and in the distance I see people falling and I say, 'This is like a fucking movie! I've seen this before – I'm in a Russian movie!'

I was a scout. I had a gun. I wasn't much good with it because of my astigmatism but I had no reason to fire it yet because we were nowhere near the enemy. When they're firing artillery shells at you they are quite a distance away from you. Next scene, a group of officers at battalion headquarters say, 'We've got to know what's behind that rise over there. We need a scout. Frye! Go beyond that rise over there and make us a drawing of what you see.' 'OK.' There were no 'yes sirs' in our army. That was because we were an army of comrades, an army of brothers, except that some were more brothers than others. I start going forward and I hear funny sounds. Pschee, pschee – it's bullets passing my ears – somebody is firing at me. I said to myself, 'I'd better hit the dirt.' I hit the dirt and I rolled over and I zigzagged – just like I'd been trained to do – and I got up and I ran and I hit the dirt and I rolled over and I zigzagged and ran and I finally got to the hillside. I was with a group of others, the other scouts. But I was the one who could draw. I crawl up on the hillside and I look over, over the rim and there's a steep drop on the other side of the hill. In the little valley there sits a town. The other side of the valley there are emplacements, enemy emplacements. I can see enemy soldiers.

I draw the situation. There's a big church tower sticking up. I put that into the drawing because you can orientate

yourself when you have a big object like that on the horizon.
And I start making my way back. Pschee, pschee – the bullets
are whistling by me. Hey! they're aiming at me, so I say, 'Hit
the dirt!' I hit the dirt and I roll over and I zigzag and get up
and hit the dirt and roll over and zigzag ... I'm getting
terribly out of breath and the bullets are going by, pschee,
pschee. Finally, after what seems to me an endless time – it
may have been five minutes but it seemed like an hour of
running – I get back to battalion headquarters. All the
officers are standing there – the battalion commander and
the company commanders – waiting for my report. I can't
... catch ... my ... breath ... I ... can't ... catch ... I'm lying
there panting. Eventually I gasped it out and explained the
sketch and they said, 'That's very important. All right, fine.'
Then they give the commands and what seems to me like the
whole fucking army – it was just a brigade but it may have
been a thousand men – start moving forward in different
positions, in the centre and on the sides. I'm still lying there
catching my breath.

The battalion commander, Hans Amlie was his name, a
Swedish American, said, 'OK kid, come along with us.' So I
am marching with the *commandatura* and with all the officers
– I'm going into battle and I'm part of the general staff!
Towards the end of that day, I had rejoined my group. We
had put ourselves into position where we surrounded the
town but we weren't strong enough to invest it. The idea was
to put the town under siege until we could find a way to
break into it. That evening at the end of the day, as the dusk
was falling, I'm with my group of scouts, Group A of Section
A of the first company (that's the point group). My commander was a sergeant by the name of Ray Ticer – a fisherman
by profession and here he was a sergeant in Spain – and he
said, 'Let's move forward on this piece of ground. We don't
know what's on the other side so be careful.' There were
nine of us in the group. I was at the extreme left-hand end of
the line. We walked up a little incline then we came to some

flat ground which was a traditional threshing ground. We are walking along the threshing ground and there doesn't seem to be any opposition. Remember that it's dusk – we're not seeing terribly clearly any more. There's the tower of the church ahead of us, we're closer now than we've been all day. We see it looming above us, growing taller as we advance.

We're going forward quite slowly, deliberately. All of a sudden, 'rat-tat-tat-tat', a machine-gun opened up on us from the tower of the church. Every one of the men was hit except me. Why? Because the minute I heard the sound, bang, I hit the dirt. Bang, I rolled over. Bang, I moved in a zigzag and I was the only one of the nine who wasn't hit. The lesson I'd had that day when I was training paid off.

That was the first day of the battle of Quinto.

The second day we were given orders to march in this direction and then in that direction. Where were we marching? Nobody really knew. We got to the end of where we were going, then the order came down, 'March back,' so we marched back. The enemy must've been maddened by what he saw – troops marching back and forth. 'My God, there must be thousands of those goddamn Communist Republicans!' We don't know what effect it had on them but we kept joking, 'We're going to frighten them to death. If we keep marching back and forth like this, they'll be sure that there's a vast army here making different manoeuvres in order to surround them completely.' That's how the second day passed.

On the third day, we got orders to go down the hillside into the town of Quinto. There wasn't much resistance – the Fascist forces were retreating because we had a big encircling movement on the entire Aragon front.

'Frye, take the machine-gun and shoot at that window at the top of the church tower!'

'OK.'

Our entire company had one machine-gun. We knew

from the various propaganda stories and from sad experience that the Fascists had about one machine-gun to every
four men. We had one machine-gun to a company, which at
full strength was a hundred and twenty men. One machine-
gun. Now *we* had the little machine-gun because we were the
point group. It was a Russian Dykterov. It was, for its time, a
somewhat advanced gun because it was very light. We used
to march along and we used to calculate, 'If so and so gets
hit, and if this guy gets hit, and if on Thursday that guy gets
hit, on Monday, I'll get the gun.'

Whether this was Monday or not, I do not remember but I
got the gun. I was sent on this mission to go into a house and
find a proper angle to shoot at the window at the top of the
church tower opposite. I get into the room and I do
everything that they taught me in the two weeks of training
that I had. And everything that I learned in the movies. We
took the mattresses off the bed and put them in the window
and we found the right angle and we placed the machine-
gun and we were going to fire at the church. We get into
position: 'OK. Ready. Aim. Squeeze. Fire!' *Trach* – nothing.
Nothing. Pulled the trigger, nothing happens. Why does
nothing happen? We don't really know because we have no
training with a machine-gun. We had been trained to use a
rifle – five bullets each, but we had not been trained to use
the machine-gun. Nevertheless, we sit down, we take a
blanket off the bed and put it on the floor, and we
disassemble the gun to see what's wrong and we find that
the firing pin is worn out. After all these preparations we
didn't fire at the church. I hadn't yet fired my rifle. I'd been
a scout, I'd drawn maps, I'd marched up and down to
frighten the enemy but I hadn't shot my rifle yet. This was
my great chance to fire the machine-gun – *gornischt*, nothing
... We said we might as well get the hell out of there – and
we did.

While this little drama was going on, the rest of the
brigade had moved into the town from a number of

directions and we had captured the town. The only place we hadn't cleaned out was the church and its tower. We're standing around and somebody has a bright idea: 'Let's collect straw from all the barns and start a fire at the bottom of the tower and smoke them out.' That was done, a fire was started. We could see the smoke climbing up because it came out through windows all along the height of the tower. Finally, we saw the smoke coming up from the top window and we heard shouts of surrender. The fire burnt itself out and about thirty young soldiers of the enemy came down and surrendered, hands in the air. I'm one of those standing in a circle around them with guns at the ready to control them, lest they should try to change their minds, and attack us.

The colonel, Colonel Copic, one of the commanders of the brigade, comes into our circle, looks at these prisoners whose faces are blackened with the smoke and who are dying for a drink of water. One of our guys came forward with his water canteen and passed it to the enemy soldiers. Copic says, 'Don't give them your water, you'll need it.' This guy moves back and these enemy kids are standing there – they're kids just like us. Copic says, 'Sergeants and corporals, forward!' Of the men in the group, six step forward. He said to them, 'March!' and pointed a direction, then he turned to us and said, 'Shoot them!' I am horrified. I watch this as though in slow motion. I see some of our boys lift their rifles. I see these enemy lads walking along, looking behind them, terrified. Trat, trat, trat, trat, trat, trat! and the sergeants and corporals are dead.

Next order, 'March the prisoners back to division head-quarters.' It is now a hot August afternoon, the temperature must be 100 degrees Fahrenheit and we're marching. These boys have had no water, so we sneaked water to them, we pass around our canteens and they give us back the empty canteens. As we walk along I catch the eye of one lad, extremely handsome, the traditional Spanish long thin face – they look a little like horses, very beautiful horses. I look at him and he looks at me, and we are both marching in this incredible heat. This lad, as he marches, is tearing the stripes off his shirt. He is a non-commissioned officer and he's trying to tear them off and I watch him. He looks at me and I don't say anything. He is not succeeding in tearing off the stripes so he unbuttons the shirt, takes it off and drops it as he's marching. He's marching bare chested.

After a very long march we get to divisional headquarters. Now I definitely know I'm in a film. It's a scene of epic proportions. Divisional headquarters is on the side of a hill which is part of the foothills to a little range of higher hills. At the top of the ridge, we see thousands of people dressed in black. These are the people from the town and the surrounding villages who escaped while the battle was going on. They're standing at the top of the ridge outlined against the afternoon, livid sky. Down here at the foothills, the place is lousy with men going back and forth. There are asbestos tanks which have been sunk into the ground and are filled with water. An officer gives the order, 'Let somebody collect all the canteens of the prisoners and fill them up.' We gave them water, for which they were very grateful. They're getting their drink of water and trying to wash their faces which are still covered with soot, and up comes one of our generals, General Walther. I saw the back of his neck, he had a big crease of flesh at the back of his neck. He was a fleshy man, a big, broad fellow, strutting like a cock. I said to myself, 'That's Eric von Stroheim, this is a film with big stars.' He looks at the prisoners we're guarding. Meantime we've been joined by other prisoners – there were masses of them. He says, 'Corporals and sergeants forward.' Oh my God, the same thing's going to happen again. This time they've had experience, they don't want to come forward. Men in the ranks of the prisoners point at other men, their own comrades, corporals and sergeants. My boy, without the shirt, without the marks of his rank, is pushed forward. He comes forward and he raises his fist in the Communist salute and he says, '*Yo no soy fascista.* I am not a Fascist. *Soy communista, camaradas, soy communista.* Comrades, I am a Communist.' The general pays no attention, he says to them, 'March!' and they go off. Again he says to our boys, 'Shoot them.'

This time, I'm in the firing squad. I'm in the group that has to march after them and shoot them. The next thing I know is that I'm falling and somebody has grabbed me by my collar and is holding me up. I hear the shots of the rifles and I hear the groans and the cries of the dying men. Then one of our young lieutenants goes to the group of dead men on the ground and gives them the *coup de grâce* with his revolver, and that's the last thing I remember. I had fainted. General Walther, the general himself, had grabbed me by the collar and held me up and then he let me down on the ground. When I woke up I was on the ground in a state of shock. The general didn't say anything to me, none of the other officers said anything to me, nobody made any comment about it.

Now we're on a truck, going back to where the rest of our troops are. Our troops were still surrounding the town to make sure we would hold it. I get onto the truck and in the truck there are two huge aluminum pots of food. One of them has rice pudding in it. I'm sitting in the truck with five or six other guys and with the battalion commander, Hans Amlie. Everybody is very hungry so everybody digs his hand into the huge pot and digs out a handful of rice pudding and feeds himself. Me, along with the rest. I am weeping. I'm sitting and weeping and eating the rice pudding.

Hans Amlie is sitting near me, he says, 'We had to do it because we had captured more prisoners than we had troops. There were more of them than there were of us. There were three thousand people standing on the ridge, members of the town. We had to make a show of strength.' He said, 'This is what happens in a war.' I said, 'We are fighting for democracy and brotherhood, this is not what we should be doing.' I'm weeping and eating rice pudding. And Amlie says, 'You'll understand it, in time you'll understand it. Don't worry about it.' And that was the only thing anyone ever said to me about my behaviour. This Hans Amlie was a very, very sweet man.

I never did see my darling Juanita again. She never got her *cosas*. And all my life I have wondered, 'Shouldn't I have gone back somehow, I don't know how, but somehow, to try to find the child, to apologise, to give her *cosas*?'

*   *   *

War is war. It doesn't really matter under which banner you fight, soldiers behave like soldiers and one of the traditional things that soldiers have been doing for millennia is looting. The town was captured. The citizens weren't allowed back into the town immediately so our boys started to go through all the houses to see what they could find – I amongst them. What was I looking for? Two things: I wanted a clean pair of socks so I went into some houses and opened drawers until I found a pair of socks. I also wanted a real plate to eat off, all I had was an army issue tin plate and tin fork. 'My next meal,' I said, 'I want to eat like a *mentsch*.' I went into a house and into a kitchen, found a plate and a fork and put them in my knapsack. That was the extent of my looting.

Not entirely. I'm not very proud of it so it's hard to tell, but I have to tell it. Our kitchen unit had uncovered a trove of barrels of Spanish brandy and when I lined up for my breakfast, instead of the usual coffee and bread they were doling out brandy. The boys were filling their water flasks. It was very good brandy. Six o'clock in the morning, standing on the road, drinking brandy until I must have been quite high. Maybe I can use that as an excuse for the next story I have to tell.

I was wandering in the town in which we had been fighting in the streets. While I was busy taking apart that machine-gun, the rest of the battalion was fighting house to house, looking for Fascists. Some of our men had been killed in the streets. I walked through the streets of the town and saw dead soldiers in peculiar positions. One in the corner of a doorway, sitting up as though he'd gotten tired, but he was dead, one of theirs. Just outside the town there was one of ours lying in the blazing August sun, his body already bloated, his face turned purple. I did something of which I'm terribly ashamed. I went through his pockets and found a wallet with his identity card, his paybook and about four hundred pesetas in cash. He must have been a good poker player because all we got was ten pesetas a month so how could he have accumulated four hundred pesetas? I took it. The four hundred pesetas. I put the wallet back on the body, so that the burial detail could identify him. With that four hundred pesetas burning a hole in my conscience I went to where they were doling out the food. I had seen the lunch wagon coming up, they were dishing out a hot meal, the first we'd had in four days. I wasn't going to miss that, especially as I was full of Spanish brandy. I pulled out my porcelain plate, my china plate and my good fork, and went to get my meal. It seemed to me it was one of the best meals of my life. In reality it was no better or no worse than the usual crap the field-kitchen fed us.

On the trucks again, moving into new positions, disembark. Move through the fields, our commander appears and says, 'Boys, I promise you our air force is active and will deter any enemy planes.' Famous last words. No sooner had he gone away after this splendid announcement than we heard planes in the air – not ours. Ours never showed up, all we saw were enemy planes dropping bombs. We were moving into position through irrigation ditches. We were keeping off the roads, which are covered by the enemy who is in the town which we are investing. Belchite. They can see us, and are firing at us. You hear the bullets going by.

When you're mounting an offensive, you don't just push into one town, you are pushing along a whole frontier, a whole border line, you have to move your troops as quickly as possible from one place to the next to put on the pressure as soon as you find their weak point. We come to a battalion of young Spanish soldiers, on our side. Boys. Fifteen years old, sixteen years old, very poorly equipped. A young Spanish officer with that wonderful long, horse-like face and a young little moustache – an audacious moustache, looked like Douglas Fairbanks senior. He was exhorting his soldiers. I didn't understand all of it, but it was clear that they didn't want to go forward and he kept repeating, '*Adelante*, Forward!' They were afraid to stick their heads up out of the ditch so he got up. He went up the side of the ditch and stood at the top and said, 'You see, nothing. Nothing.' And, bang, suddenly he fell down, the bullet had just hit him in the earlobe. He said, 'It's nothing' as the blood was streaming from the ear. He felt it, he said, 'It's nothing. *Es nada*.' He climbed up again on the ditch and he stood there with his arms spread out wide like a crucified Christ and in just about as long as it takes to tell, he was crucified. He was shot down, his dead body fell into the ditch and then the soldiers were surely not going to move.

The command came to us: 'Get over the edge of the ditch and move forward into the next ditch.' We said, 'But these Spanish kids are in there.' 'Walk over them. Crawl over them.' They wouldn't go into battle, they were frightened. We were frightened too, but we simply were more disciplined, and we had faith in our officers. They were guys, just like us. Charlie Nusser in command of our company, you met him. Just a nice guy. A guy like me. He'd been promoted to officer in the field. We climbed over these

Spanish kids and we moved forward. We didn't get hit because we didn't stand up, we were on the ground. We were crawling on our stomachs, zigzagging, doing what they had taught us, and we got into another ditch. We kept crawling forward all day until we got to the edge of the town where there was a road. On the other side of the road was a Spanish church, tremendous tower, big enough for a cathedral. The lack of balance is very startling when you see a small church with a huge tower. We paused to rest for a while. Our soldiers on my right as I face the town had occupied a barn on our side of the road. The town was across the road.

We had been informed that we were going to launch an artillery barrage. Our artillery was going to soften up the town by lobbing a lot of shells into it and then we would be given the command to move forward into the town. One of our young officers, Lennie Lamb, a slender, good-looking Jewish lad, a New York boy, Lennie was guiding the artillery. He held a field telephone which was connected to the artillery in our rear. He was with us on our side of the road. He wanted them to hit a garage which was on our left side as we faced the town, there were snipers in there and they were shooting into our flank. Lennie started to give them directions, 'On the left, on the left!' but he got excited and turned around to face the artillery and he kept pointing with his left hand ... 'On the left, on the left.' But left was now right. He was pointing to the barn on the right that our boys were occupying. The artillery shifted, started to lambast the target on the right – eight of our boys were killed.

By the end of this artillery barrage, when we were supposed to move into the town and attack it, dusk fell very quickly. It was too late to advance so we lay around and waited for the food. As usual the food trucks hadn't kept up with our advance and we were hungry. Me, I'm up front. So is Charlie Nusser. Charlie says, 'Hey guys, I think we got to do a night patrol.' 'Yeah. OK.' He says, 'Frye, you're a scout, you go and the sergeant and two other guys.' Four of us. OK. We start to put on our gear. We had taken off our haversacks because we were resting, because it was dusk and there was no place to go. Now we're putting them on again, we're checking our rifles, we're getting ready to go out on night patrol. I say, 'Hey Charlie, what is this night patrol?'

'The way I figure, we got to go out and check our flanks. We've got to contact the enemy.'

I said, 'Yeah, OK.' We're just about ready to go and I say, 'Hey Charlie, how do we know when we contact the enemy?'

He says to me, 'Don't worry, kid, they'll be shooting at you.'

We went out on that night patrol. As we went along we discerned that there were people on our left, on our side of the road and suddenly we hear, 'Who the fuck goes there?' 'OK guys it's us.' As they had said, 'Who the fuck goes there?' it couldn't be anybody else but our guys. The enemy is hiding in the town on the other side of the road. They weren't shooting at us so we didn't contact the enemy. We returned. In the morning the firing starts. It comes from behind the church. It comes from the top of the tower of the church. It comes from the garage which we had tried to eliminate the day before and which by mistake was saved. There seems to be a machine-gun nest somewhere in front of us – someone is very well ensconced in a position where he is not discernible to us, firing a machine-gun at us which prevents us from getting up and moving into the town.

Roman Kendzierski walks around and says, 'Give me your grenades.' He collects everybody's grenades and puts them inside his shirt above his belt. Takes out a grenade, pulls the pin, transfers it to his left hand; takes another grenade, asks somebody to pull the pin, holds the clamp in his right hand – he's got a grenade in either hand and he goes forward to wipe out the machine-gun nest. All of us are watching him and we think it's an act of tremendous bravery, and it has something to do with wiping out the shame of his brother's dishonour. He gets pretty close to the church and all of a sudden we hear the ominous tut-tut-tut-tut-tut-tut-tut-tut of a machine pistol – and Roman is blown up. The bullets hit the grenades across his waist and he was simply blown up. That's the end of the story of Roman Kendzierski. When you see something like this with your own eyes it becomes part of your existence. You cannot possibly forget it. He had tight blond curls on his head, he had a Slavic face with high cheek bones, a straight nose and blue eyes. A good looking kid, feisty little bastard, he reclaimed the honour of his family.

Shortly after this, it was decided that we would move back two or three hundred metres and re-group, order another artillery attack and then move forward again under our artillery. That's called a lifting barrage where you fire the shells and then keep lifting them. That is to say you enlarge the range. During the night, despite our night patrol, the enemy had crossed the road and was firing into our flank. They were behind us and they were shooting our men down one after the other. I'm crawling in the irrigation ditches, trying to keep my head low. I've got my rifle in my right hand. I put my right hand forward and then pull my body up, resting on my right elbow, and all of a sudden I'm hit and there's a strange sensation in my arm, my hand becomes useless, the rifle falls out of it . . .

My arm was dead, completely numb, it was paralysed, although I didn't know it at the time. I couldn't pick up my rifle and I started to crawl on my left elbow, pulling myself along, trying to get to the rear where maybe somebody could look at my arm, tie it up or do something. As I go along I feel that on my left leg my leather legging had opened up and my wallet which I kept inside the legging had fallen out. In the wallet was the four hundred pesetas which I hadn't had time to spend.

Now listen to a piece of insanity. Wounded, paralysed right arm. I can't strap up the legging with my right hand, so I struggle to fix it with my left. I turn around and crawl back the way I had come – they're shooting all around me – to find my wallet. I was not going to give up that money. It had been enough of a crisis of conscience that I had stolen if off a dead body, I wasn't going to lose it like this, that would be adding insult to injury. I crawled back maybe fifty metres, found the wallet, stuck it inside the other legging, turned around again and continued to crawl to the rear.

I reached a little declivity where there were half a dozen other soldiers, all wounded. Somebody pulled out my shirt tail and pinned it up to form a sort of sling. They said, 'The ambulances should be over there, if you can get there, somebody will take care of you.' With my arm in this improvised sling, my wallet in my legging, I continued to crawl on my left side, very tortuous. I get to a road and there is the ambulance. No stretcher bearers. Nobody volunteered to come forward and pick us up because we were being picked off on all sides – there were a lot of wounded that day. I heard much later that we won that battle. We captured the town of Belchite and also thousands of enemy soldiers and much equipment, machine-guns, ammunition ... when you're fighting and you're hit, when you're in the middle of it, you don't really give a shit about victory or defeat, you are fighting to preserve your own life. That's all you care about at that particular moment. It wasn't until later that I had patriotic feelings about having participated in the victory at Belchite. That was the extent of my military effectiveness ... I was not a good investment as a soldier. They lost money on me.

I got to the ambulance which was a lorry manned by Red Cross male nurses. The improvised ambulance drove away from the battle. After an hour's ride we stopped at a roadside café. 'We'll stop here for five minutes, who ever is thirsty, get down and get a drink or have somebody fill your canteen.' I got off the lorry and I bought cakes and candy for every man in the ambulance. I spent a hell of a piece of the four hundred pesetas. I didn't want it on me any longer. The ambulances moved all the way back to the Mediterranean coast to a hospital north of Valencia at Benicasim. Before the outbreak of the war, Benicasim had been a beach resort of the wealthiest families and now the luxurious villas had been confiscated and converted into clean, comfortable hospital wards.

A bullet had gone through the biceps muscle of my upper right arm and had badly damaged the ulnar and the median nerves which meant that my right arm was paralysed and I had no function in my right hand. I was experiencing the worst pain I have ever experienced in my life, certainly before then and since then. If someone walked across the room on hard leather heels that clacked on the tiled floor, my arm would respond to every clack. If someone went out of the door and slammed it, I would jump because the pain was so intense. They started to give me morphine to reduce the pain. I would get an injection and would have a few hours of respite. Morphine is a lovely drug. You go into a sort of a daydream, experience the most wonderful euphoria until it wears off and then you are reminded again of the depth and intensity of the pain. That's when you start screaming for another injection. I could not explain in Spanish that I needed another shot because of the pain, I acted it out but they had their instructions as to when I got my next shot.

I don't know how many days it took for me to become addicted, but I was addicted. I was screaming and shouting and making terrible scenes. I said, 'I've got to have another injection.' One day they took me into the surgery. The young Spanish doctor, extremely handsome, talked to me very quietly. I didn't completely understand what he was saying to me. 'It'll be all right, it'll be all right. Don't worry.'

He started to prepare an injection. I was sitting in a chair, anticipating my injection, yearning for it. I looked around across my left shoulder to see that he had taken a much larger syringe than I had ever seen in his hands before, and he filled it up from a number of capsules. He came to give me the injection and said in Spanish the equivalent of, 'Are you ready?' I said, '*Si, si*,' and he gave me the injection. I felt as though someone had taken a small log of wood and banged me across the back of the neck. It was a huge blow, and I sat in the chair, not unconscious, I was conscious but paralysed, not just the paralysis of the wounded right arm, but my whole body was paralysed. He called the nurses and somehow or other they got me back to bed and laid me out. I knew at what time he had given me the injection, it was ten o'clock in the morning. I lay on my bed paralysed for the next twenty-eight hours. Unable to move, unable to urinate and that hurt badly. The pain was even greater than the pain of the wounded arm. I didn't have nightmares, I didn't have daymares, I was just lying there felled, like an ox. Finally it broke. I was able to get up and ran to the toilet. The pain in the arm came back with an enormous pulse of painful sensation. I got back to my bed and I must have been weeping. I called the nurse I said, 'This is impossible, I need an injection.' She said, 'No more injections.' They got hold of the doctor and he explained to me in Spanish that he was not going to give me any more morphine, he had given me a huge dose in order to break my addiction, and that from now on I would have to manage the pain without morphine.

I said, 'What am I going to do?' I was weeping, like a child, just sitting there weeping. 'Get drunk!' he said.

'The nurses don't allow me to keep liquor in the room.'

'You can keep as much as you like I'll tell them,' he said.

There was a *cantena* at a distance of maybe one kilometre from my villa at Benicasim. Over the course of the next days I developed a routine: to the *cantena* in the morning where I drank a hot milk with rum drink, but drank enough so that the pain was alleviated. At noon I walked back to the hospital and had lunch, then walked back to the *cantena* and started to drink Spanish brandy through the hours after lunch until supper time. By this time, I not only felt no pain, I didn't know where the hell I was. Supper time, back to the villa, supper, back to the *cantena* where I started to drink Spanish champagne. Only a man in my condition could consume that much Spanish champagne, which was lethal. I drank so much that I didn't know where I was at when the canteen closed. There was a curfew, a certain hour when you had to be back at the hospital. I wasn't observing the curfew, I didn't give a damn. A number of times they found me on the road dead drunk and picked me up and brought me back to the hospital. Nobody said anything.

'What is going to happen to my arm?' The chief surgeon, Professor Kisch, said to me, 'It is possible to operate in an attempt to clean up the injury and possibly rejoin the nerves. However,' he said to me very quietly, 'the thing to do now is to try to get repatriation and have the operation done in America where you will get better care than here.'

I gave up the continual drunkenness. I became more aware, I made friends. I walked along the beaches. I was sunburned. I had lost a tremendous amount of weight because the food had not improved. One day a friend from New York turned up – one of the nurses in our hospital was his girlfriend – Herbert Kline. He knew me as a young actor who had come out of The Workers' Laboratory Theatre, I knew him as the editor of *New Theatre* magazine, a brilliant publication – some of the best critics wrote for it and Herb was a great editor, an excellent reporter. Herb turned up – energetic, voluble, extremely active, and things started to hum. He came with a young French photographer who was his cameraman – Henri Cartier Bresson, who was later to achieve world fame – he is considered one of the best photographers in the world. Herb was a maker of great documentary films. The title of this one was going to be

Return To Life. How the Republic cared for young soldiers from all over the world who had offered their lives and were now battered and wounded.

When Herb arrived I was in bed. I used to spend a fair amount of time in bed because I found that the more I rested the less reaction there was from my arm. I was still experiencing pain. Herb came up to me, 'What the hell are you doing in bed?'

'I've been wounded.'

'I can see that but that's no reason why you can't get up and be active. I want you to help me in my film.'

'Doing what?'

'You've still got one hand, you can *schlep* the cameras. Come on.'

That same day I was Herb's *schlepper*. I *schlepped* cameras, I *schlepped* lights and I *schlepped* cables and got very involved in the making of the film – very curious, trying to look into the camera every chance I got. Cartier Bresson was a very businesslike chap, there was not much fooling around with him, but I would plead with him, 'Let me take a look.' And he'd let me look into the eyepiece of the camera and I would watch Herb to see how he lined up the shot, what he was shooting, why he was shooting it, how he directed it ... Herb didn't know this, but I was his co-director on this film. He put me into a scene where a group of wounded men were watching a football game, played by wounded soldiers. He put me into a very good position and so, at last, I was also a film star. That generous, friendly gesture of Herb's turned me around psychologically ... for the first time I began to think that there was a life for me after Spain.

After moving from hospital to hospital, in 1938, I am in Barcelona waiting for some papers to be signed which will permit my repatriation. I have no passport so unless I get some piece of formal paper from the Spanish government, I can't budge. After a couple of weeks my papers came through. I was put on a train which took me from Barcelona to Perpignan, the French port town, down by the Spanish border. I was out of Spain, I was in France.

When I arrived in Paris I telephoned Cartier Bresson, who had said to me in Benicasim, 'If you get to Paris give us a call' – he spoke good English. He was most friendly. 'Where are you staying?'

'In a miserable place...'

He said, 'If you like you can stay here with us, I have a big studio, and we can put up a camp bed for you.' I moved into his home – 77 Rue des Petits Champs ... the street of the little fields. It's one of those old Parisian buildings where you walk up five or six or seven flights of wooden stairs.

I stayed there about a month. He was living with an Indonesian girl, they called her Elie but her Indonesian name was Retna Moerindiah and she was a Javanese dancer. She was exotic, she was oriental, and she was a firm believer in the transubstantiation of matter. She took me out shopping – she took me to spice shops and introduced me to spices that I'd never heard of before. For me it was all new and exciting, she used to buy a little of this a little of that and we'd come home and she'd cook something with that spicing. Henri was not very voluble, he was given to long silences. But he was very polite, very good to me. I was a guest in his house, I was eating at his expense. Eventually I was in an office of the Canadian Embassy in Paris, where a very sympathetic young consular official made out a new passport for me. I told him my passport had been stolen in Paris. Herb Kline, who used to visit Cartier Bresson, had bought a green tweed suit – a Donegal tweed – which didn't fit him. He said, 'Look, kid, I would give it to you, but I need the money. I'd like to sell it to you. I think it will fit you, because you are so thin.' I bought the suit from him for some very nominal amount of francs and I went home to New York in Herb's green Donegal tweed suit. It was very green.

I sailed back to the US on the *Queen Mary*. When I had left

New York, May had been at the dock. I can still see her standing there forlornly waving to me as the ship moved out towards the ocean. She was there to meet me when I came back.

*   *   *

THELMA
I'd like to add something to your Spanish story, Peter. You often said to me, 'My greatest ambition is to march through the streets of Madrid in a victory parade. If, by that time, I'm in a wheelchair, promise you will push me.' Your Spanish experience informed your whole life – not only because of the wounded arm, but casting the die that you would spend your life as idealist and fighter.

After forty years' dictatorship, Franco died and a Socialist government was democratically elected, which was what you had fought for. As 1986, the fiftieth anniversary of the outbreak of the Spanish Civil War, approached you felt that something must be done to organise your victory parade through the streets of Madrid. You offered to go at your own expense to meet Felipe Gonzalez to get the thing rolling. We contacted MPs, all those we knew in the left wing movement in England, but had no response.

One day you asked me to buy you the *New Statesman* and inside we found an advertisement announcing the dedication of a statue on London's South Bank in honour of the British Battalion of the International Brigades. We went and this was the first contact you had made with fellow veterans. From Bill Alexander, who runs the organisation of British veterans, we got the address of VALB (Veterans of the Abraham Lincoln Brigade) in New York. You wrote, saying that if they were planning any sort of celebration in 1986, we would like to join them.

Almost immediately we received a most excited reply. Your letter had been opened by Charlie Nusser, the same

Charlie Nusser who had been your commanding officer fifty
years earlier. He wrote back in great excitement saying he
remembered you as a good soldier, always doing what you
were asked without question. You were amazed that anybody should remember you that way ... and very proud. He
wrote to us that, under the leadership of VALB, a reunion
was planned in Madrid for as many veterans, friends and
family as possible, in October 1986.

We went. And they came from all over the world – some
three thousand people, about six hundred of whom were
veterans. Men and women – women served mainly as nurses
and ambulance drivers, but they came to Spain in 1936–39
in their thousands. All the vets, of course, elderly men and
women in their seventies, eighties and nineties with their
wives, children and grandchildren. Of the forty-five thousand volunteers who went to Spain, half were killed, many
more killed in the Second World War, most of those not
killed were injured. Those who had come to fight in Spain
from Fascist countries and couldn't go home fought throughout the war in the Underground – with the partisans in
France, in Belgium, in Holland, in Poland, in Nazi-occupied
Ukraine – wherever they could sabotage and demolish
German war-materiel and the German butchers who used it.
Here in Madrid were the handful of survivors. Many chil-
dren and grandchildren of those who had been killed. The
International Brigade was the greatest force of international
volunteers in history, the first fighters against Hitler and
Mussolini, a generation of young, brave idealists ... you lost.
But now you felt you had won, and you had come back to
Spain to celebrate.

You didn't have your victory parade. Felipe Gonzalez
didn't want to open up old wounds and so the government
gave no official backing to the event. But the cities of
Madrid and Barcelona and, above all, the people of Spain
were overwhelming in their welcome. Dolores Ibarurri,
known as La Pasionaria, was still alive, a frail old lady in her

nineties, and she greeted the veterans, as she had promised forty-eight years before. La Pasionaria was an Asturian Communist member of the Cortes who had been the inspiration of the Republican soldiers. She rallied the men and women of Spain at the outbreak of the rebellion with: 'It is better to die on your feet than live on your knees!' When the International Brigade finally had to withdraw in 1938, she said to them, 'Comrades of the International Brigades! Political reasons, reasons of state, the welfare of that same cause for which you offered your blood with boundless generosity, are sending you back some to your own countries and others to forced exile. You can go proudly. You are history. You are legend. You are the heroic example of democracy's solidarity and universality. We shall not forget you, and when the olive tree of peace puts forth its leaves again, mingled with the laurels of the Spanish Republic's victory – come back!' You came back and she was there for you.

The veterans all wore a badge which said that you were from the International Brigades, so on the street dozens of people came up to us, shook you veterans by the hand, hugged you, kissed you saying, '*Hermanos* ... Brothers! Thank you, thank you!' Buying a ticket for the underground, the ticket-seller came out of his booth saying, 'I'm not going to let you pay' and he embraced you with the tears streaming down his face.

What magnificent people, remarkable human beings those veterans were and are. Like you, they have continued to fight wherever they see injustice. There were receptions, meetings, banquets. In both Madrid and Barcelona the largest hall in the city was filled to overflowing when they had their special tribute events. In Madrid, where there were many young Spaniards in the auditorium as well as those old enough to remember, the entire audience joined hands, raised the hands in the air and sang the song of liberty; Ed Balchowsky, a pianist who lost his right hand in Spain, sat at the piano with his flowing grey beard, singing and playing with his left hand; a group of beautiful young Spanish singers sang the Republican songs of the Civil War and, unplanned and spontaneous, the veterans went up on the stage at the end to be cheered, each one holding a red carnation which Israeli veteran, Salman J Salzman, had brought specially from Israel.

At the first big banquet in Madrid in a huge room with thousands of people, you spotted in the distance a man, whose back was turned to you, with large ears protruding on either side. 'Good heavens,' you said, 'that's Gabby. He was next to me in the trenches and I begged him not to shoot his gun so close, that he was deafening me. I am sure that is why I have to wear two hearing aids today.' You walked over to look at the man's face: 'Gabby?'

'Yeah?' It *was* Gabby – Herman Rosenstein from Los Angeles – and *he* was wearing two hearing aids!

PETER

I had fought in that terrible war and I knew then what had been happening to me and to those around me, as I still know it now: war memories are not easily forgotten. But coming back to Spain in October 1986, fifty years later, I was to learn a great deal about my war that I hadn't known before. First, that I had really been a volunteer in an *International* Brigade, for here they were, all around me, the pitiful remnant of the boys and men of more than fifty nations who had volunteered to defend the infant Spanish Democratic Republic. I had known it before in my mind. I knew it now in my guts. Because here they were and I was shaking their hands and embracing them.

The experience was overwhelming. The history of the International Brigade in the Spanish Civil War is of vast importance in the history of our civilisation. The world ignored it, to its cost – maybe it will finally understand it now before it is too late.

THELMA

For two days, between Madrid and Barcelona, we toured the battlefields. In Quinto you stood with Charlie, your commanding officer, surveying the area for miles around, remembering. Belchite. The town has been preserved exactly as it was after the two battles which devastated it. Franco had a plaque at the entrance as a memorial to the evil of the left-wing Republican government, which of course was removed when Franco died and the town now stands as a reminder and memorial to the evil of all wars. On a burning hot dusty October day I walked through this ghost town with the men who had fought there nearly fifty years before – rubble, twisted balconies, ghostly churches, ruined shops and houses. As we drove away you saw some irrigation ditches opposite the ruin of a very big church. 'That's where it was,' you said, 'that's where I was wounded...'

On the last night in Barcelona we all went to the Pueblo Espanol, a perfectly re-created Spanish town built on a mountain overlooking the harbour of Barcelona. As the sun began to set, a band started to play and the large square was filled with all we old folk dancing – some in couples, some in circles, some with great energy, some gently. A girl with a throbbing, deep voice led us to join in the great Civil War songs – if we hadn't known them before we arrived, we certainly knew them now. Once again the liberty song, with everybody joining and lifting hands, hundreds and hundreds of us. I found myself holding Ed Balchowsky's stump where the right hand used to be. Afterwards there was a final dinner for the Abraham Lincolns – every vet was presented with a certificate and a bronze medal especially struck for the occasion ... the first and only evidence you ever had that you fought in the Brigade. As Charlie Nusser handed you your medal he said, 'Pete, you're discharged!'

Peter's parents, Jack and Celia, on their wedding day. Montreal. 1913.

Peter and his younger brother Bernard. 1917.

Peter and his little love Juanita. Spanish Civil War. 1937.

Peter in Spain during Civil
War. 1937.

Erwin Piscator, the German
director.

Peter as a young man.

At a cousin's wedding in Montreal 1950. Back row: Peter, Batia (his second wife), Bernard (brother) and Stip (brother-in-law). Front row: Father and Mother, sister Sylvia.

Peter with his little daughter, 1956.

Taken at a rehearsal at Habimah Theatre.

Thelma"s father, Louis Wigoder, 1928.

Paula Ruby, Thelma's mother, in the C. B. Cochran revue THIS YEAR OF GRACE, 1928.

Thelma with brother Geoffrey.

With mother.

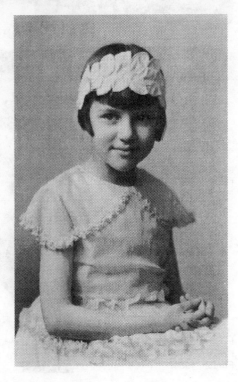

Bridesmaid, Aged 9.

Teenager in America, 1941.

In Christopher Fry's A
PHOENIX TOO FREQUENT,
Frinton, 1950.

Prince Charming in
CINDERELLA, Hull 1952.

With Tyrone Power at the wedding of Jimmy & Nina Thompson, 1956.

With Tyrone Power at the Palladium in the NIGHT OF 100 STARS. Back row L. to R.: Jean Kent, Peggy Cummins, Brenda Bruce, Tyrone, Joan Sims, Sheila Sim. Front row: Dulcie Gray, Thelma, Anna Massey, 1956.

With grandmother and mother in Thelma's dressing-room at the Palladium. THE SLEEPING BEAUTY, 1957.

Thelma with her parents. 1960.

Jay Lewis directing Richard Attenborough and John Mills in his film THE BABY AND THE BATTLESHIP, 1956.

Thelma with Maurice Denham in the film INVASION QUARTET, directed by Jay.

With John Gregson in the film LIVE NOW, PAY LATER, directed by Jay, 1965.

Thelma with Jay.

With Paul Eddington and Michael Malnick in the musical JORROCKS at the New Theatre, 1967.

With Judi Dench in the musical CABARET at the Palace Theatre, 1968.

First West End
appearance. In THE
WHITE DEVIL at the
Duchess Theatre, 1947.

As the Empress of
Morocco in TURN AGAIN
WHITTINGTON at the
Palladium, 1960.

As Mrs Peachum in THE
BEGGARS OPERA, 1979

As Mrs Trapes in the same production of THE BEGGARS OPERA, 1979.

In the revue HIGH
SPIRITS, 1953 London
Hippodrome Theatre.

With Bill Kerr in ONCE
UPON A MATTRESS.
Adelphi Theatre, 1960.

With Kenneth Williams
in THE BUCCANEER.
Apollo Theatre, 1955.

Thelma doing her
cabaret act.

In first film WHERE THERE'S A WILL. L. to r.: Thelma, Kathleen Harrison, Leslie Dwyer, Dandy Nichols, Ann Hanson, George Cole.

Thelma with Keith Baxter and Orson Welles in CHIMES AT MIDNIGHT. Dublin, 1960.

With Hugh Paddick in FOR AMUSEMENT ONLY. Apollo Theatre, 1956–58.

As Lady Hamilton in THE
HERO RISES UP.
Edinburgh Festival and
Nottingham Playhouse,
1969.

Singing 'Do you love me?'
with the Japanese Tevye.
Tokyo, 1980.

With Michael Flanders at the midnight premiere of the film THE ADMIRABLE CRICHTON, 1957.

SO HAUNT ME. BBC television, 1993–94. L. to r.: Tessa Peake-Jones, George Costigan, David Graham and Thelma, the bride.

With Topol in FIDDLER ON THE ROOF. Apollo Victoria Theatre, 1983.

Thelma as Golde in FIDDLER ON THE ROOF, 1970.

Filming with Sir John Gielgud in Yugoslavia, 1986.

Peter with Topol in TV film MR KNOWALL, 1987.

Peter in MOMMA GOLDA, 1980–88.

In the film KING DAVID.

With Golda Meir, 1978.

Peter and Thelma's wedding. With Thelma's parents, 1970.

Peter and Thelma with Candy, 1970.

Thelma and Peter in their cooking programme THE BETTER HALF on ATV television, 1971.

Peter with
Emperor Haile
Selassie.

Peter with the
young Itzhak
Perlman.

Peter and Thelma with aunt Mona, 1989.

Peter with Oded Teomi. Tasting different varieties of malt whiskey, 1990.

Thelma and Peter in their home in Wimbledon, 1991. The year of Peter's death.

THE ROSE AND THE RING. Greenwich, 1973. Thelma starred and Peter directed.

Book IV

The Launching

ENSA

THELMA

I feel proud that you went to Spain, part of that selfless upsurge of idealism which inspired a generation of young men and women. It is hard to get back to my story. You have arrived back in America in 1938 and I have arrived back in England in 1944. England in October 1944 was a very different place from the New York I had just left. I came back to a country of blackout, shortages, war, bomb-sites, exhaustion, fear, and the new horror, the V1 and V2 rockets being sent over to scare us into submission. You could hear the V1 approaching and when the engine cut off you ran for cover. The V2 just exploded with no warning and if you were still alive when you heard the explosion, you knew you had survived until the next one. Sometimes I wondered if I had been sent to America for four years to be in safety, only to return to become a victim of the rockets. Once, in Knightsbridge, London, I ran for cover when I heard the V1 engine go quiet and after the explosion I looked up and saw I was standing under a glass canopy. I was lucky to reach the end of the war uninjured.

The reunion with Dad was joyous. Always the most unselfish of men, he had endured four years separated from his adored family because he believed it to be the best thing for us. There was still conscription for every man and woman over eighteen, and I was nineteen. I didn't want to work in a factory, I didn't want to go into uniform or become a landgirl on a farm. I wanted to use the fine theatre training I'd received – to do something, anything, connected with theatre.

We discovered that the ENSA headquarters were at the Drury Lane Theatre in London. ENSA was the organisation which sent out entertainment for the troops – entertaining the troops was designated war work, so that was where I wanted to be. Mother came with me to London to see the head of the Drama Section, a well known actor called Henry Oscar. ENSA had taken over the entire, historical and very beautiful Drury Lane Theatre, and the dressing-rooms were turned into offices. I told Henry Oscar I had just returned from America and I mentioned the names of plays I'd been in at Finch and Yale. 'I follow what goes on in the American theatre closely,' he said, 'where were these plays produced?' I told the truth. He was kind. 'I'm so sorry,' he said, 'I can't engage a totally inexperienced actress.'

I felt that bottomless pit of bleak disappointment I was to know only too often when wanting a job desperately and not getting it. Mother, in her quiet, well-modulated voice, spoke up: 'While we were waiting backstage to come up to your office, we saw that they were auditioning on the stage.'

'That's for the variety entertainment division,' said Henry Oscar.

'Could Thelma audition for that?'

Henry Oscar said yes.

We stood in the wings watching the auditions. It was late in the afternoon. An elderly lady sang, 'All Things Come Home at Eventide' and a sad-looking man did a violin solo. Then a baritone sang, 'On the Road to Mandalay'. The only music I had with me was 'I Caint Say No' from *Oklahoma!* which I belted out in my loudest, vulgarest voice. *Oklahoma!* was playing in America, it had been a sensational breakthrough in the musical theatre, and I had done a production at camp. I always wanted to play the comedy part, Ado

Annie, and 'I Caint Say No' was her song. I saw the little group in the stalls sit up, take their feet off the chairs in front of them, start to smile. I think they had all been fast asleep until my belting woke them up. When *Oklahoma!* opened soon after the war in London, it played at the Drury Lane Theatre and was a smash hit but I claim to have been the first one to sing 'I Caint Say No' from that stage.

As soon as I had finished, a man came running round onto the stage. His name was Cecil Harrington and he asked us to come at once to his office. He explained that he was in charge of the Hospitals Division and he wanted me to join a troupe which started rehearsals the following Monday. 'Our groups entertain wounded and sick soldiers. We go into hospitals, convalescent homes ... anywhere housing disabled or sick servicemen and women.' I was over the moon – at last, a professional job.

'You'll be the soubrette,' he explained, 'comedy songs like "I Caint Say No". What is your name?'

'Thelma Wigoder,' I replied.

'Heavens, you can't have such a difficult name – nobody will be able to spell it or pronounce it. You must choose a stage name.'

I wasn't prepared for this. If I had to change my name, I rather fancied Thelma Leeds, as that was my home town but before I spoke up Mother, again, in her musical voice, *'My* stage name was Paula Ruby.'

'Very good,' said Cecil Harrington, 'that will look good on the posters and programmes – Thelma Ruby. See you on Monday.'

That is how I became Thelma Ruby ... I had reservations about the name because Ruby didn't seem to me to be a real surname. Years later, when Jack Ruby jumped into prominence for killing Lee Harvey Oswald, I felt a bit better about Ruby being my surname!

In our concert party there were six of us plus a pianist. I quickly gathered together a repertoire of American comedy songs. I was to be paid £7 a week, £3 a week rehearsal money. We started rehearsals on 27th November 1944. Between rehearsals and our opening on Christmas Day we had a short break and I went up to Leeds to Mom and Dad. For the rehearsal period, I had stayed with friends outside London. I booked digs in Camden Town for my return from Leeds. When I returned to London after seeing the folks, Mom gave me sandwiches for lunch on the journey, as wartime train journeys were difficult. No sort of refreshment, the trains were very slow, very crowded and very cold. I spent many hours on the train and arrived at Kings Cross in the early evening in pitch black and fog – still blackout, remember – and icy cold on Christmas Eve. My suitcase was heavy and there was no sign of a taxi. I lugged my case into the Underground and was very relieved when a soldier offered to carry it for me. He got out with me at Camden Town station, and then carried it quite a long walk to the digs. I was full of gratitude, and gave him the last sandwich and bit of cake left over from what Mother had given me and said goodnight.

I rang the doorbell. A lady answered and when I said who I was she said, 'I didn't expect you today, I thought you were coming tomorrow.' For several minutes she kept me outside in the cold but eventually she allowed me inside and took me upstairs to my room, brought me a cup of tea but no food – and I had given my last crumb to the helpful soldier – and I was starving hungry. She left me with no heating, no bedside light, no hot water – a dark, depressing, freezing room in which I spent one of the most miserable nights of my life. 'Christmas Eve,' I kept saying to myself, 'surely tonight of all nights the landlady will relent and discover within herself the milk of human kindness.' My feet were like ice – I have always had poor circulation in the feet, as well you know from when I dig them into your warm body to thaw. But never were they colder than Christmas Eve 1944. Lumps of ice. I sometimes get the circulation going by soaking my feet in hot water but there was no hot water, no hot water bottle. I tried wrapping them in my coat, I tried sitting on them, rubbing them – nothing helped. Not only my feet – my legs, my arms, my nose. I could not sleep.

Next day, Christmas Day, we did our first performance at a charming hospital in the country in a place called Wargrave and, to my great relief, were invited to stay overnight. So, at long last, I was launched as a professional performer.

We travelled all over the country in a minibus carrying a strip of footlights, and stayed at ENSA hostels. Each show in a different place. Sometimes we had a stage, sometimes on the same level as the boys, sometimes among the beds in a ward. We travelled to the most beautiful stately homes in the country. They had been converted into convalescent homes and often the stately families were there to run the place. We played to an entire audience of boys who had been blinded, another that was limbless. The boys who had lost both arms and both legs were perched on a couch on the front row, just a trunk and a face. We played to the mentally disabled, to boys just returned from prisoner-of-war camps, emaciated and barely alive. An important part of our job was to talk to the boys after the show, try to make them feel human and alive and not like freaks. This was a big effort for me. I have always been squeamish about anything medical but I said to myself quite firmly, 'If these boys can suffer like this, the least you can do is quell your fear and aversion and show all the compassion, humanity, cheerfulness and humour that you can summon up.' And I did.

VE day – the end of the war in Europe – was 8th May 1945. That evening our show was a few miles outside Chichester. There was a famous surgeon called Archibald McIndoe who specialised in plastic surgery and he was doing remarkable work for the air force boys who had been shot down in

flames and badly burned. He had a hospital in East Grinstead.
The boys had to have many operations to reconstruct their
faces and bodies, and this place outside Chichester was a
centre for them to recuperate between operations. Looking
out into the audience I saw some of the most horrific sights
of the entire tour. Whole faces burned off – ears and nose,
eyes and mouth disappeared, hands burned off – but the
euphoria of that night was fantastic. They laughed, they
screamed, they cheered, they loved the show and afterwards
in the bar they put their handless stumps through the
handles of the beer mugs and we celebrated together until
one o'clock in the morning. My heart was bursting with
admiration for their courage.

On the way back our coach broke down three times.
During one breakdown a policeman came over to us and
said, 'I think all the Jews should go over to Germany
immediately and inject a pint of their blood into every
German.' From Portsmouth we saw bonfires, flares and
flashes and the fleet lit up. By the time we got back to
Chichester it was the middle of the night. Nobody on the
streets. But after six years of blackout, Chichester Cathedral
and the ancient cross in the middle of the town were
brilliantly floodlit in green and red, the first lights for six
years. We wept for the beauty, the profound relief that for
us in Britain the war was over.

Return to Life

PETER
March 1938. I'm back in New York. It's early springtime and
it's chilly. With a paralysed right arm. I wore a lined, leather
glove on my right hand because the circulation was so poor
that the hand used to get terribly cold. Not as cold as your
feet, but bad enough. I was wearing a Catalan beret – a wide

beret which sticks out all around about two inches away from the skull. And my green suit. I looked like hell, very thin. May was taking care of me, she'd given me a bed in her apartment.

One night I went backstage at a Broadway theatre, where the Group Theatre was performing Clifford Odet's play *Golden Boy*. Luther Adler was playing the Golden Boy, Elia Kazan was playing Fuseli. I knew the whole cast from the time I was a Group Theatre apprentice. John Garfield, whom we used to know as Julie, had a small part. They were marvellous. They were certainly the best theatre company that America had ever seen. They were all shocked to see me because of the starved look and also because of the right arm hanging from the shoulder, the right hand enclosed in the black leather glove. Some of them thought I had lost my hand, or had an artificial arm.

I made contact again with my old life and pals got me an interview with Julie (Jules) Dassin who was directing a play called *Medicine Show* co-written by Oscar Saul. Julie gave me a part in the show. The name of my character was 'Pete'; I was a Polish steelworker. *Medicine Show* was a Living Newspaper about the need for social medicine in America. I was one of a group of fifteen men and woman who were all condemned to death by the statistics. Also May got me a job at Modern Age Books and taught me how to do book manufacturing – it's an interesting profession. Then I moved on upwards from that into the design of book jackets, the paper sleeves of books. And record sleeves. Although I am right-handed, I learned to do all this with my left hand.

May insisted that we get married and I said, 'May, what do you need me for? I'm no good to you.' She said, 'Of course you are. I love you and I want to take care of you.' That really tore it, that last line. I don't know what it was, some mistaken sense of pride, when she said, 'I want to take care of you' – I resented it. I had been with May off and on for a number of years. I left her to go to Spain, and now I was back with her and she was helping me. She thought we should formalise the relationship and get married. I resisted. I didn't want to marry May. Not because I didn't like her. As you know from meeting her – we always remained friends – May was an absolutely delightful person. She was then, as she remained, a charming girl with a great sense of humour, but she was older than me and the lightning had not struck. But psychologically and physically I did need somebody to look after me. Finally I said, 'All right, we'll get married' and we fixed a date. On a certain day she took an extended lunch-hour and we were supposed to meet at 11.30 a.m. in downtown New York in the municipal building to go through the civil ceremony. I came an hour late, and that was not my usual habit, I was normally very punctual. I did not want to get married, so I came an hour late but got married anyhow.

May was a good companion and a good friend, generously devoted to my improvement. It was arranged by one of the Spanish Aid Committees for me to have an operation; a very kind young Jewish surgeon at a hospital in Brooklyn would attempt to do a nerve graft on my arm. In 1938 that was a relatively new technique, a technique which was not really worked out until the terrible days of the Second World War when surgery made great advances all over the world. The young surgeon operated on me. He must have done something right because in time I did regain the use of my arm and partial use of the hand – the first three fingers of my hand function. I have, according to doctors' estimates, only thirty per cent of normal function in that hand. The last two fingers are totally useless and only get in the way. But now that my left arm and hand are useless I am all the more grateful to the young Brooklyn surgeon.

After my recovery I was appointed to the job of social director in Camp Unity. I worked there for two seasons – the summers of 1938 and 1939. It was a summer holiday camp run by the Communist party under some pretended independent framework. It was a camp for 'workers'. There were little bungalows, a big dining room, a social hall with a fairly well-equipped stage at one end. People came for their holiday at reasonable fees and a liberal-progressive cultural ambience. It could hold as many as a thousand guests simultaneously, a big operation.

I took the job because it flattered me. I was twenty-four years old and I was going to be in charge of a staff of twenty-seven people and responsible for all the entertainment and education programmes of the camp every day of the week. Like you some years later, I was in charge of the music, the theatre, lectures, athletic events, social games. I directed plays and when possible I acted in them. On the staff were George Kleinsinger, who became a well-known composer, one of his most famous compositions was *Tubby the Tuba*. And Earl Robinson who wrote *Ballad for Americans*. We did a musical called *Life in the Day of a Secretary* by Alfred Hayes, who later became a well-known and well-paid Hollywood screen-writer.

I had a group of six professional actors, all good singers, and I would augment that with guests who had some amateur theatre background. I had a technical director, in charge of scenery and construction. Earl Robinson was the music director. The following year I had Dean Dixon, a black man as the musical director. He also became famous as a conductor. It was a fascinating experience but what is interesting to me now, fifty years later, is how did I function in this framework which I had already learned to hate in Spain. This 'Communist party dictatorship of the proletariat'. I began to understand what had happened in the Soviet Union long before most other people. I was not anti-Communist. I was anti-the-Communist-Party which is quite a difference. How did this square with my conscience – that I was in charge of this programme which had to be vetted by the commissar. Everything I did, every programme that I planned had to be vetted to make sure that I wasn't straying from the party line.

I chose plays that were tendentious. I did an early one-act play by Bertolt Brecht called *Signora Cararras's Rifles*, a little one-act play about Spain – Brecht at that time was following the party line and I followed Brecht. When I chose a play, I chose a play of social content. Irwin Shaw's *The Gentle People*, which talks about some helpless, innocent victims of gangster-ism in the Brooklyn docks – the gentle people, by co-operating, manage to overcome the machinations of the gangster. They push him out of the boat and he drowns. That was for me! That had positive social value – it was also an entertaining play.

One weekend I brought out a man by the name of Huddy Ledbetter, known in the world of folk song as Ledbelly. Ledbelly was a convicted murderer who had been freed because he had become famous as a composer and player of folk music. American negro work-songs, folk songs. The entire camp was entranced by this really remarkable figure. He was very primitive, he was very crude, but he had a marvellous singing voice and he sang all his own songs. The visit of Ledbelly was a highlight of my programme that season. His records were being sold, stories were being written about him and he was a startling and unusual figure on the American cultural scene. He'd been taken up by the left wing.

I hired Shelley Winters, whose name was then Shirley Schrift. At the time she was about sixteen years old and was quite incredibly beautiful. I guess I didn't really hear the crudeness of her speech – it was a real Brooklyn accent. I guess mine wasn't all that good either. I hired her. She was a total disaster from beginning to end. She couldn't do anything right. She had no experience, she hadn't been trained, all she had going for her was that unbelievable beauty. She had a gorgeous figure, she was tall, she was slender – magnificent bosoms, an angelic face, curly blonde hair, but that was it. She was so bad that the manager of the camp, a good old party-liner by the name of Louis Pasternak, came to me and said, 'We've got to fire this girl.' I said, 'Louis, it's not her fault, she's just a kid.' We had a long argument but in the end Louis said: 'All right, OK, if you think you know what you're doing...' She stayed and didn't suffer the dishonour of being fired from her first job. And thus I saved the career of one of Hollywood's future queens!

I was a good master of ceremonies. I had all kinds of *shtick*, some of which, when I think of them now, make me hide my head in shame because they were so crude but they worked. They liked the fact that I was a veteran from Spain and they liked the programmes I gave them. I pushed Earl Robinson to complete *Ballad for Americans* and to conduct it, with actors, with singers, in Camp Unity. The first performance ever. The crowd went mad about it as the rest of the nation did later on when it was brought to their attention. I was very proud of that. George Kleinsinger's *The Whitman Cantata* – a choral setting for orchestra, soloists and chorus of Walt Whitman poems – magnificent! Performed first time at Camp Unity. We were progressive, we were avant-garde, we were social-minded and, artistically, we were people of integrity. We believed in what we were doing and we did it with loyalty and with enthusiasm.

At the end of the 1939 season the Soviets signed the Nazi-Soviet pact and that crisis resulted in people leaving the Party in droves. Most American Communists couldn't accept it. No matter what the comic stars tried to explain – saying this was the party line and we had to defend the Soviet Union even when they did things we didn't understand – it was no longer sufficient, it didn't work. This was all beyond me already because I had long defected from any sense of loyalty to the Party line. At the end of the 1939 season I left Camp Unity and the Communist Party for ever.

Starting a Career

THELMA

I left ENSA and was sent to Edinburgh to replace a girl who had taken ill, but who recovered before I arrived. I had finished my acting training at Finch and Yale in 1943, yet here I was in 1945 without having acted.

At this point, Miriam Warner, an agent who was a friendly, cockney, gruff-voiced, ample lady, got me my first legitimate job in a legitimate production – a musical called *The Three Waltzes* starring Evelyn Laye who was a big star of the musical theatre. She was glamorous and famous and I was greatly in awe of her. The show had been running fourteen months in the West End, and I joined them on tour for the last eight weeks.

I wasn't a chorus girl – no singing or dancing – but I was one of a group of five girls who kept turning up as different characters in different costumes. One of these girls had to leave, and I was brought in to replace her. The show was in three acts: the first act was in the Victorian era, the second in the Edwardian and the third was contemporary. Evelyn Laye played a mother, daughter and grand-daughter who, in the last act, is making a film about the life of her grandmother. Stirring stuff! Not exactly the important social-conscious drama with which you, Peter, were connected.

I had one line. Evelyn Laye's characters were all actresses. In the Edwardian sequence she is performing offstage to an audience that includes King Edward. I ran onto the stage which, in the play, was the side of the stage, the wings, and said to the dresser, 'Mrs Evans, Mrs Evans come quick. Katie's doing an encore, the King stood up and clapped!' That was the first line I spoke on the professional stage.

There was no doubting that Evelyn Laye was the star. Every other part supported her, showed her off at her beautiful best. When she made her first entrance in a huge crinoline dress, the audience would applaud. She ignored the actors on the stage and dropped into a deep curtsey to the audience. She was aware of everything that was happening, onstage or off, and was in complete control. She showed great kindness to me, the lowliest member of the cast, giving me encouragement and advice.

Our stage director, a tall, impressive man called Frank Royde, stood in the wings all evening making sure everything ran smoothly and at the front of the stage, supervising every scene change. He would tell us off if a curl was out of place, or if we let the train of our dress drag on the floor offstage – we had to lift the train the moment we made an exit. Evelyn Laye taught me how to handle a train. I was learning – things I hadn't learned in drama school. Every night I watched the whole show from the wings.

Four weeks before the end of the tour an actress who had a speaking part in the third act left the show. It was decided that, with such a small part and such a short time to go, they would cast the part from among the five 'chorus' girls. Frank Royde auditioned us. We read from the script. When I had finished my reading, he asked me to do it in a different way. I explained to him why I had read it the way I had and what I was trying to achieve. Then I went ahead and did what he asked. He called me to his room. 'I am going to give you the part,' he said, 'but I nearly didn't. If you want to be an actress there is a rule you must learn – if the director asks you to try something, do it without comment, question or explanation. If, after you have tried it with all your concentration and enthusiasm, it doesn't work for you, if you are not happy with it *then* is the time to discuss.' It was good advice.

Then he added, 'Being too pushy, that's one of the problems I've always found with your people.' It was the only hint of anti-semitism I can remember in the British theatre but it must have hurt – why else would I remember it so clearly and still feel a twinge of pain.

A real part in a real production on a real stage with a real star. I was impressed by the panache with which the seasoned actors handled anything which went wrong. At the last matinée, Evelyn Laye brought on a package of garlic sandwiches to an actor called Charles Goldner and they both sat, supposedly at the edge of a river, solemnly eating every last sandwich while improvising a scene. To me that was the height of professional sophistication.

When I came back to England, I started to read the *Daily Herald*, the daily newspaper of the Labour Party. I became very friendly with a couple called Esther and Leslie Joseph – they were both supporters of the Labour party and through them I became enthusiastic and joined myself. The war in Europe was just over. Such horror and fear would never again strike the world, this was the moment to build a fair and just society for everyone. During the 1945 campaign I worked for the Labour Party, campaigning, distributing leaflets, attending meetings. Esther was in hospital with rheumatoid arthritis and we transferred the excitement of the campaign to her hospital bed, infecting the fellow patients, trying to persuade them to vote Labour.

Imagine our excitement when Labour won – the celebrating with Esther and Leslie! We didn't expect Labour to win because of Churchill. The great hero Churchill was still leading the Conservative Party and we naturally thought that the entire country would vote for Churchill through gratitude to him. But to our amazement, there were enough people who said, 'Let's have a new world, and let's have a better world and let's start the post-war period with more concern for the people at the bottom of the heap.' I feel sad now, remembering that euphoria – the Nazis defeated, the war won and Labour elected to govern the country. We thought we would live to see a finer, more caring peaceful world. At last, when I was twenty, I became a left-winger and a socialist. Like you. Preparing, maybe, to fall in love with you twenty-five years later.

In 1946 I got a job in repertory with Harry Hanson's
Court Players and I stayed with him for a year as his leading
lady. As was the custom in those days it was twice nightly,
weekly repertory. Good parts, big parts. I arrived in Stockton-
on-Tees which was the first town we appeared in, and
couldn't find any digs. I booked into a hotel on the very
wide main street which was full of stalls on market day. It
was what was called a 'commercial hotel', meaning that it
was full of travelling salesmen. I had a tiny room, barely
furnished. The second night – don't forget I was still very
virginal and very young for my age – one of the salesmen
that I had talked to in the lounge came and knocked on my
door, put his head round and said, 'Can I do it with you?'
'What?' I said.

'I'll give you a pound!'

'Get out!' Maybe I should have said yes, it would have
helped me to pay for the room!

During the second week, when I had already rehearsed,
learned and opened in *Night Must Fall*, another man struck
up a conversation with me in the lounge. He was charming,
a travelling salesman from Manchester. The next day he
took me out for lunch. We had a good meal and at the end
he searched for his wallet and couldn't find it. 'I must have
left it at the hotel – could you lend me the money, I'll bring
it back to you tonight at the theatre.'

That evening, after the show, a knock on the door, there
he was and he said, 'Thelma, a most terrible thing has
happened, I've lost all my money. My wallet's been stolen. I
have searched everywhere. I've been to the police. Could
you please ... I've got to pay the hotel and I've got to get
back to Manchester and I don't have any money, and I've no
one to turn to. Could you lend me the money? I need £9.'
Which was my whole week's salary. 'I'll send it back to you
tomorrow, as soon as I get to Manchester.' I lent him the
money.

Two weeks later, I got his address from the hotel and

wrote a desperate letter because I desperately needed the money. Eventually I got a letter from his wife saying, 'I'm terribly sorry to inform you that my husband has been conning people and borrowing money all over the country. The police have at last caught up with him and he is, at this moment, in jail. There is no way I can return your money.' More things I was learning that I didn't learn at drama school.

I moved into digs with Mrs Blakeston. My £9 a week was a good salary for those days as a leading lady. The digs cost three guineas a week with all food included. Theatrical landladies were marvellous people who loved the theatre – they cared for you and spoiled you. They would give you good food, stay up late at night to give you a hot meal after the show, in return for which you had to listen to how they buried their husbands and the tales of the big stars who had stayed with them. All for three guineas a week! I had a landlady in Edinburgh who gave me a huge breakfast and tea as well as lunch and supper, and insisted on giving me sandwiches in case I got hungry between meals. The digs in Chester have left an indelible memory – the toilet was at the bottom of the garden and the bathroom was in the basement, which had a stone floor and no heating. And no taps. You heated the water in a large copper container heated by gas, then ladled the water into the bath. This cost extra.

I played so many parts: Eliza Doolittle in *Pygmalion*, a mixture of farces, thrillers, West End successes. No Chekhov, Ibsen or Shakespeare, but plenty of Emlyn Williams, Terence Rattigan, Nöel Coward and J B Priestley. We rehearsed in the day, did two shows in the evening and Tuesday, Wednesday and Thursday I stayed up all night learning the lines. I'm not a very quick study and I used to get very tired. Some way had to be found to stay awake and I started to smoke, to give me something to do to try and stay awake. I looked at myself one night and said, 'I don't like smoking. It's going to cost me a lot of money that I can't afford. I've got to find some other way of staying awake.' So I stopped the smoking and started eating fruit. I'd eat apples, I'd eat oranges, I'd eat a whole bowl of fruit to try and keep me awake during the night. For nine months.

I struggled to create a character. I remembered what my wonderful teacher at Finch, Frances Pole, had taught me. I tried to use the Stanislavsky method – remembering from my own life when I had felt a similar emotion. Remembering all the little physical details surrounding that happening, and then waiting for the emotion to come flooding back and I could use that in the situation in the play. If you had to play a murderer, you had to remember being on a picnic with a wasp buzzing around and around until you had only one passion – to kill the brute. I tried. I stayed awake.

After three weeks I thought, 'To hell with Stanislavsky! Let me learn the part as quickly as I can, use my instinct, my intuition and get on with the play!' Natalie Kent, who was the character actress in the company and with whom I shared a dressing-room, used to say, 'Darling, you've got three performances if you are very talented. Each week when you read the play say to yourself "Is it Number One out of the bag, is it Number Two out of the bag, is it Number Three out of the bag?"' That's all you need to know.' Never any question of digging into the character, of trying to understand the play, the background, just pull Number One out of the bag, Number Two out of the bag, or Number Three. Quick thinking. Improvising. They are all tools of the actor's trade, and are learned by doing. The year in repertory taught me many valuable techniques, despite the totally inadequate rehearsal time. It also gave me the confidence I badly needed. The same people came to see the shows week after week, and they had their favourites, and whenever you made your first entrance, you got a round of applause.

Twenty-one, starting a career. I learned that one of the

most precious bonuses of being an actress is the deep friendships you make, the camaraderie, the laughter, the caring, the feeling of belonging to a very elite group of people who really love their work. Very little Equity protection in those days – working long hours day and night, no rehearsal pay, primitive digs and dressing-rooms. We felt it a very small price to pay for the privilege of working in the theatre.

Shining Stars

PETER

Let me go back to 1941. I'm twenty-seven years old and I moved into a new phase. I started to attend acting classes in the Michael Chekhov studio in New York. Beatrice Straight, a sensitive and talented benefactor, was a young, extremely handsome actress belonging to the aristocracy of American wealth – five or six generations of inherited American wealth; they were already, in those days, millionaires who counted their millions in the hundreds. Her mother and stepfather, Dorothy and Leonard Elmhirst, had bought an estate called Dartington Hall in England and Beatrice Straight invited Michael Chekhov to Dartington Hall, where he laid the foundation of his new theatre. When the war broke out in 1939, Chekhov and his devoted followers moved to the US. Michael Chekhov – Mischa as everybody called him – had already taken New York by storm when he did a season there in 1935. I was taking classes with Michael Chekhov and Beatrice studied along with us. In those classes were some people whom I had already known before, including Elia Kazan and Morris Carnovsky of The Group Theatre, Sanford Meisner, who later became one of the best teachers in New York, and Marion Seldes, who is now in Hollywood.

THELMA
Was Michael Chekhov the only teacher?

PETER
When you had Michael Chekhov, you didn't need anybody
else. Born in 1891, died in Hollywood in 1955, he was one of
the most extraordinary actors and teachers of the twentieth
century. The nephew of the great Anton Chekhov, he had
been a student in one of the Stanislavsky studios. Stanislavsky
often referred to Chekhov as 'his most brilliant student',
although Chekhov radically challenged Stanislavsky's System
of modern acting. Chekhov was a successful actor, director
and teacher in Russia but, by 1927, was officially denounced
as an 'idealist – a sick artist, alien and reactionary' and was
marked for liquidation. But, in 1928, after receiving an
invitation from Max Reinhardt to perform in Germany, he
was given permission to emigrate. He lived in several places
in Europe, building a reputation as a director but, most
important, he was a fantastically brilliant actor. He was a
little man – I don't think he was more than five foot three,
with a high-pitched voice and a potato nose like Karl
Malden's, only much smaller because he was a much smaller
man.

When I was accepted into Chekhov's classes I was called in
to have a talk with him. I told him about my Russian
background, that my parents were Russian Jews. He assumed
that *I* was Russian. Thus, when he was giving his classes –
and he spoke in a very heavy Russian accent – he would
say:

'Peeterrr, telll mee, eez clearrr hvhatt I amm sayingg?
Peeterr, pleasz to trrahnslate forr mee, hvhatt is...' He
would burst into Russian and I was expected to translate. I
didn't know what he was saying but I could make a
reasonable guess. In this way it was established that I was
Michael Chekhov's translator. I have only just discovered
and am very proud that there is a chapter in his great book

Lessons for the Professional Actor which records our class on 8th December (I think that was the date of Pearl Harbor). Like this book, it is a duologue about acting technique between Michael Chekhov and me.

I had a wonderful time in those classes. I remember one improvisation in which I was partnered with Morris Carnovsky. Chekhov used to stage big, orgiastic improvisations where thirty people in the class were all in one improvisation, which used to become free-for-alls. Drunken sailors in a whorehouse in Marseilles! It was in one of those I remember Morris Carnovsky grabbing me by my jacket – it was winter time, I was wearing a tweed jacket – and he pulled so hard that he tore off all the buttons from the front of the jacket. But I was learning something about acting ... so what's a few buttons. For me these classes were a turning point because I had been ashamed of my crippled hand and felt I couldn't be an actor any more. I was overcoming that feeling here because I was involved with Chekhov and his thinking and his exercises which were brilliant. As a teacher I go into an acting class now flooded with memories of the things I learned from Chekhov.

In all my teaching I used a great deal of what I learned from him and I'd like to give you just a flavour. We would start by 'crossing the threshold', stepping out of our every-day world into that special, magical, ineffable space, the field of energy and vitality that radiates from the actor's creative work, that special and powerful atmosphere of the stage. That space which loves us.

The main difference between Chekhov's technique and that of Stanislavsky was that Stanislavsky's method is based on sense memory and emotional recall. He taught, as you have just told me, that the actor should dig down into his memory and personal experience, remember all the circumstances which provoked this emotion and let the emotion come flooding back and in that way you build your performance. Chekhov said that it should *not* come from your personal experience, but from your imagination. For example, to capture the sensation of sadness, imagine the grieving sounds of a rural family mourning the accidental death of a boy and girl; walk through the atmosphere of a flood-devastated village or sit and stand with a quality of sadness. Chekhov felt his performers could produce more powerful and individualised emotional expressions without having to evoke difficult-to-control memories of personal experience. Chekhov would say, 'Stanislavsky ... he tell you: in order to play this scene you must to remember your own grandfather. I say, no, no, no! Please to remember *all* grandfathers!'

His technique is based on developing imagination and concentration, a feeling of form, of beauty, of ease and of your relationship to the whole, including the importance of ensemble playing. We worked on developing a 'psychological gesture' for the character, which was not seen by the audience but which we could conjure up just before going onstage to give the *feel* of the character. We learned to have a centre either in or outside of our bodies to work from, which fitted the character – an inquisitive person might have it in the nose, a drunk swaying above the head, a noble person in the chest etc., and all movements flow from this centre. Oh, I can't teach you the Michael Chekhov technique in ten minutes, but he was great.

After some months in the class, Chekhov's assistant, Zhdanov, came to me and said, 'Mr Chekhov wants to know would you like to play Duke Orsino in his production of *Twelfth Night*. We have a tour of universities in the Southern States of America.' I didn't know then that Orsino is one of the most thankless roles in all of Shakespeare. It is terribly difficult to play, because there's no real scene anywhere.

This was my first Shakespeare. Except that I had done a piece of *Hamlet* when I was a boy. I asked my English Lit teacher at Baron Byng High School, Percival Algernon Gilchrist Clarke, permission to do the ghost scene from

Hamlet in the manner in which I conceived it. He agreed. I
sat on a pile of orange boxes which I had covered with an
old green velvety curtain. I had on a trench coat with the
collar pushed up under my wavy dark hair, and I sat
ensconced in a crevice between boxes, deep in thought.
Harry Davis, who was my side-kick in those days, was playing
the Ghost, which was an offstage voice. In my avant-garde
production he didn't appear – I was the only one on the
stage. The Ghost's lines emanated in my conscience – I was
hearing my father's voice in my mind – my replies were a
stream-of-consciousness soliloquy. Comes the performance,
I was supposed to answer him ... but not a word came out of
me, because I had exhausted myself doing the setting and
the lighting and the stage managing. Harry spoke the
Ghost's lines and waited for the reply ... and there was no
reply! So he spoke my lines as well! Every here and there I
would hold up my head and repeat something he had just
said ... to show that I was still with it.

Now I'm playing Duke Orsino in Chekhov's production.
Come to think of it, that rounded out my career as a
Shakespearean actor. The part of Fabian was played by Yul
Brynner who was a lovely companion. He was full of fun,
extremely charming and very, very good. Very athletic, very
strong body, and a wonderful, rich speaking voice. It was a
good cast, a lovely production and it put me smack, right
back into the middle of showbusiness again. I had overcome
my shame about having a crippled hand on the stage.

I wanted to develop my directorial ability, especially in
comedy. So I got jobs directing mostly comedies in summer
stock. In Pennsylvania I did *Design for Living* by Nöel
Coward, one of the great comic dramatists of the century.
There I had my first encounter with a star personality and
there I was blooded. The star was Ilka Chase, who was a
Hollywood star and was travelling the summer circuit. I
come to my first rehearsal – no star. 'Where is she?' 'She
doesn't arrive until two days later because she has just

finished a week playing the same part in another summer theatre; you rehearse the other characters and then she'll fit in.' There are six or seven characters in *Design for Living*, and I started to lay out the staging. Monday goes by and no Ilka Chase, Tuesday goes by and no Ilka Chase and Wednesday she arrives. Ilka Chase was a tall, slender, rather good looking woman with a terribly posh accent. She was American but she was trying desperately hard to sound British. She arrived with her two leading men – I had been directing the subsidiary characters. We started the rehearsal and she said, 'Listen everybody, it's quite simple, when I stand you all find places and sit, but when I sit down will you all please stand. For this scene I sit over here so you all stand, and darling, you here and you here,' and I'm helpless. This did not check with anything in my experience. I had never been man-handled by a star before. I didn't know what to do.

The rehearsal finished and I went to a bar near the theatre to have a drink with the other members of the cast, who were just as flabbergasted as I was. She had changed everything. The first thing I did was get plastered, which was very helpful because it relieved the tension and the worry. The second thing, I said to myself, 'Either I break this lady, or she breaks me. I'm going to sit down tonight and write a little script of what I will say to her tomorrow.' My script said, in effect, 'You don't have a clue as to what is proper stage behaviour. I don't know where you got your training, but you cannot come in and ride roughshod over a cast of actors the way you did yesterday and I am certainly not going to allow it. You are going to do as I tell you. You're going to take direction from me, or you can take this job and stick it up your dittybox.'

Next morning she arrived a few minutes late and said, 'Good morning, darlings!' I launched into my tirade. Quietly, calmly, with a strong voice. She stood there ... she said, 'Why darling, why darling...' She didn't know what else to say – everybody was darling to her. Even though I was insulting her I was still darling. I said, 'If you are ready, we will now start the rehearsal and you will do as I ask you to do.' She was so flabbergasted that she did. Saturday night the show opened and the managers of the theatre came to me and said, 'That was absolutely brilliant,' But Miss Chase wouldn't talk to me … I wonder why! When I went backstage she very obviously snubbed me even though we'd had a terrific reception.

I directed a play at the Barter Theatre in Virginia. Here people did not pay admission in cash money, they brought what they could from their farms – a hen, a dozen eggs or some vegetables – and this food was used to feed the actors. I directed an original play by Sherman Ewing who, with his wife Marjorie, were well-known producers in New York. Sherman's play was about Voltaire and the French Revolution. Ernest Borgnine played the Emperor Frederick and Hurd Hatfield played Voltaire. Two splendid young actors who went on to great careers in Hollywood. The importance of this production is that it led to Sherman Ewing coming to me a few months later saying, 'I've been invited by ANTA, the American National Theatre and Academy, to do a play for their fifth anniversary. We've decided to do Bernard Shaw's, *Getting Married*, with an all-star cast. Will you direct it?'

I bought a new suit of tobacco-brown tweed and a pair of fancy shoes – Church's English shoes – of brown buckskin which I thought went very well with my brown tweed suit! The cast was going to include Peggy Wood in a central role. She was a star – a very beautiful woman with a rather haughty acting style, which the audience seemed to like very much. She was a doyenne of the American theatre. It was a great cast: John Merivale, John Buckmaster – a real bastard – and Arthur Treacher. I made sure that I came to the first day of rehearsal well prepared. I started to stage the play and everybody was very affable and very willing. Arthur Treacher was a very funny man. When I gave him a direction, he'd

say, 'Quite right old boy, in the future give it to me by the
numbers.' I said, 'What do you mean Arthur?' He said, 'Just
say number thirteen, and I'll give you what's needed.' What
he meant was that if I found it necessary to say something to
him, then obviously what he was doing was wrong, but he
would fix it himself. He didn't want to be told how to do it.
That's how I directed him, by the numbers. I'd say 'Arthur,
thirty-five.' He'd say, 'Righto' and continue. He was very
good and very funny and a great addition to the cast.

The others were actors with whom I got along very affably
and everything was fine, except for Peggy Wood who didn't
come to the first day of rehearsals because her part didn't
start until somewhere near the middle of the play. She came
on the second day and, like Ilka Chase, she started to give
directions to everyone. By now I was experienced, and I
handled her similarly to the way I had handled Ilka Chase. It
worked again. Arthur Treacher was standing in the back
giving me the high sign – 'You've done well, me laddie,' and
the rest of the cast was standing there beaming. The
production opened at the Helen Hayes Theatre on 52nd
Street. I'm glad to say it was considered a brilliant production and got wonderful reviews. Sherman was very
proud of me.

These stories about 'breaking' the stars. Was that the right
way to do it, was it fair? Was I wrong? Did I behave badly?
I've had it on my conscience – not to the point where I had
sleepless nights about it, but I have needed to convince
myself I was right. The answer is startlingly simple: a
director directs. If he doesn't direct he isn't a director.

The West End

THELMA
1947 was the year of my first West End appearance. The play

was *The White Devil* by John Webster, directed by Michael Benthall and starring Robert Helpmann. What a thrill. This was the first production of a projected season of classical plays at the Duchess Theatre. Do you hear those words that made my heart sing? West End. Stars. Classics.

My part could have been bigger for my West End debut. I played an old lady with blacked-out teeth, The Keeper of the House of Converted Whores – the whores had been converted to Christianity. My one and only line was to Robert Helpmann while he pressed bribe money into my hand, 'Should it be known the Duke hath such recourse to your imprisoned sister, I were like t'incur much damage by it.' My main task in the company was to understudy Martita Hunt, who was already firmly into, to put it kindly, her middle age, and I was twenty-two. Martita Hunt was a formidable lady, well-known as a lesbian. She used to invite me into her dressing-room and pour tea for me from a black teapot into black teacups, and then give me speech lessons. She would take my hand, slap it onto her middle and shout, 'Feel my diaphragm!' After the show there was always a crowd at the stage door waiting for Robert Helpmann's autograph. Martita would stride out, wearing trousers, and nobody knew who she was. So she would grab the autograph books and say, 'You want my autograph, don't you?'

She was a good actress. The rest of the cast were also superb: Margaret Rawlings, Hugh Griffith, Andrew Cruikshank, Patrick Macnee (*The Avengers* star), and a 16-year-old in her first part, Claire Bloom. I had one line, Claire didn't have any. I shared a dressing-room with another lovely actress, Joan Schofield, at that time married to the popular film star Dennis Price. Our tiny dressing-room became the social centre for all the company. On matinée days we gave great tea parties with cakes from the best shop in London, Floris. What a squash – I perched on Hugh Griffith's knee because there was nowhere else for me to sit. He told Joan once he thought that I'd fallen for him because I sat on his knee – but I only sat there because there wasn't anywhere else for me to sit, unless he sat on my knee. Just the men in the company ... we never bothered about the girls in the show. The production was a great success with audiences and with the critics. *The White Devil* is a bloody melodrama from the time of Shakespeare and Benthall directed it with panache. Robert Helpmann was famous as a ballet dancer but this established him as a damn good actor. He and Michael Benthall, who were 'a couple', were the artistic directors of the season at the Duchess, and for the second production they chose *He Who Gets Slapped* by Andreyev. They engaged Tyrone Guthrie to direct it.

To my joy, I was invited to stay with the company to play a small part in the new production. Tyrone Guthrie, very, very tall and thin, was one of the most talented and famous directors of his generation. My part was non-existent, no more than a walk-on. Yet Guthrie found the time and deemed it important that my character should have a name, Edie, and the part grew through improvisation. By making us small part actors feel important he enriched the fabric of the production – surprisingly this is a rare quality in directors. Most of them concentrate only on the leading players.

In this case the leading actors alongside Helpmann were an old actor of repute, Ernest Milton, a magical young actress, Audrey Fildes, and a French actress, Suzy Prim. This time I was the understudy of Suzy Prim. *He Who Gets Slapped* is a circus story, and I was understudying the lady lion tamer, Zinaida. On the first morning of rehearsal we sat around to read the play. Guthrie turned to me: 'Thelma, Suzy Prim has sent a message from Paris that she cannot be here this morning, so would you please read the part.' Next day she didn't arrive, so I continued to do the part. Helpmann and Guthrie started to worry. Helpmann phoned Paris and was given the message, 'Miss Prim is in the South of France with her dying mother.' He phoned Paris daily, and was given the same message. For two weeks. Meanwhile I had this valuable experience of rehearsing a major role with Tyrone Guthrie.

By this time in panic, Helpmann phoned a friend in Paris and asked him to go around to the house to see if he could find Suzy Prim. The door was opened by a maid who said, 'Miss Prim has just gone out shopping, she'll be back in half and hour.' That was the end of Suzy Prim! Tony Guthrie, as he was known, was charming. He took me aside, praised my efforts highly but said that I was much too young for the part and they would have to get somebody else. They brought in an actress called Margaret Diamond, and they extended the rehearsal period to five weeks, unheard of in those days. Great play. Brilliant production. First night. Ernest Milton, who had a large part, came onto the stage – and dried. He couldn't remember the line. He was prompted, but by then he had fallen apart completely and he couldn't remember *any* of his lines. Every single line had to be fed to him in a loud voice by the stage manager. Bobby Helpmann said afterwards, 'I didn't pray, "Please God let Ernest Milton remember his lines," I prayed, "Please God, let Ernest Milton drop down dead, then we can carry him offstage and get on with the play."' It was agony. It was disaster. The owner of the Duchess Theatre, watching from the back of the circle, made a phone call before the final curtain and booked in another show to open in two weeks' time.

The second night Ernest Milton knew every line and was brilliant. The show was a sensation. The audience gave us an ovation. Too late – we were given our notice. Word got around the theatre-going public and the theatre was packed every night, cheers every night – it was heartbreaking. After the closing performance, Robert Helpmann stepped forward to make a speech. It took him some time to quieten the audience, who were going crazy. 'I wish you all to know that, as artistic director of this season, this production is being withdrawn tonight without my knowledge or consent.' The crowd went wild, they rushed onto the stage, huge crowds at the stage door – but it was the end. Not only of this production but of their plans for the rest of the season. It's not fair that one actor going to pieces on one particular evening should torpedo an exceptional, important, brilliant production which has taken years to write and mount. I don't think there should be one First Night, but a week of premieres with the critics coming on different nights. As it is, many of us are in terror on the First Night and give an inferior performance, knowing that not only the production but our entire careers are at stake.

A young actress in London in the late 1940s – looking back, it was a period of endless excitement. I didn't sit at home waiting for the phone to ring. I would go up to the West End – the small area around Piccadilly, Shaftesbury Avenue, Leicester Square. Packed with theatres, cinemas, restaurants, coffee bars, theatrical costumiers, second-hand bookshops, new bookshops – and friends. Like being in a village. I used to 'do the rounds', as it was called. Call in to the agents, or if something was being cast, just turn up and hope for a chance to interview or audition.

Auditions are so frightening. The preparation for them, the diarrhoea, the journey to them with pounding heart often from the other end of the country at your own expense. The feeling of worthlessness as you wait with crowds of other hopefuls, stepping onto an empty stage lit by work lights with an anonymous voice from the stalls telling you to start. 'Thank you – next!' You've worked for days if not weeks, you have spent money on rehearsing, if it's a musical, with a pianist. And a choreographer to help you to set the number. Had your hair done specially in the West End by an expensive hairdresser. Unable to sleep or eat. 'Thank you – next.' Auditions never stop, even when you are well known, even when you are older. There *must* be a better way to cast a play than to put actors through such agony and expense. We are all so vulnerable and eager for even a crumb of praise. We are not playing a violin, or painting a canvas, we are exposing our deepest and most private inner self for assessment – we must be crazy! There is no escape. Nearly all my jobs were from auditions. When the miracle happened and I got a job in those early days, I would take the new script and go to Taylors Coffee Bar on Rupert Street which would be full of actors – their delighted congratulations tinged with envy. Olivelli's in the basement at night, crowded with pros – still flaunting the new script.

I also went through periods of inertia when out of work. I could not get out of bed, It was a big effort to get up and get to the bank before it closed at 3.30. I never had any desire to undertake any other kind of work and if I couldn't act, all other activity was meaningless. Sometimes I tried – for a while I grew sweet peas. I wish there had been an Actors Centre in those days where I could have taken courses, tried to improve my acting. It wasn't that I was actively unhappy, I just shut myself off from living. I slept the time away and now I am furious I didn't make better use of my time. In my twenties I opted out of politics, social work, involvement with Equity, serious conversation. I was a loyal friend and a good daughter – but, oh, how I wasted my time.

My next West End part was in a play called *Four Hours to Kill* by Norman Krasna at the Saville Theatre. A huge cast, headed by a Hollywood gangster film star, Jack La Rue, and directed by a Hollywood director, Noel Madison. The action takes place in the foyer of a cinema and many stories intertwine. Again my part was small, again I was understudying, this time the leading lady who was the girlfriend of the backer, neither of them heard of before or since. It was not as straightforward as you think, getting the job of the understudy. Noel Madison, the director, asked me to go to his hotel suite where he would hear me read the part and then decide if I could have the job. You would think that by 1948, nearly twenty-three years old, I would be a little bit wise and wary at such an invitation. Not I. And I was still 'saving it'! 'I can't quite decide,' he said, 'the understudy job is between you and another girl in the company. It depends which of you is nicer to me.' Then he fell upon me with the object of seducing me, and I fought him off. I escaped intact, shaken but pure! The other girl did have an affair with him but he gave me the job of the understudy.

After the first performance in London, we got a polite reception from friends in the stalls, but loud 'boooohs' from the gallery, with added catcalls and whistles when a huge bouquet of flowers was presented from the backer, Saul Harris, to the leading lady, Barbara Blair. The next day the dreaded announcement on the notice-board. 'We regret that this production will close in two weeks.' Only a two-week run so there were no understudy rehearsals. The Monday night of the last week, I was making up twenty minutes before the curtain was due to go up when the stage manager rushed in, 'Thelma,' she said, 'you are going to have to play Barbara Blair's part tonight. She has just phoned to say that she has fish poisoning.'

I ran quickly down to the star's dressing-room. Barbara Blair wore a very expensive gown in the show made by the top designer, Rahvis – pale turquoise raw silk thickly hand-beaded with black jade, strapless with a tight straight skirt, and high platform shoes to match. She was size ten, I was size fourteen. By wearing nothing at all underneath, the dresser and the wardrobe mistress hauled me into the dress and fastened the zip which went all the way up the back. She was also five feet two to my five foot seven, so the skirt which reached the floor on her barely covered my calf. No rehearsal, hardly able to breathe in the dress, wobbling on the high platform shoes, I was half carried onto the stage.

I threw myself into the performance, anxious to make the most of this unexpected chance. I was doing fine until it came to a love scene and, tenderly looking into my lover's eyes, I felt the zip starting to come undone. Under my breath I said to my lover, 'Pretend you're making love, put your arms round me and try to do up the zip!' The poor man tried, but it needed at least two people to haul up that zip – and he failed. I played the rest of the act facing the audience with my arms held up in front of me to stop the whole dress collapsing around my ankles. I think the audience was fooled but the entire company were behind me and had a view of my naked back extending very low. The curtain came down for the interval and they all exploded with laughter. I walked off the stage and fell with a thump – the bloody platform shoes! I limped and gasped my way to the end. I was given a solo curtain call, the cast all applauded onstage, it got into the papers – 'West End ovation for Leeds actress', said the *Yorkshire Post*. I thought that was my one night of glory and that it was over. But Barbara Blair never was seen again. The next day I was taken to a costumier to hire a dress and shoes, and I played the part for the rest of the week, until we closed.

Teaching and Improving

PETER
Late 1945 I got a job in New York teaching acting at the American Theatre Wing, which had established a school for American actors who had served during the war and who were now being demobilised and felt that they needed a refresher. Amongst the teachers there were Martin Ritt and another friend by the name of Joe Anthony, who later became a well-known director in New York. We would get a group of between twelve and twenty students and we had volunteer actresses to play the women's parts, including Jean Stapleton, who later became very famous and Eileen Heckert, who has had a wonderful Hollywood career.

We invited agents, directors, theatre people. That's how

Lee Marvin got his start, out of one of my showcases. Lee Marvin in those classes was remarkably similar to the persona he revealed later on the Hollywood screen. Tough, iconoclastic, hard to handle. A powerful, inner-directed young man. He didn't want to hear about the philosophy of acting or the social function of the theatre arts. He was the total pragmatist. If your suggestion worked for him he bought it. Everything else was bullshit. He didn't whisper, he said it out loud, I learned to cope with him, we parted friends.

We would work on acting exercises but mainly I encouraged the students to start working on scenes. We would analyse the scenes, I would encourage them to push ahead and complete the scenes – direct them, rehearse them over and over again to remind them of the demanding discipline of professional theatre work. This was a very exciting period in my life. I was getting a reasonable salary. I put in a lot of volunteer extra hours to make the thing go. For one thing I had great sympathy for these individuals, for another I was very loyal to the idea. This is the way society should work – cooperative self-help. The American Theatre Wing had been formed during the war years to do what you did in ENSA. Then, when they realised that the men were coming home, someone came up with this very bright idea of retraining classes and it worked beautifully.

In 1946 I am called in to talk to Mr Erwin Piscator – millions of people don't know today but he was probably the greatest director in the world – who was going to start a new drama school at the New School for Social Research, to be called the Dramatic Workshop. I came to see Mr Piscator, preceded by my reputation as a teacher at the American Theatre Wing. He said, 'Would you leave the Theatre Wing?'

'No, I don't think I would like to leave the Theatre Wing.'

'Could you manage to give me a certain number of hours of teaching in my school?'

'I'm sure we could work out a reasonable schedule,' I replied. He hired me.

Piscator then said, 'I'm giving a party for the staff of the school. I think it is a better idea to give a party at the beginning of the term rather than wait to the end, because if you wait until the end, we might not want to have a party.' I came to this party at the New School for Social Research – there were drinks, there was food. 1946, I am thirty-two years old. I didn't drink very wisely, I drank too much, and I got pissed. I'm a very pleasant drunk – I become so sweet and good! In my drunkenness, I go up to Mr Piscator and say, 'Herr Piscator, tomorrow I have to start teaching and I don't have a clue of what I'm going to teach.' He beckoned me over with his index finger and he said into my ear, 'Herr Frye, alvays teach vat you don't know.' I staggered home, rather bemused. In the morning I had to show up at the school to teach, that line of his ringing in my ears. Always teach what you don't know. I didn't understand it.

I came to the school fifteen minutes early, knocked at the door of Piscator's office and said, 'Mr Piscator, last night, when I was drunk, you said something to me which sounded very good at the time but I don't understand it. Could you explain it?'

'Vat did I say?' he asked me.

'You said "Always teach what you don't know."'

'Ah, *ja, ja, ja.* If you will teach what you already know, to you it will not be interesting, therefore to the students you will not make it interesting. But if you teach what you *don't* know – I rely that you have natural curiosity and you will propose the subject to the students in such a way as is suggested by your curiosity and you will make them curious, and together you will learn what both of you don't know.' I have remembered this line all my life, and I would say that I based my philosophy of teaching on this line. I always reminded myself every time I started a new class in different situations in New York and later on in Tel Aviv: 'Alvays teach vat you don't know.'

The government had developed a programme of scholarships, something called the GI Bill which was an appropriation to pay all veteran soldiers for a certain number of years of schooling so that they could work their way back into civilian life. This was very good for the schools because it kept them afloat during this period, and it was very good for the students. At the Dramatic Workshop some of my students were Rod Steiger, Nehemia Persoff – known as Nicky, Martin Balsam and, for a brief period, Walter Matthau. And Jean Sachs, later a very successful director in New York. Piscator arranged special scholarships for girls: I worked with Patricia Neal, Elaine Stritch, Beatrice Arthur – now very popular in *The Golden Girls* and Elaine Dundy who became a best-selling author.

When Patricia Neal arrived, she stood in the doorway of my office looking absolutely gorgeous and she said to me in that low, snakey, seductive growl, almost like Talullah, 'Mr Frye, do you think I can do anything in the theatre?' She had a heavy Southern accent. I just looked at her and said, 'Honey, you can do anything in the world you want to do!' I accepted her and put her into a play I was doing at the time, *The Scarecrow* – a nineteenth-century American play. She was a member of this class which included Martin Balsam, Nicky Persoff and Lee Bergere, who played the butler in *Dynasty*.

I then did a production of *Of Mice and Men*. I developed an idea of a singing wayfaring stranger who links the scenes. You remember I told you about bringing Ledbelly to Camp Unity? I had learned a lot of his songs and used them. One of the songs I learned from Ledbelly was 'Goodnight Irene' and I put that into the show as one of the choruses of the wayfaring stranger, and then it was picked up in a scene-change by the whole cast as they played a horseshoe game. There were no real horseshoes, but they played a game of pitching horseshoes and singing 'Goodnight Irene'. The production was an enormous success. We had moved into a little theatre, off Broadway, The 48th Street Theatre in which Piscator mounted a series of productions which were the rage of New York. Everybody came to see them because they were brilliant, they were stunning. He did something called *All the King's Men* adapted from the novel by Robert Penn Warren, a very successful American writer of the period. He did Jean-Paul Sartre's *The Flies* and *Les Nuits de la Colère* by Armand Salacrou. We continued to perform *Of Mice and Men* as part of the repertoire. The Dramatic Workshop Theatre was the toast of New York.

Piscator decided to spread out his school and rented a second theatre in downtown New York called The Houston Street Playhouse It had a much larger stage than the one on 48th Street, in a very old building. The school was expanding so rapidly he needed more classrooms, more space. He decided to open the season at The Houston Street Playhouse with my production of *Of Mice and Men*.

People come, people go, and we had to put in replacements to the cast. I had had a fairly well-known American folk singer doing my wayfaring stranger on 48th Street – Jerry Reed – red-headed with a freckled face and a sweet singing voice. He left. Among my new students was a tall, slender, very beautiful black boy, and I said to him one day, 'Harry, can you sing?' He said, 'I don't know, I've never tried.'

'Can you carry a tune?' I asked him.

He put his hands together as if carrying a weight and said, 'Carry a tune, I don't know.'

'I'm going to teach you a song and then you try to sing it back to me.' I taught him, *a capella*, the first song that I used in my show which goes like this:

> Times are getting hard, boys.
> Money's getting scarce.

If times don't get no better, boys,
I'm going to leave this place.

Take my true love by the hand,
Lead her from the town.
Say goodbye to everyone,
Goodbye to everyone.

I went through it with him a couple of times. He picked it up and started to sing. I said, 'Son, you have got a beautiful voice.'

'I do?'

'Yes, you do!'

'I didn't know that,' he replied.

'I'll teach you the rest of the songs in the show, and I'd like you to play this part,' I told him.

'I hope you know what you're doing!'

And that was the beginning of my work with Harry Belafonte. He appeared in this show – he was stunning. He was seen by some agents and picked up immediately and put into a nightclub. That was the last I saw of him. But when Harry Belafonte put out his first recording, he dedicated it to me. On the label of the record it said, 'To my teacher Peter Frye'.

When I was teaching at Piscator's Dramatic Workshop, I met Reiken Ben-Ari. He had been a student in one of Stanislavsky's studios in Russia, and then joined the Habimah Theatre studio in 1921. He was one of the beggars in Vachtangov's famous production of *The Dybbuk* which toured all over Europe in the twenties. When the show came to America there was an internal squabble and some members of the Habimah company stayed behind in America, the others went to Palestine and founded the National Theatre. Ben-Ari was one of those who stayed in America. Amongst other activities in the scramble to stay alive he got a job teaching at Piscator's School. Ben-Ari boiled down the whole Stanislavsky system of acting to three questions. When you are on the stage you must ask yourself: '1 Hwherrre do I cahmingk frromm? 2 Hwherrre do I gohingk? 3 Hwhatt thah h'helll I'm doingk h'heerrr?' Ben-Ari was absolutely right.

Ben-Ari asked me to direct a group of actors who wanted to do a play in Hebrew. One of the leading figures was a lady by the name of Shifra Tzemach who had collected a group of actors of very varied experience, most of whom had survived the Holocaust after having been caught in Europe during the war years. When I met them, they said: 'We've found only one text translated into Hebrew – *The Merchant of Venice.*'

'You're crazy!' I said, 'in 1947 you want to play *The Merchant of Venice* in Hebrew? A play which is fundamentally anti-semitic?'

Someone said, 'It isn't anti-semitic, it depends how you interpret it.'

'I will not direct for you *The Merchant of Venice* in any language, but if you are willing to enter upon a period of improvisation, I would like to create a play – based around the Shylock scenes in *The Merchant of Venice* with a dramatised discussion about the meaning and significance of the play. We will reason out why we are doing these scenes from *The Merchant of Venice* today in New York in 1947.'

We started to build a play in which a group of players from different backgrounds, like *their* backgrounds – out of the concentration camps, out of a Catholic monastery, out of war-shattered Europe – come together in New York and want to do a play in Hebrew, and the only text they've got is a translation of *The Merchant of Venice* – should they do it? I drafted Nehemiah Persoff who had been born in Palestine and spoke Hebrew fluently. He played Bassanio and was a great help to me because he was accustomed to my techniques of improvisation. He also became my translator because at that time I knew no Hebrew. I insisted that in addition to the play being in Hebrew, every here and there we break out into the native languages of the different people involved in the play – French, Russian, Italian – and Yiddish. The play was peppered with phrases from all of these different languages. It had music – I found, for example, an English song of the fifteenth century which approved and celebrated the anti-Jewish massacres in York.

I called the play *Shylock '47*. It was centred around the question: Was the creation of Shylock only the creation of an anti-semitic character or are there redeeming features in the character that make him an archetype of universal application? I divided the play into three acts – the first act as it might have been performed in the Shakespearian London of the sixteenth century; the second act as it might have happened in Germany, after the Lutheran Reformation in the seventeenth century. The third act was performed as it might have taken place in Cyprus in one of the British concentration camps where they held the poor Jews taken off the illegal boats on their way to Palestine. You can imagine how emotive this was for the people in the cast and for the audiences that came to see it.

In different scenes I reversed the actors playing Shylock and Antonio. I wanted to show how little was the difference between the Jewish and the non-Jewish merchants of Venice. Ben-Ari played the traditional conception of Shylock as an evil, greedy little man, driven by his feelings of revenge to kill his arch-enemy Antonio and Miguel played Antonio as a hero. But when they reversed roles, Ben-Ari played Antonio as a cunning merchant and Miguel played Shylock tall, proud, unashamed, saying, 'Yes, I want to exact my revenge because revenge is something I learned from you.'

I hired an old Jewish actor called Mr Shochat from the Yiddish theatre in 2nd Avenue to play a priest in the courtroom scene, there to administer the last rights to Antonio when Shylock insists on his pound of flesh. I wanted him to make the sign of the cross, but before he can begin his prayer, Portia comes in with her speech 'The quality of mercy...' But Shochat had come to rehearsal with the prayer memorised in Latin and insisted on speaking the entire prayer. I kept telling him, 'No, just make the sign of the cross.' Every rehearsal he insisted on reciting the entire *Domini Pobiscum*. On opening night, I arranged with the actor playing Antonio to stumble into him when he had made the sign of the cross and shove him into the wings where a stagehand grabbed him and pulled him off. While being dragged off, Shochat shouted the prayer at the top of his voice. Fortunately he was old and his voice didn't carry out front.

We played for a month to full houses, in small theatres, I grant you, but it was a tremendous hit. A critic came from the *New York Post* and wrote, 'If you want to see a really splendid anti-Fascist play, you'll have to take a quick course in Hebrew and go to see *Shylock '47*. It is the best play in New York right now.' The famous actor of the Yiddish Theatre, Jacob Ben-Ami saw it and wanted to buy the rights to translate the play into Yiddish. Jacob Ben-Ami, the great Yiddish actor whom I had adored since I was seven years old. I foolishly refused because he wanted to play only Shylock, not Antonio, and I thought it would spoil my conception that there is no real difference between the noble Antonio and the evil Shylock – that they can be interchangeable and if only one actor played Shylock the point would be lost. When Portia comes into the court and says: 'Which is the merchant and which is the Jew?' in my production both of them stood up simultaneously. There is no Christian, there is no Jew. There are human beings who get trapped in human situations. There are human motivations like revenge and you cannot say that Shylock will always behave like Shylock because he is a Jew. Shylock will behave like Shylock because he is a human being who has suffered a great deal at the hands of the Christians. And you must think carefully before calling anybody a 'Shylock', thereby stereotyping Jews as greedy and bloodthirsty.

Playbill

THELMA
In 1948 I got my first real part in the West End – not a small part and understudy, a part in my own right. A new play by Terence Rattigan called *Playbill*, starring Eric Portman, Mary Ellis and Marie Löhr, directed by Peter Glenville. An evening of two short plays, *The Browning Version* and *Harlequinade*.

I was in *Harlequinade*. The setting is a provincial theatre in the north, a dress rehearsal for *Romeo and Juliet* led by a middle-aged Donald Wolfit style actor-manager and his leading lady wife playing Romeo and Juliet. In the middle of the rehearsal a girl – me – wanders onto the stage with her soldier husband and a pram with a baby. My opening line was, 'Can I speak to me Dad, please.' It transpires that as a young actor the leading man had an affair with the land-lady's daughter in this Yorkshire town which he has completely forgotten about. I am the result of this liaison and have come with my husband to meet my dad and introduce him to his grandson. Romeo with a grandson! Mine was a lovely part – I kept appearing at odd moments and in odd places, at one point finding myself on Juliet's balcony and getting vertigo.

First reading. The New Theatre, now the Albery Theatre. The special excitement of the cast assembling, all strangers, sitting in a semi-circle on the stage. Next to Peter Glenville sat the handsomest man I had ever seen – tall, blond, perfect features, a sweet smile … Terence Rattigan. Wow, could I have fallen for him but I was on the wrong side of the fence. What a loss for womankind! I was seeking a man to share my life with, and whom do I meet? Robert Helpmann, Michael Benthall, and in this show – Terence Rattigan, Peter Glenville, Eric Portman...

I had been given the script of *Harlequinade* but not of *The Browning Version*. I listened while that play was read aloud for the very first time. It was an hour of special theatrical magic that was never repeated ... a sort of perfection. I wept, was deeply moved and thrilled. In the entire rehearsal period, not a word was changed – maybe unique in working on a new play. It was exactly right the way he wrote it. Among the cast was a huge man, middle aged and with a very upper-class speaking voice – Campbell Cotts. My part was in a Yorkshire accent which, of course, is second nature to me. He had the part of the front-of-house manager of the theatre, also with a Yorkshire accent. Campbell came up to me after a few days and said, 'I'm having trouble with my Yorkshire accent – could you help me?' Thereafter, when-ever we both had a break in rehearsals, we went into an empty dressing-room and I coached him in 'Yorkshire'. One day he said, 'Do you think we could continue this over lunch?' It is an unwritten law among actors that if you go out to eat together, everybody pays for himself. Campbell steered me to a very fancy club with astronomical prices. I blanched. To my relief, at the end of the meal he said, 'Put your purse away. I insist on paying. It's the least I can do to thank you for all your help.'

A few days after our lunch I discovered that Campbell Cotts was really Sir Campbell Mitchell-Cotts, the premier baronet of Great Britain and owner of a major distillery in Scotland. He had been a barrister, Parliamentary Private Secretary to Duff Cooper, a missionary in Africa, and now decided he wanted to be an actor. He was also in *The Browning Version* playing the headmaster. He had a scene when he enters the room where Eric Portman, a school-master, is tutoring a schoolboy, and Campbell's first line was, 'Ah, Crocker-Harris, I've caught you in.' As a joke, one of the cast said to Campbell one day, 'Wouldn't it be awful if you got it wrong and said, "Ah, Crocker-Harris, I've caught you out"!' Campbell got into a state of near-hysteria and panic that he would make the mistake and night after night he went down on his knees just before his entrance, beseeching God to help him to say the correct line. Finally, he could stand it no longer and left the show!

We took *Playbill* on a pre-West End tour before opening at the Phoenix Theatre. The last week of the tour was at my beloved Grand Theatre, Leeds. You can imagine the pride and delight of my parents, the publicity in the local papers. Mom and Dad invited the entire company to a party at home on the Thursday night after the show. That very morning at rehearsal, Mary Ellis complained that one of the actors, Anthony Oliver, was getting more laughs than she was in *Harlequinade*. Such is the power of stardom, the laugh lines were given to her. That night the laugh lines were delivered by Mary Ellis – complete silence! Not a single laugh. At the end of the show we were all asked to remain onstage – obviously this was a crisis, only three more performances before the London opening. Eric Portman had the huge Number 1 dressing-room and he went into it followed by Mary Ellis, Peter Glenville, Terence Rattigan, Stephen Mitchell, the producer who was presenting the show. Mother and Dad were at home with the party all prepared, we had ordered taxis to bring the company which were waiting at the stage door. There we were, left standing on the stage, still lined up for the curtain call. After ten minutes Marie Löhr, a splendid old actress, big and tall, of the Edith Evans school, with a beautiful, ringing voice and the air of a duchess, said in her most sonorous tones, 'I'm not waiting a moment longer. I'm going to Thelma's party and I suggest you all join me. Come along, everybody!' She swept off the stage, we quickly followed and off we went to the party. About an hour later there arrived the gaggle who had been in Eric Portman's dressing-room – all of them. None of them was talking to anybody else. Their smiles were frozen – and so was the atmosphere – as they ate the food Mom had spent days preparing.

We opened at the Phoenix the following week. Needless to say the laugh lines went back to the original actor. There are many theatrical superstitions. Marie Löhr believed in all of them. A green dress had been designed for her. There is a little-known superstition that green is unlucky and she made them change the colour. A better known superstition is that you mustn't have fresh flowers on the stage. There were no fresh flowers on the stage, but Marie was very upset because the stage manager, who stood in the prompt corner, was wearing a corsage of fresh flowers which had been given to her. 'Disaster,' said Marie, 'something terrible is going to happen!' The end of *The Browning Version*, enthusiastic applause. All through *Harlequinade*, tremendous laughter. At the very end of *Harlequinade* there is a blackout, the lights are supposed to fuse for a second, and when the lights come up Eric Portman is seen with a large pot – he has been trying to find the correct place to put it throughout the play and at the very end he finds the perfect spot. Curtain. On the first night there was some confusion, and the curtain came down during the blackout, cutting out Eric's last moment of placing the pot. About thirty seconds early. An explosion of applause, cheers … we are lined up for the curtain call and Marie said to me, 'I told you it would be disaster.' At last I was in a big hit. I stayed with *Playbill* for a wonderful year.

Three Sackings

PETER
At about the same age as you were beginning to succeed in the West End, I got a job as the stage director of the St Louis Municipal Opera, an open-air theatre in a forest glade.

There were two very beautiful huge oak trees which were incorporated as part of the stage and they were part of the scenery of every show. The designers would very skilfully weave the scenery in, around, behind, at the side of these trees and they were always part of the show and beautifully lit up. It seated twelve thousand people, but that didn't scare me because I had directed in Madison Square Garden. It had an enormous staff of electricians and carpenters and scene painters. What was a stage director? Not like yours in *The Three Waltzes*. There was John Kennedy, the overall director of production, a very aristocratic looking stage designer with a fine Roman nose, a conductor of the orchestra, a conductor of the chorus. There was a ballet master who choreographed the ballets and a modern dance director who choreographed the jazz numbers. And there, at the bottom of the heap, was I, the stage director.

My job was to direct the little scenes of dialogue which came between musical numbers and between extravaganza production numbers. The opening of the stage at the St Louis Municipal Opera is enormous. If you have to get an actor to make a quick entrance and bring him to the centre of the stage you have to put him on roller skates to get there in any sort of timing. 'The way to solve this problem,' said I, 'is not to act everything at centre stage.' When I decided to direct the actors to play what they thought were vital scenes at the side of the stage, they rebelled. They also refused to start their dialogue at any time between appearing onstage and reaching their distant destination downstage centre. They really were antiquated. The actors went to John, the production director, and complained. 'We always come down front and centre and then we start to talk.'

John was very nice to me, he really did his best for me, but during the third show the pressure became too great and he spoke to me, 'Look kid, I'm going to have to let you go at the end of the week. There's too much resistance to you amongst the actors.' This is the first time in my life I've been sacked. I can tell you it is not pleasant, very hard to absorb. You look for self-justification, you try to rationalise yourself out of it but the fact remains you were sacked. From what was considered a rather prestigious job.

My agent in the William Morris office sent somebody to me to talk about directing a play called *Crescendo*. Johnny Cline, the producer, gave me the script. I started agonising, should I do this piece of shit, because it was a really thin script. Some sort of Hollywood-style melodrama with a classical pianist who was also a murderer. Badly written, badly constructed, but I had been sacked in St Louis and this was a chance to recover and to do my first commercial show on Broadway. I said, 'I'll do it.'

Then Johnny Cline sprang his great surprise on me, 'Do you know who I got to write the concerto? (The play is built around a concerto) Sigmund Romberg!' We had a pianist at all rehearsals and at the critical moment the action in the play would stop and the pianist would play the concerto, which was a real pain in the arse because it had nothing to do with the dramatic development of the script, it only held it up. We're into the fourth week, and we are approaching dress rehearsal time. Johnny Cline says, 'Today I got a surprise for you, Sigmund is coming to the rehearsal.' Sigmund Romberg was a very wealthy man. He wrote *The Student Prince* and *The Desert Song*, he composed over seventy operettas and his songs were sung all over the world. He came to the rehearsal and at a certain point, to get things started, I said to the actors, 'Let's move it, let's get the show on the road. Where's the pianist – let's get on with this goddamned concerto.' Slip of the tongue. I'd forgotten that Sigmund was there, and that you can't say 'goddamned concerto' in his presence because he thinks he has written a master work.

At the end of that day's rehearsal, Johnny Cline said to me, 'Stay behind, I've got to talk to you. My boy, I'm sorry I've got to let you go.' I asked him what was the matter.

He says, 'You're stupid. Why did you say goddamned concerto in front of Siggy. That's clever, you think?'

'No, I don't think it's clever. Did I say that?'

'Sure you said it, you stupid son-of-a-bitch.'

I'm fired. My God, coming on top of the previous experience, the second time in a row, at a critical moment, I'm fired. I almost got the show finished, and I'm fired. Johnny Cline didn't pay me, not one single cent of the two thousand dollars we had agreed upon. They got Orson Welles to take over from me, but even he couldn't save it. It opened and closed in Philadelphia in one night. I suppose Orson did it because he needed the money. The two thousand dollars that I should have gotten Orson owes me, except he won't pay it either because he's dead.

I was separated from May. Not the first separation we had in our married life. We were technically married for thirteen years, but I don't think I spent six years out of those thirteen with her. It was a wrong marriage but I always remained friendly with her. Recently May died and I found out for the first time that she was eleven years older than me.

There remains one more disaster to tell about before I went to Israel for the first time, and this was a play called *Forward the Heart* by a man with the name of Bernard Reines. I got the job of directing *Forward the Heart*, a play with a very good central idea. A young American army officer comes back from the war blinded. He had been an amateur sculptor so his mother and his uncle, who were very wealthy and from an aristocratic American family in Boston, said to him, 'Why don't you try sculpting again?' On the stage there's a little sculptor's studio and we see the blind man feeling around, going mad with the frustration of not seeing what he's doing. There's a fourth character who is a black girl who works in the house as a maid.

The sculptor is introduced to the girl by her name – he isn't told she's black, he just knows her as the maid – Florrie. He complains and speaks of his frustration.

'Why don't you go out into the garden and pick some flowers?' she suggests.

'How can I?' he replies.

'You can tell what their shapes are. I'll go with you the first time and I'll tell you what you're touching. After a while you'll recognise them. You can smell them and you can arrange them.' Gradually the boy realises he's in love with this girl and he discovers that she is black. He is particularly bound to her when she tells him that she lives with an old grandfather who is also blinded. When he falls in love with the girl Mamma and the uncle are horrified, and they fire the girl. In Bernard Reines' play, at this point, the boy plans and carries out a successful suicide.

I said to him, 'Bernard, you are destroying the thesis of your play. You call the play *Forward the Heart*. Why doesn't the bloody heart go forward? Why does he have to tear out his heart, why does he have to destroy himself?'

'You read the play, you said you were going to direct it, you're going to direct it the way it's written and you're not going to ask me for any changes,' he replied.

'But Bernard listen to what I'm saying to you. You have a golden opportunity to be in the vanguard of American playwriting and to say it is possible for a white American to live with a black American and to make a life together, and you'll be saying a very revolutionary thing.' He wouldn't hear of it and the argument raged. I told the producers: 'It will be the making of the play.'

That night I went home and wrote a suggested new ending. In the morning I went to rehearsal and gave out copies. All hell broke loose! Reines got hysterical. He was screaming, he was shouting, he was weeping, literally weeping tears, saying, 'Get rid of him. Fire him.' My God, again! I'm fired! The producer completed the direction of the play which opened and died immediately.

Three in a row. St Louis Municipal Opera – sacked. *Crescendo* – sacked. *Forward the Heart* – sacked. I am utterly convinced that if we had strengthened that ending so that they walk out like Charlie Chaplin, the tramp with his little street waif, into the sunset, it would have brought the house down. But this was 1948. Long before Martin Luther King and the great developments in the black and white relationships in America. On the other hand, it was after the war in which American negro soldiers had served with great heroism in all the battles of the Second World War and for the first time there were negro officers and even a black general. There had been great advances, but they came back to the same discrimination and hatred of blacks which has been characteristic of America from the beginning. This was a period in 1948 when we could have made a strong statement and a certain part of the audience would have accepted it. But he didn't have the guts. He didn't and it didn't and it wasn't, and there I was not having finished a production for the third time in a row.

Diary of an Actress

THELMA

More and more I was becoming known as a comedienne. One day I went to a party at the home of my great-aunt Cissie and met a woman called Betty Alvarez, a bird-like little lady who was a pianist-accompanist. 'Do you sing?' she asked. 'Oh no, I don't sing, my *mother* is a singer.' I never thought I had a voice. I had never learned singing and I'd never tried to sing, only the 'point numbers' I had done years before in ENSA. I didn't want to be compared to Mom.

Betty said, 'Listening to you talk I'm sure you've got a singing voice. Come to me, I want to see if I can help you. I coach singers.' Isn't it curious how a chance meeting completely changes our lives. Is it all ordained on the day of our

birth? Only by meeting Betty Alvarez at great-aunt Cissie's
birthday party did I start to sing and only because of Betty's
encouragement did I go into musicals. And in musicals I had
my biggest successes. My first job in a musical was to play
Prince Charming in the Pantomime *Cinderella* in Hull. How
I loved striding across the stage showing my legs and all the
nonsense that goes on in Pantomime.

In May 1951, aged twenty-six, I kept a diary for one week.
It gives a picture of what I was like at that age. I was in the
middle of trying to break off a romance.

1951 May 9th. Three years ago existing became living. I
suppose most people fall in love, and everyone feels their
experience to be unique in the history of the world.
Suddenly no incident is ordinary – it becomes a heightened
adventure waiting to be put into words to share with
another. A bus journey or buying a loaf of bread –
everything becomes acute and dramatic and exciting until,
propped up in bed and faced by a clean white sheet of
paper, the day crystallises clearly to be communicated.
Writers and artists do not need love to make them alert and
aware. They are constantly watchful and sensitive so that
they may interpret life and the longings within their souls
for the benefit of mankind. But I am not a true artist.

Now – because no relationship between two people can
exist without constantly changing character – that door is
closed to me, and I can no longer write in letters what
burns to be said. When hopes and joys and longings and
fears and experiences are locked up inside a person,
psychiatrists say it is dangerous. Now I am *not* contemplat-
ing suicide and I am *not* going mad – I am afraid (and
rather sorry) I am too normal and ordinary for that. This,
perhaps, will be the diary and private outpourings of a girl
who has just missed the boat.

Since my college days I have not written one word that
was not a letter. Letters – what worlds of joy they have

brought to me. They are usually the temptation with which I bribe myself out of bed. They are the intimate contact, unhampered by speech and bodily inhibitions, between me and one other. Once I knew I should see that handwriting each morning – it was the *only* period in my life when I have gladly and without effort risen early.

  You see, I am lazy. I sleep my life away. Ever since I can remember, I have done only what was essential. I have little initiative and no drive – I am a failure. I am also a great dreamer – the two usually go hand in hand. And so, before I sink into a permanent daze of detached lethargy, I shall try and enter something into this notebook every night. Perhaps, in time, I shall be able to explain to myself the knotted confusion that alternates with the apathy in my heart. And, who knows, I may even learn to write.

10th May. Since this journal was 'inaugurated' last night, it has more than justified its existence. My mind is alive and receptive once more. I have never been noted for qualities of dogged perseverance, so I do not anticipate that this will last for long. I give it three weeks at the *most*!

  Today (and please, do not ever breathe my secret) I went for the first (and probably last) time in my life to a fortune-teller. Down a little street in Knightsbridge. I found a gaily painted black and yellow door flanked by garages and a builder's yard. I went up two flights of carpeted stairs – the walls were hung with delightful 'Cries of Old London' etchings, the windowsills gay with flowers. Through a kitchen and down a passage, all spotlessly clean, into a charming lounge. This was not what I had expected. I had visualised draperies and hangings, an aura of mystery, incense, all the trappings and paraphernalia one connects with such an occasion. Instead, here was a bright and tastefully furnished drawing-room, round which I immediately spotted three elegant French clocks and a fine bronze.

There to greet me was a little woman dressed in black, with a face as white, unshadowed and unlined as a mask, and faded auburn hair scraped back and tied with an emerald green chocolate-box ribbon. And her voice danced with the leprechauns and fairies of Ireland. I liked her. There was a warm friendliness, an instinctive humanity, a simple faith and a direct look in those piercing eyes that broke down barriers and warmed my heart – and oh, that wonderful brogue!

We sat in front of the gas fire and chatted. Then she took my pearls, asked my birthday and started to talk. I record here some of what she said so that, for interest, I can look back later and see if any of it came true.

She saw at once that I was an actress. 'You will get a big opportunity soon, and you will seize it with both hands. Someone will drop out and you will leap into the breach. You will work on films – in fact on three branches of theatre work. Things will begin to go right for you, and your best years will be between now and 1953. You will marry within two years – someone much older than yourself, and I don't think your family will approve – but you will be very happy and will have two children, a boy and a girl.

'You have a charmed life, and always avoid accidents, sometimes very narrowly. You will have a long life, but you must seize out with both hands and grasp it. And remember, silence is golden.' So don't dare speak, dear Journal. That is the gist of what she said. I shall not record the rest, in case this ever falls into alien hands.

Frankly, amazing though much of it was, I cannot believe that my future will be so rosy. Tears and anguish and frustration have figured so largely in my life for so long now, I cannot envisage a sudden 'turn of the tide', as she termed it. 'You need not worry' she said. Well, she is paid to say that – it is what most people want to hear. But I keep my tongue firmly planted in my cheek.

Incidentally, she said I was immune to contagious

diseases ... I have just discovered five spots on my legs, which could, I suppose, be some food that has disagreed with me!

11th May. I like to think I take after my grandmother's family. What an unusual and lovable family they are. Four of them are still alive – three sisters and a brother. The three 'girls' are widows and the brother a widower. Today I spent with three of them – only my grandmother was missing.

What a family household they must have been when they were young – all musical, artistic, talented, intelligent and with an overwhelming, bubbling, indomitable sense of humour. They were raised in the rose-tinted, gracious Victorian age and each of their lives is a romantic and fascinating story. Each has had one great love – each has had to live through the death of that love. Their lives have woven varying patterns, but always a strong crossthread has been their devotion to each other. And now, their ages ranging from sixty-eight to seventy-five, they are alone and cling to each other.

Being with them is a rejuvenating experience. The sparkle of their personalities flares up with a brightness that is dazzling. For a while they will be still, and their beautiful faces in repose, minds cast into the past, eyes sadly smiling will be old. Then something strikes them as ridiculous or stimulates that mad, precious sense of humour, their eyes are alight, their cheeks set to chuckle and they are ageless and magnificent.

12th May. Green-letter day – which means a softening of the features and steadying of the heart. Not until it arrives do I realise that for days there has been a frown, an unformulated worry clogging the throat, a tensing of the muscles, a slight unsteadiness of the hand. Then it is there and, for a while, the heart is assuaged...

13th May. Whit Sunday. Traditionally this is a British holiday. In America they had never heard of it. And for me today is utter quietness. Occasionally I switch on the radio – non-committal and pleasing programmes not listened to with any concentration. The Sunday papers are savoured. Relaxing in a hot, scented bath I listen to *Family Favourites*. I study and think deeply about the part I start rehearsing this week. Outside it is dull and windy, so I have no conscience to fight with ... 'You *ought* to be out in the sun, you know.' There is an unearthly peace – never experienced here before. Even when I have been alone there has always been the undeniable and lively presence of Shep, our dog. But today there is no dog, no telephone bell has cut across the Sunday stillness. From within my hermit's cave there has been only one contact with the outside world – the milkman seeking to be paid and delivering cream for the first time for many, many years. But this silence is not empty. Not only do the neighbouring radios impregnate the walls, dully and persistently, from all sides, but my mind is given every opportunity to wonder, imagine, meditate, reminisce, create ... fill the rooms with longings, disappointments, hopes, reproaches. It is not often given such scope, not often, in fact, given its head!

And it frequently lights upon the contrast between this Whit Sunday and last Whit Sunday. Then the notion of peace such as this was unimaginable. Then I was in the midst of the most intensely lived, intensely felt period of my life. Then the sun *was* out, and through the heat mists there hammered sickness, death, great decisions, heartbreak, anguish ... with all its bitter unhappiness, there was a glory about those days which makes me glad they formed a part of the pattern of my life. Only through enduring such a baptism of fire can I find my true self, and the truths of those around me. It was a test, a challenge, and the climax of a year's gathering storm clouds. Now it assumes a shape and purpose ... just a year ago ...

That diary was written during the period when I found it hard to get up each morning. I don't know when the realisation of mortality hit me. For many years now I have been enormously energetic, sleeping little, leaping out of bed in the morning, never enough hours in the day, you begging me to take a little afternoon rest, remembering the quotation from Ecclesiastes which Frances Pole taught me all those years ago at Finch: 'Whatsoever thy hand findeth to do, do it with all thy might. For there is no work nor device nor knowledge nor wisdom in the grave whither thou goest.'

Jealousy and Failure

PETER
Despite the fact that there is a difference of eleven years between us and despite the fact that you started professionally somewhat later than I did, our careers have been amazingly parallel. We've had careers on the stage, on the radio, in the cinema and on television. I am wondering whether in one sphere the pattern is similar – the sphere of jealousy.

I confess freely that I lost a great deal of time in my life and a great deal of energy in feelings of jealousy against my peers. I will give a specific example. Martin Ritt and I grew up together in New York. We moved in the same circles, politically we were of the same ilk and later tarred by the same McCarthy brush, so there is a great similarity in the development of both our careers. We both became directors at a fairly young age, and we were both talked of as the 'coming young directors'. I'm ashamed to say that every time Marty had a success I was jealous. It reached a point where I was poo-pooing Marty at every opportunity. I said, 'Yeah he's quite talented. He's not as good as I am.' This went on for a long time and it made me sick.

THELMA
When you saw his films?

PETER
Before. In New York, when he did things on Broadway before me. I got sacked and he was successful. It was Shakespeare who so wisely understood that Othello, because of this fault of jealousy, was going to destroy the only thing he loved, his Desdemona. In the end it would destroy himself. I think that I would say that jealousy is the most destructive emotion that I have ever felt and I felt it more than once. I gave one example, but over and over again I would die a little death every time somebody amongst my peers had a success. Has this affected you in the same way?

THELMA
I don't think that it's eaten me up as much as you but it's there – resentment, jealousy – and it is a very unpleasant emotion. For example, Maggie Smith. She and I started in revue at about the same time. I made a hit in *For Amusement Only* and she made a hit soon afterwards in a revue called *Share My Lettuce*. One paper described her as the second Thelma Ruby. She said to a mutual acquaintance who reported it to me, 'I don't want to be the second Thelma Ruby, I want to be the first Maggie Smith.' Maggie Smith went on to become a big star of theatre and film and I didn't. I think she deserves it but then so do I. My stomach will churn while I'm thinking, 'Why couldn't those chances have happened to me?'

One of the early TV jobs I had was in a series called *Puzzle Corner*. The host of the show was Ronnie Waldman, who was also a high executive in the BBC. As the name implies, there were all sorts of puzzles which the viewer had to solve. My section was called 'Guess Which Year' which combined headlines and songs from a certain year – there was a tenor, a soprano, and I sang the popular song. The soprano was a fresh and glorious young teenager called Julie Andrews. She used to travel up from the family home in Walton-on-Thames by train and sometimes she would be held up and be late for rehearsal. The producer used to get angry and call her 'Little Miss Bighead, she'll never get anywhere in this business'. Most unfair as she was as charming and natural and spirited and talented as a girl could be. What happened to Julie's career was what I consider a complete success and I am happy for her because she deserved it. So did I! Am I jealous of Julie? Yes. It's not something that burns me and I wouldn't tear her down but it rankles. It eats away that you started together, that you know you have talent, the same as they had talent – and you didn't make it.

PETER
It eats away at your self-confidence, and instead of fighting your own battles, you are busy feeling jealous about someone else. You're using up emotional energy, you're using up your creative ability. You put that into the feelings of jealousy which should be going into work and advancement.

It took me a long, long time to overcome this terrible defect of character. At different times of my life when I thought about it, very often I would blame it on my mother. She was eaten up with jealousy of my father's family – the way they adored him and looked down on her. So I have comforted myself with the thought, 'It's not my fault, it's in my genes.' Of course, now I don't think that has anything to do with the case. I imagine that top stars are jealous of the success of stars who are even greater than they are. I think it is a basic part of the personality structure of people in this business. It is such a struggle to survive, it is such a struggle to succeed that even when you are successful, you are

194 DOUBLE OR NOTHING

envious and jealous of anyone else who makes a success because you want it all for yourself. Are you jealous of your friend Judi Dench?

THELMA

No, because we are of different generations. But I am envious of the way she has had the chance to work constantly, doing interesting, important and challenging roles, while I have sat around for months, sometimes years, waiting for the phone to ring. I feel cheated and deeply regretful that I did not have the chance to develop, as an actress, in the way that I longed to. But nowadays I do not sit around day after day when I'm not working eating my heart out as I used to. Before you, my career was all important and between jobs I suffered from frustration and jealousy. But with you in my life there aren't enough hours in the day. Who has time to be jealous?

PETER

I don't want you to think that I have been a walking disaster area, giving off fumes of jealousy wherever I went. It wasn't like that but it was a problem and I am glad to say I faced myself with the problem and trained myself out of it. More serious is the basic feeling about myself that I am a failure. Not because I didn't become famous enough to appear on Oprah Winfrey. But because I believe I was born with excellent gifts, that I had a magnificent potential, most of which I have not realised. In that sense I feel that I am a failure. Mine has been a life spent swimming upstream – against the current all the way. The system didn't reward me because I fought the system. Now I look back and see so many things I started and didn't finish. So many things I should have tried and didn't. I don't think I'm the only failure in the world – the world is full of failures, many more failures than successes. Even the great successes feel somewhere, perhaps, that they have failed.

All my life I believed that everything I was doing in the art of the theatre was an attempt to grope towards a higher level of humanity, to become more aware, to become more concerned, to become more knowledgeable, to develop more feeling for my fellow humans. I believed in the perfectibility of the species. But in most of the work we have to do in order to stay alive in our profession, that is not the motivation. It is 'Get paid, take the money and run'.

My youthful idealism has not been entirely impaired. But in this period of tremendous social and political change in the world, certain beliefs that I held in the earlier part of my life that I thought were absolute are now seen to shake like in an earthquake, perhaps lose their roots, fall away and die. Have they failed? Have I failed? My basic perception of life is still the same, to wit – if mankind could only learn the simple lesson: It is easier to cooperate than to compete. If they could only learn that. I believe that cooperation is just as much an instinct basic to our survival as is greed. Greed at the moment is all-powerful. Cooperation is something that the psychiatrists talk about or the social workers – talked about but not practised.

Now that I do not work any more, I truly feel a failure. I think I'm still bright. My memory isn't what it used to be but I know which rehearsal to go to, which show I'm working on. I know what idea I'm dealing with. I know how to talk to people. I know how to bring people out – and it is all wasted. I sit here with my detective stories and my political journals and my *Time* magazine and my *Economist*, and the television. I try to run the world from these mountain tops. Hah! I make sure that I see all the news programmes on the television to see whether they are following my instructions. But whom am I kidding? I am an unemployed, rejected director.

THELMA
Just as I'm an unemployed, rejected actress.

PETER
But I got you.

THELMA
And I got you.

PETER
Maybe it's better that we are successful 'might-have-beens' rather than a couple of sated, cynical has-beens! It is clear, as we say in Yiddish, it was *bashert*, it was ordained that our lives had to be led the way we led them so that we could meet, so that we could marry, so that we could continue together. I've been married to you for twenty years – the most glorious years of my life. The most fulfilling. Even though I face terrible problems: 1 of growing older. 2 of unemployment. 3 of severe disablement. 4 of despair at not getting my share of glory. Despite all this, the joy that I have had in living with you makes everything that came before seem necessary and purposeful and self-fulfilling.

Book V

The New Country

Adventure

PETER

1948. I am thirty-four years old and I've just had three
disasters in a row and I am saying, 'Oh my God, what
next?' I was low. As the Americans would put it – I was
lower than a snake's belly. Then, in the fall of 1948, I
received a letter from Yosef Millo, who was the artistic
director of the Chamber Theatre, inviting me to come to
Israel to direct and at the bottom it was signed 'With
comradely greetings, Yosef Millo.' This is for me! He
signs with comradely greetings! I write back immediately:
'Yes, I would be glad to come, but you haven't said
anything in your letter about the arrangements of how I
am to get there.' The war was still going on – Israel's War
of Independence `didn't finish until the spring of 1949.
The reply came: 'You have to get to Rome. There is no
direct flight to Israel from New York but when you get to
Rome we will give you the address of a man and he will
see to it that you get to Israel.' It begins to be very
exciting.

February 1949. On the plane, landed at Roma, have the
name of the man to contact. I found the man whose
name is Danny Agronsky. He introduced me to his wife,
Katia Levi Agronsky. Danny says, 'I'm supposed to get
you to Israel, which is not so easy because there are no
planes going to Israel, nobody wants to land a plane at
Lod Airport. Leave it with me for a couple of days. Katia
will look after you.'

The following day I talked to Danny. 'When do I go to

Israel?' He says, 'Take it easy, take it easy. Stick around a couple of days. Katia will take care of you.'

The third day I'm in Rome I meet him at the hotel – we're having a drink – he says, 'Tonight.'

'What, tonight?' I ask.

'I think I've got something arranged for you.'

It was very mysterious, very exciting. I was never one to turn down adventure. I'm not such a great hero but I'm not a coward. I'm not afraid of trying new things, never was. 'OK. Where do I have to be?'

'Stick around the hotel and around midnight I'll take you out to the airport.' Which he did.

I said goodbye to Katia. We get to the airport. Midnight. Big, empty, high-ceilinged halls – the Italians love to build in a grand style. I don't see *nothing*. I don't see passengers. I don't see pilots. I don't see customs. I don't see ticket takers. What the hell *is* this? Danny says, 'Just be patient, wait,' and off he goes. Suddenly I turn around and there in a corner of the airport is a crowd of people dressed in Arab clothes. The men wore long robes which later I learned to identify as gallabiyas and the women wore long skirts and trousers, and it was a cluster of about a hundred people. There were policemen and there were customs officials and there was a lot going on and I saw money changing hands, going from one policeman to another and from one customs official to another and Danny circulating around the group. What the hell is going on? Danny runs over to me, 'Come on, come on, we're loading.' I'm loaded onto a plane with these people. In charge is a young lad who is their *shaliach*. He was a messenger sent from Israel to bring this group of new immigrants from Tripoli to Israel. They had flown from Tripoli, the chief sea port in Libya, to Rome, to the airport. They were collected at the airport and put on a plane to Israel, a secret plane, not belonging to any airline – some black market arrangement that the Israelis had made to fly planes into Israel. This was part of what they called in Israel *aliya bet.* The second immigration. This was going on all the time from ports in Italy and from the Black Sea, from Romania and from Yugoslavia. There were refugees collected from all over Europe and from North Africa and they were being brought to Israel, either in ships or in planes.

I'm sitting on the plane with these people dressed in Arab clothes who are speaking Arabic amongst themselves. The little *shaliach* is speaking English, Hebrew, Yiddish and Arabic. I don't think he knew much Arabic, and mainly he's saying, 'Shh, shh. Quiet, I want you to be quiet. Please, I don't want any noise.' He was very excited, very nervous, a little hysterical. What the hell difference would it make if they were noisy on the plane! He said, 'Shh, shh' all the way. There were quiet conversations, there were women sitting with children on their laps and there were old men chatting with each other. It was a small plane. It carried about a hundred passengers and the reason Danny hadn't told me about it earlier was that he wasn't sure he had a place for me.

The women weren't exactly veiled, they wore scarves over their heads. They had Arab customs because they had been living in an Arab country and they looked like Arabs. Sitting in front of me right by the window is a very ancient old woman. I say now that she was ancient, she might just have been forty-five or fifty, but with the clothes she looked very old to me and she sat and prayed all the time in Hebrew, I'm picking this up and I'm trying to sense the atmosphere of this trip. Suddenly I am an immigrant to Israel. I just came to direct some plays at the Chamber Theatre, but I'm an immigrant to Israel. The flight from Rome to Tel Aviv is a couple of hours. Propeller planes in those days – maybe three hours. As we approached the coast of Israel the *shaliach*, the messenger, says, '*Nous approchons.* We are approaching the coast of Israel and the pilot will fly at a low altitude so that you can see the lights of Tel Aviv. We will turn out the lights inside the plane.'

Dawn was breaking. The lights are still shining from the city and the pilot flies over Tel Aviv – he flies in a circle so that everybody gets a chance to see it, you know how the plane banks and there is the city lying below you at a very funny askew angle. Then he completes the circle and the other side can see it and this little guy in the plane keeps saying, 'Shh, shh.' The people can't contain themselves – they start to applaud. They applauded Tel Aviv from the air. They were returning to their homeland and me with them.

In the letter from the Cameri, the Hebrew name for the Chamber Theatre, the comradely greetings said that there would be somebody to meet me at the airport. I have to go through immigration and then I look around for the somebody who is supposed to meet me – *Gor Nisht!* Nothing. No Yosef Millo, no comradely greetings, no delegation, no taxi, no flowers, no nothing! I hang around waiting, but after a while I thought, 'There's not much point to this.' I asked somebody, 'Can I get a taxi to take me to Tel Aviv to Number 1 Aliyah Street?' 'Sure,' he said.

Seven o'clock in the morning I arrive at the office of the Chamber Theatre in a crummy old building. I climb up the stairs in a rather filthy hallway and I look for ... everything is in Hebrew and I don't know Hebrew, I don't read Hebrew, I don't speak Hebrew. I find somebody to ask. 'Cameri Theatre?' 'Oh, Teatron Hacameri, here, this is their door.' Maybe it's seven-thirty in the morning by now and I knock on the door. Nobody there!

I'm carrying a suitcase. I put it down, sit on it and wait outside the door. At eight o'clock, yes, a girl comes and says, 'Who are you?'

'At this point I am not really sure, but I am the man from New York who was supposed to come to the Chamber Theatre in Tel Aviv to direct some plays.'

'Oi, they were supposed to meet you!' Eventually somebody arrived and took me into the centre of Tel Aviv to a room they had rented for me in a private flat on a street called Beilinson, a few doors from the Ohel Theatre, of which I was later to be the artistic director. I am brought to the room. I'm tired, I'm sleepy, I'm dirty, so I have a wash and I open my suitcase and have a shave – at that time I was beardless.

Lunchtime I was taken to a restaurant in a private home – a family had turned their sitting room into a restaurant with four or five tables and they served home cooking. Everything was all right except that there was no food. This was the time of *zena*, which means austerity, fasting. Available were egg plants – they had a great supply of egg plants – and a pretty good supply of frozen fish fillet from Iceland or Greenland. They serve me a basic meal – it's well cooked, it's home cooking, it's pleasant – and they're talking to me in a *mélange* of languages. Some English, some French, some German, some Yiddish and, of course, Hebrew. They are all talking Hebrew amongst themselves. Fortunately I enjoy food of practically any kind. I particularly like aubergine in any form whatsoever and aubergine can be cooked in many forms. I even like fish fillet, so I had no problem adapting myself to Israeli austerity. I was sitting with a group of people who were the leaders of the theatre. They had greeted me with comradely feelings. They behaved very nicely, very warm, very open – Israelis make that impression when you meet them. They're not a closed people, they're not a suspicious people, they're not a hard people. 'We'll take you around, we'll show you a little bit of Tel Aviv,' which then was a small town. It had great charm. 'This evening you are coming with us to the first Purim party since 1936.'

Purim is always a celebration in Israel, particularly for the children – they dress up in costumes and masks and parade through the streets. Grown-ups go to Purim parties which are costume parties. I am taken to the rehearsal hall of the Habimah Theatre where the party was being held, but the party was given not merely by the Habimah Theatre, but by the Tel Aviv municipality and all the artists of Tel Aviv were going to appear, and they said this will be a wonderful opportunity for me to meet the artistic community. I thought to myself – how I'm going to meet anybody without a language?

I was under the impression that I was travelling to a tropical country so I had only tropical weight summer clothes and the weather was freezing. Somebody lent me a sweater which I put on under my tropical weight jacket and I came to the Purim party – and it was a party! There were hundreds of people – the artistic community, the Bohemian community, they were all there. One of the few people I knew in Israel was Gershon Plotkin, who had first recommended me to the Cameri Theatre. At a certain point he was standing with me on my left side when someone from the Chamber Theatre came towards me with a beautiful girl in tow – tall with a very interesting sort of oriental face. Somebody said to me, 'That's Batia Lancet, who is one of our leading actresses. She speaks good English.' I met Batia Lancet. She was then twenty-seven, in the full flower of womanhood and she was a beautiful woman.

A group of us then retired from the Purim party to a restaurant off Ben Yehuda Street – the Dolphin Club where you could get strawberries in February. I wound up sitting with a dark, attractive girl by the name of Ofra Burla. There was fun, there was laughter, there were speeches in Hebrew which I didn't understand and Ofra was translating to me in my ear and then it came time to go home. I said, 'I'll take you home. Do we get a taxi?' 'No, not at this time of the night. You won't find a taxi. I'll walk you home,' she said. As Ofra and I walked home we passed a central crossroads, the corner of Frischmann and Dizengoff. Dizengoff at that time already was the Broadway, the Piccadilly of Tel Aviv. At that corner there was no vehicular traffic. There was a big bonfire in the centre of the crossroads and there were people dancing the *hora* madly around the bonfire singing.

Somewhere, somebody had an accordion and was playing. We walked to the corner of Dizengoff and Gordon and there was another bonfire and another circle of dancers. We walked around and saw this at all of the major crossroads and I imagine the same thing was happening all over Israel. People dancing in the streets. Celebrating Purim, the first Purim in an independent Israel, celebrating their independence. I was deeply moved and felt the urge to become a part of this torrent of joy in the establishment of a new, independent, Jewish, Socialist country. It had been only that morning that I had seen those Jews from Tripoli kissing the ground at the bottom of the airplane steps.

Three Hits

I had come to Israel with two scripts in my suitcase that I wanted to do – firstly the play by Armand Salacrou which I had seen at Piscator's Dramatic Workshop *Les Nuits de la Colère*, *The Nights of Wrath*. They were very pleased at the Chamber Theatre with this choice of play. They wanted something new, fresh, European and perhaps even American. On my second day in Israel I was taken to lunch and in the company of the people who came with me was Batia Lancet. Before long a romance blossomed and I moved in with her. When the play opened, Batia read and translated the reviews to me, which were good and spoke positively of the work I had done with the actors. The show was a success.

My second show was *Born Yesterday*. I had seen this in New York and thought it marvellous, beautifully directed – Garson Kanin, the author, had directed it himself. I went backstage to talk to Judy Holliday, the star of the Broadway show, whom I had already met before when she was a night-club entertainer down in The Village in a nightclub called

The Village Vanguard. She was a member of a quartet which included Betty Comden and Adolf Green. Judy Holliday was an absolutely delightful personality. She had this funny little baby voice and it wasn't put on – that was her voice and that's the way she talked – and she had such a Bronx Yiddish expression.

I went backstage and said to her, 'You've been in this show for five years. How do you stand it? Five years of acting in the same show?'

'It's never really the same show twice. Every night there's something different.' That wonderful Bronx accent.

'I'm coming to see it again tomorrow,' I said. I came to see it a second night and I laughed like a madman, it was even funnier the second night than it was the first night, for me. I went backstage again: 'What did you do?'

'It's the same, it's always the same, but it's different.'

'What do you do to make it different?' I asked her.

'I just pretend it's all happening again for the first time.' She was brilliant. I saw it eight times. And every night she was slightly different – she didn't do anything obvious. She just played it each night with that wonderful excitement and energy of the first time. Stanislavsky talks a great deal about this in his book – the necessity to play it each night as though it were happening for the first time. That was a great lesson for me.

I come to Israel with this play, *Born Yesterday.* They read it at the Cameri and say, 'What has it got to do with us? It's about Americans and junk dealers who become wealthy men who scream at their competitors and try to screw everybody and about this little girl who is sort of a tramp because she is living in sin with this multi-millionaire junkman, Harry Brock, but *we're* not like that.'

We argued for a few days and I said, 'Let me start rehearsals and you come and see what it's like. If you insist that you don't want to do it, we won't do it, and you'll suggest something else to me, but I'd like you to look at it.'

We are rehearsing in the little Mograby Theatre, which is now a cinema. At that time it was being used as a stage and Mr Mograby, who was a Jew from North Africa, had his office in the building. He was the Cameri Theatre landlord, and he was doing everything he could to get them out of the theatre because he wanted to turn it into a cinema. They had been having a terrific running fight with him for years. At rehearsal one day we heard an argument going on in the office and the door opened and somebody came running out and Mr Mograby is running after him and he's cursing him, shouting in Arabic and in Hebrew, calling him a thief. I said, 'What about him? Is he a Harry Brock?' That convinced them.

Born Yesterday was the greatest success the Cameri Theatre had had until then – it was a real hit. Hit in Israel means … when a show runs more than fifty times it's a hit – we're talking about a small country. This play started to run and run and run and it passed the hundred mark and it passed the two hundred mark – nothing in their history had done what this play did. Israel is a great theatre-loving country. You can get into a taxi and the driver will recognise you … and you are a director, not an actor … and he'll say, 'I saw your last show, I liked it very much except in the second act, there was a place where…' and he knows what he's talking about, he knows what he likes.

We were now looking for a third play for me to direct during which time I am travelling around seeing the country. Wherever I went they said, 'This is the guy who was in the International Brigades', and I was accepted everywhere as a 'fighter'. I was having success and fame and public acceptance, everything that had been lacking in the recent period in New York. I was working for expenses, an absolute pittance. They were poor and still living in the wartime state of austerity. I didn't care, I hadn't come to Israel to get rich.

I decided to do an Israeli edition of my New York
success *Of Mice and Men*. My adaptation of Steinbeck's *Of
Mice and Men* was inspired by Greek tragedy – I didn't do
it as a cowboy story. I didn't change the text, it had been
dramatised by Steinbeck himself. But using the text as it
was written, I added certain elements of Greek tragedy.
As in America, the wayfaring stranger, which is the title
of an American folk song, was the Greek chorus, and I
wound him through the show. I was beginning to learn
some Hebrew from sitting at rehearsals and listening to
the actors repeating text which I knew in English. After a
while it sank in, and I could speak whole passages of text.
I completed *Of Mice and Men*, we had several successful
public dress rehearsals and it was put on ice until the fall
so I said, 'I'm going back to New York.' What I had in
mind was to try to get a job in television. All my friends
were getting jobs in television, which was then just opening
up. 1950.

I went back to New York and the following day I went to a
party at a Park Avenue home. Harold Clurman was there
and a lot of other New York theatre celebrities. I came home
late from this party, where I'd had a lot of fun, about three
o'clock in the morning. There was a message by the telephone from my landlord. 'Please call operator 321 in
Montreal.' 'Your father is dying, come as soon as you can.' I
didn't go to bed, I didn't change my clothes. I packed some
underwear and socks and took a taxi to the La Guardia
Airport, which wasn't far from where I lived. I arrived in
Montreal at eight o'clock in the morning and went straight
to the hospital.

My father was under an oxygen tent. My mother, my
brother and my sister were in attendance and they looked
absolutely exhausted, this was the third day that he'd been
under oxygen and they hadn't had any rest. 'Look,' I said,
'I've just come and I'm relatively fresh, you go home and get
some rest. If there's any change, I'll call you.' They went and

I was left there with my Pa. I reached in under the oxygen
tent and took his hand, a big, horny hand, he'd worked for
years as a presser and had developed callouses. I put both
my hands under the oxygen tent and stroked his hand. I
kept talking to him. 'Papa, it's Peter. Pa, do you hear me. I'm
here. I came to see you, Pa. Pa, do you hear me.' There was
no reply, and I sat there for hours, his right hand in mine.
Suddenly he put his left hand to his mouth and made a
sound, he put his hand to his lips but I couldn't understand.
I don't exactly know whether he knew I was there. I stroked
his hand 'It's Peter, Pa. I came, I came to see you.' Suddenly,
he had an enormous haemorrhage and died.

What I'm going to say now is not particularly original
or unusual. As I stood there looking at my dead father I
grew up, in one moment I grew up. I was the father and
he was the child. The memory of that morning when I
was the one left in the room when my father died with
his hand in mine is one of the most powerful memories
in my life. It's so ironic. I was the prodigal son who had
been away all these years, which is the meaning of my
father's original name, Pribluda, but he died with his
hand in mine and not in my brother's hand, not in my
mother's hand, not in my sister's hand. I think Bernard
never forgave me for the fact that I sent him home and
stayed there with Papa until he died.

As you know I have always regretted so terribly that I
never really talked to my father after I'd grown up. After all
the arguments, all the pain I had caused him – rejecting his
beliefs and trying to convert him to mine. Now I wanted so
badly to say, 'Papa, you were right and I was wrong. You
knew it better than I knew it, but at the time I thought I
knew everything.' I had never been able to say this to him;
since that painful day in the hospital I conduct long conversations with him which are very illuminating, we keep
going over all the meagre little scenes of our life. The one
shortcoming of these colloquies is that he can't reply and I

must reply for him. I put my questions to him as the son and I give his answers as the father. I know him better in his death than I had ever known him in his life.

The Blacklist

They had a fabulous opening of *Of Mice and Men* in Israel. It was a sensational overnight success and I wasn't even there. I went back to New York from Montreal and got a job in television at CBS. 1950. In those early days of television when it was live there were no video tapes. There was not even a good system of reproduction. They recorded the television programme on what was called a Kinescope – it was miserable, very poor quality, not suitable for re-broadcast. There could be only live television. It was like making a movie, except that there was immediate, spontaneous, simultaneous directing, cutting, editing. It was very exciting. I took to it immediately. First I did a TV programme about Paul Robeson with just still-pictures and sound. Then there was a period where they put me on a show with a pianist with one camera and said, 'Go ahead, get the hang of it.' There was no zoom lens and the camera sat on a wheeled tripod. You could pan left or right, tilt up or down, dolly in or out. That was it.

I stayed with that for three weeks, then I was moved up and got the directing job with a show called *Lamp unto my Feet,* a quotation from the Bible. It was a Sunday public service show, the religious broadcast. The formula was that each week we would deal with either a Protestant story, or a Catholic story or a Jewish story. Fifteen minutes of 'drama with a moral' followed by fifteen minutes of religious discussion led by a pastor a rabbi or a priest. I found myself working with the writers and telling them what I wanted them to write. I worked with writers Ted Apstein, who is by now an old best friend, Horton Foote, Norman Rosten, Raphael Hayes. One day I said to Raphael Hayes, 'I'd like you to write a modern adaptation of John Bunyan's *Pilgrim's Progress*. You have to tell the story of the adventures of Christian, the central character.' In a couple of weeks he came back with a fifteen-minute adaptation, in verse, of the *Pilgrim's Progress* by John Bunyan, which was splendid and which I put on television. I used the possibilities of television as they hadn't been tried before. For example, Christian goes through the Slough of Despond and then he comes to Vanity Fair – I had a scene where there was a 'cooch' dancer, a practically naked dancer, who appeared dancing her sexy dance in Christian's forehead. I had to work it out. Technically, you have a big close-up of the boy playing Christian and then an extreme long-shot of the 'cooch' dancer on another stage with another camera, and you had to get the proportions right so that when you overlap dissolve you can put the figure of the gyrating seductress inside Christian's forehead.

In another script, by Horton Foote, I used a coat tree, you know, a coat hanger with metal hooks. That represented a tree in the garden. I used it with such angles and shots that people began to believe it *was* a tree. That was important because the tree figures symbolically in Horton's story. The vice-president in charge of my show was a man called Charlie Underhill – a big six foot two, blond, blue-eyed American, gorgeous to look at, had been a football player in college, a really nice guy. I started to get telegrams from him every week, which means he was watching my show. Charlie's telegrams would say, 'Peter, this is great'. Next week, 'Peter, keep it up'. 'Wonderful. Peter, this is television.' These telegrams were delivered into the studio every Sunday afternoon right after the live broadcast.

I got offered another TV job to do a one-hour adaptation of *Macbeth*. They said to me, 'Can you prepare this show in thirteen days?' That is to say adaptation, casting, set up designs, rehearse it and get it on the air in thirteen days from now. First I cut the play. Immediately I set up appointments with the production staff and outlined the design of the show. I wanted to do the play in modern clothes. Macbeth, Banquo, Duncan, Macduff, all the leading figures, were clothed in costumes made up of different uniforms of different armies. This is after the putative first atomic war, where almost everything has been destroyed. I was saying that even after the final devastation caused by man, survivors will continue to be jealous, greedy, ambitious murdering bastards. I decided to substitute for the barren heaths of Scotland the rubble of the city of Rotterdam. I used all kinds of tricks with lighting – without scenery and mostly with projections. For the sets I needed just a few simple platforms and screens, furniture for the banquet scene and props for the three witches, which in this case were played by three men in the tattered remnants of uniforms.

Macbeth was played by John Carradine, a wonderful Hollywood character actor. He was the preacher, Casey, in John Ford's film *The Grapes of Wrath*. Lady Macbeth was a Canadian actress, Judith Evelyn. I used five cameras on the show. In those days when you did a show live you are fighting time. I *had* to finish within the hour. At rehearsals John Carradine had said to me. 'One thing you are not going to cut and that is "Tomorrow and tomorrow and tomorrow!"'

'John, I promise nothing! I have to finish the show on time – I finish it on time or I get bounced.'

He pleaded, 'Don't cut that monologue.' When we came to it, I look at the clock and I see that I simply do not have time for the one minute and three seconds that the mono-logue is going to take. I give the signal to the floor manager ... I talked to him on his earphones, 'tell Carradine to skip "Tomorrow and tomorrow and tomorrow".' Carradine got the message and looked straight into the camera with a look in his eyes – 'you son of a bitch!' But he cut it and he went right on and he was marvellous.

We did have one mishap. I had decided that Banquo would be killed by two murderers with the baling hooks used by longshoremen. Banquo was foully murdered and he decided that the scene was over and he got up but the cameras were still on him. So what you saw was the death and second coming of Banquo, all in one shot. Oh well, that's death – there is life after death on television ... Despite Banquo's unscheduled reincarnation the show got fantastic reviews. One of them I still have – they put me in a class with Stanislavsky and Reinhardt and Orson Welles. 'There's a new director in television who has a style of his own. Peter Frye.' From the *Christian Science Monitor*. When I consider, it is rather pathetic, but I've been flashing it around for the last thirty years. It was estimated by CBS that the show was seen on that one night by eighty million people.

Shortly after this I get a call from Charlie Underhill's secretary, 'Pete, Charlie would like to meet you at five-thirty today at Louis and Armands.' This is 1951. There were two restaurants on 53rd Street between Madison and Park in the same building as CBS. Colby's where you could meet all of your colleagues who who earned under $300 a week. The minute you went above $300 a week you had your martinis at Louis and Armands. I am all expectation. Am I going to be promoted?

Charlie comes in. 'What are you drinking?' 'I'd like a martini.' He says, 'Me too.' We had a martini, we had three martinis. Now three martinis was a lot for me. Charlie may have been accustomed to it, because he had been a vice-president-in-charge-of for some time, so he had developed an immunity to three martinis. I hadn't and I was getting a little bit plastered.

Charlie says to me, 'Pete, tell me, do you think there is such a thing as too much imagination?'

'Too much imagination Charlie?' I repeat myself because I am no longer sober. 'Too much imagination? No, I don't think so, I don't think anybody can have too much imagination.'

'Pete, you've got too much imagination. Pete, do you think that there's such a thing as too much talent?'

I am drinking my fourth martini, and I'm enjoying it. 'Too much talent? Is that what you said, Charlie, too much talent? No Charlie, I don't think anybody can have too much talent.'

'Pete, you've got too much talent,' Charlie told me.

'What are you talking about, Charlie?'

'I can't sell you, kid, you have too much imagination, you've got too much talent.'

I am on the ropes by now, I don't know what is happening. 'Wha ... wha ... what are you trying to tell me, Charlie?'

'I can't sell you, kid. I'll talk to you tomorrow.'

I made my drunken way out of Louis and Armand with some shattered illusions about how I was going to move up to above three hundred a week ... Somehow or other I got to the subway and went home.

The following day when I woke up, I realised that something very serious had happened to me, and I didn't know what. I went to the office and called Charlie Underhill on the phone.

'Look, kid. I've got to let you go.'

'I'm fired, Charlie?'

'Not exactly,' he said, 'but I want your resignation. I'll give you six weeks' severance pay, and that will give you time to look around for something else.'

I was fired from CBS. I didn't realise it immediately and then my friends wised me up. 'I can't sell you' was the euphemism for 'You're on a McCarthy blacklist. The commercial sponsors won't employ anyone on such a list.' My meteoric rise in television was over.

I had a new agent, Adeline Schulberg. We used to call her Ad. She was the widow of B P Schulberg who had been the president of Paramount Pictures. Ad had great faith in me. She talked of me as a director doing things on television that no one had dreamed of. She was trying to sell me to Hollywood. She told me, 'I'm negotiating a contract for you with Doré Schary at MGM and I'm sure we'll get it.'

'That's wonderful, Ad,' I said, 'my greatest ambition in life is to be a Hollywood director. Better do it quickly because I'm in trouble.' I told her the story of how I had been forced to resign from CBS because my name was on the McCarthy blacklist. There was a little book with the names of those on the blacklist – Red Channels – it was well known in the trade. Ad said, 'Don't worry about it, you've got this job in Hollywood waiting for you. It'll come off any day.'

My friends said, 'Somebody must have given your name for it to be on the blacklist.' I agonised as to who it might be, then became convinced it was a New York colleague. I thought he had shopped me, informed on me to the FBI. Twenty-seven years later I met him and discovered I was totally wrong about him. He had suffered in the same way I had and had been unable to work for seven years. For twenty-seven years I harboured a false grudge but that gives you an idea of the paranoia of the witch-hunt. It is very hard to describe how you feel when you are a victim of a witch-hunt – you go completely crazy, you don't think logically, you're frightened.

My friends stood by me. Curt Conway, Horton Foote and Yul Brynner all employed me on TV as an actor, but after each job they were informed, 'Don't hire this guy any more. He's on the blacklist.' My friends were loyal, my friends were faithful and they stood by me. It was a great help psychologically.

THELMA
Were you on the list because you'd gone to Spain?

PETER
Because I'd gone to Spain.

THELMA
Everyone who went to Spain, suffered in the same way?

PETER
Everybody I knew. The ironic thing about this was that
by now I was anti-Party. As early as 1938 I knew that I
did not belong in the Communist Party. If anyone had
asked me, 'Are you a Communist?' I would have said, 'No, I
am not.'

THELMA
Are you now, or have you ever been...?

PETER
That's the trick in the question. 'Have you ever been?'
Because if you say you had been, they say, well, as far
as we're concerned, you still are now. All the protestations
in the world don't clear you. But nobody asked me and I
wasn't invited to testify anywhere, I wasn't investigated.
I was just sacked and all doors in showbusiness were closed
to me.
   Weeks are going by. I am bothering Ad Schulberg.
'Ad, what about Hollywood?' Eventually she met Kenneth
McKenna, Doré Schary's assistant. She reported to me, 'I
told Kenneth, I said, "Kenneth, this boy is wonderful, this
boy is a genius. You've got to give him his start in Hollywood."' To which plea Kenneth McKenna replied, 'Ad, dear,
we still have some geniuses left over from last summer.'
I was on the Hollywood blacklist. That was the end of my
Hollywood contract, the end of my career as a director

on Broadway and on American TV.

1952. Batia is with me in New York and we decide to get married. We arranged to go to New Jersey and went to the office of a Justice of the Peace. Batia and I and two witnesses, one of whom was Hy Kalus who had played a witch in *Macbeth*. The judge was in a hurry. It was a Saturday morning, and he had a date to play golf. He went through the routine – 'I pronounce you man and wife. That'll be $10 please.' I said, 'No, I don't think you should get $10. You rushed through the ceremony, you're rushing off to play golf. I don't know why you have to get rich at my expense. I give you $5, that's it, take it or leave it.' So he took it. We went and had lunch with Hy Kalus and the other lad, one of my ex-students.

While I was struggling to stay alive and fighting the blacklist, a man by the name of Zvi Kolitz came to me. He was an Israeli and had heard about me. He was sure that I could make a film out of an idea that he had. 'What's your idea,' I asked him. He pulled out a scrap of paper and there were like about six sentences on it. But he had a title – *Hill 24 Doesn't Answer*.

'This is all you've got?' I said.

'Yes, that's it.'

'And you want to make a film out of this.'

'Yeah, I think it will make a very good film.'

'First a script has to be written, then money has to be raised,' I pointed out. 'Then it's a big, big problem to make such a film, because a film about Israel's War of Independence is not a small idea.'

'I'm sure it's a wonderful idea – it's the best idea I've had in years. You write it and you direct it in Israel.'

It was the best non-offer I'd had in a long time. There was nothing to keep me in the US. There was an understanding between Kolitz and me that he would produce and that I would write and direct, the film to be called *Hill 24 Doesn't Answer*. I arrived in Israel, yet again, in January 1953.

This time I had come to stay for more than twenty-eight years.

What Israel Did For US

THELMA

I was very orthodox Jewish in my teens. In New York, as I told you, I went a bit overboard and used to go with Bill Kramer to a different synagogue every Saturday so that I'd experience all the different branches of Judaism. I was interested in the trappings of Judaism. And taught Sunday School.

When I returned to England and started to work in the professional theatre, I had to drop many of the Jewish practices. I could not ask to be excused for Friday evening and Saturday matinée performances. You're in the show, you're in the show, you have to work on Shabat, the Sabbath. Then in *Playbill* Daddy asked me to get Yom Kippur, the holiest fast day, off and I tried and failed. Dad was so upset I had to lie to him. I still fasted, but I worked on Yom Kippur. It was a matinée day – that meant two shows with no food!

The following year I decided to make the break complete – not only did I eat on Yom Kippur but I bought a hat. My declaration of independence! The deep reason for this was that I did not meet many Jews as part of my life in the theatre. Always in my heart I wanted to get married and I was perfectly well aware that when I did fall in love it would most likely be with someone who wasn't Jewish, and I did not want to be hamstrung (if one can use such a word in such a context). I knew that marrying a non-Jew would break my father's heart but I thought, I have one life to live. If I fall in love with a non-Jew and want to marry ... I'm going to marry.

It goes even deeper than that. I was somewhat ashamed of being Jewish. When I met somebody for the first time I would never volunteer the information that I was Jewish. I wouldn't deny it if I was asked, but rarely was I asked. I told myself, 'My religion and my place of worship is the theatre.' That is my God.

PETER
Will it disappoint you to learn that none of this is original with you, it is the story of countless generations throughout the centuries of young Jews who outgrow the religious structure of their family, or their *shtetl*, and begin to adapt to the gentile world and they begin to feel a little ashamed of being Jewish and don't jump forward with the information. It makes no difference if they are in Buenos Aires or in Poland or in Mexico or in Texas or in Canada – it doesn't matter where: so many Jews do not stand up to the pressure of anti-semitism which, unfortunately, is prevalent through-out the 'civilised' world. None of this is original darling, it has all happened millions of times before.

THELMA
It's also true that one doesn't want to be part of a minority. One wants to be with the majority, to conform, to be part of the scene. One doesn't like to feel different.

Then, in my thirties, I met Jay Lewis, a distinguished film director/producer, and started to live with him. Jay came from a Church of England background, but we never found the difference of religion to be a problem. Neither of us was observant, which helped, but there was a posi-tive aspect. We were interested in the differences of our religious upbringing and it added a certain enrichment to our relationship. But it was the final break with Judaism for me.

When Israel became a state in 1948 I was thrilled but always I felt, 'That's for them not me. That's a place for Jews

who have no home or who have suffered during the
Holocaust, or who are Zionists and idealists. I would never
want to live there.' I still felt like that when, twenty-two years
later, our romance blossomed and marrying you would
mean living in Israel. Not only did it mean leaving my work,
my friends, my home in England, leaving my dogs and my
language, but also going to a foreign country, a strange
place. I had never been a Zionist.

When I first arrived, I referred to Israel and Israelis as
'you', not 'we'. I was not prepared for the dramatic change
in me – like the lifting of a weight, my Jewish problem,
which I hadn't realised was a problem, was solved. Once
freed of the necessary Diaspora equation of Judaism with
observing the Jewish religion, I was far more Jewish than I
had realised. In Israel being Jewish is a natural part of
everyday life. I felt part of the culture – the Jewish holidays
were the national holidays – as a girl I had hated missing
school for the Jewish holidays – Jewish music, songs, jokes
... all part of one's life. Friends, shopkeepers, plumbers, bus
drivers ... all Jewish. No more shame or biting the tongue, it
was open and wonderful. I had run away from the Jewish
ghetto of Leeds. With a few exceptions, I had found no
common language with English Jews. Here I was in Israel,
surrounded by Jews, and enjoying it. In Israel, to be a Jew
you don't have to follow any religious traditions or rituals,
you don't have to do anything, just stand up and be counted.
When the crunch comes, to say 'I am a Jew'. That was a
tremendous change in my life.

PETER
My story is only slightly different from yours because I
hadn't grown up in an orthodox home. On the contrary, my
father was an agnostic. He insisted that that's what he was,
he wanted no part of Jewish religious practices. He didn't
care one way or another about the Jewish holidays. He went
to the synagogue on Yom Kippur only because of the social

pressure around him, not because he enjoyed it or because he had any feeling for it, so I didn't have to throw off the ties of orthodoxy the way you had to. I wanted to throw off the ghetto mentality. I wanted to throw off the parochialism of belonging to a small, close-knit minority of Jews. I didn't like the synagogue. I didn't like the way the prayers were conducted. I didn't like the atmosphere. I didn't like the fact that you couldn't get into the synagogue and pray on the Day of Atonement unless you had a ticket. That seemed wrong to me. I didn't like the atmosphere of commercialism in and around the synagogue. I wanted to take my place in the world, like a citizen of Canada, the country that I was born in, with equal rights with everybody else who was circulating on those Montreal streets.

Like most Jews of our generation I experienced the desire for alienation, I wanted to alienate myself from my Jewish background. At the party I went to given by my wealthy Chicago girlfriend in her high-rise, magnificent apartment situated on the lake-front, I felt very conspicuous because my clothes weren't good enough and I was surrounded by very good-looking, tall, well-groomed, well-fed young men and women. I was introduced to somebody who said, 'Frye. How do you spell it?' I told him, 'F-R-Y-E.'

'Which branch of the family are you? Are you related to Varian Frye?' He was a high muck-a-muck in the intellectual community.

'No,' I said, 'I'm not.'

'Where was your father from?'

'Bohemia,' I said. I was ashamed of saying that my name was really Friedman and my father was from Odessa. I was ashamed that I was from a Jewish background. Where the hell is Bohemia?

I grew up in Canada in an alien, hostile environment. We were the Jews that they made fun of, we were the Jews that they ambushed on the way to school. We were the Jews whose name was on everybody's tongue – the goddamn Jews. In French-Canadian *Les maudit Juifs*. It means evil, despicable and the French-Canadians pronounced it 'modzee Juifs', 'Bloody Jews', which you used to hear at every corner in every situation when you moved out of the ghetto.

When I came to the United States of America there were jokes about sheeneys and Hymies and Ikeys. There are different ways to react to this. Some Jews become even more traditional than their own parents because they re-assert their Jewish connection, their Jewish continuity. They are proud of being Jewish. They are aggressive about it. They fight back. When somebody makes an anti-semitic joke they pop him on the nose. It doesn't matter that they get bloodied up themselves, they feel that they are doing the right thing.

I was doing what so many others do, have done and will continue to do, I was trying to assimilate. That was very difficult in my case because I started out so Jewish. I learned Yiddish and Jewish history in Yiddish, and the bible in Yiddish – you know from having lived with me, I'm *very Jewish* at heart, without being religious. So it was a dilemma.

Through chance and a combination of circumstances, I ended up in Israel, of all places. And Israel gave me something very necessary in my life. Israel settled once and for all my identity as a Jew. Suddenly, in Israel, I was a young Jew who had come to participate with other Jews from all over the world in the creation of a nationhood. In Israel, at that time early in 1949, there were people coming into the country from, oh, seventy different countries of the world. And I was part of this great thrust of young Jews who wanted to establish for themselves a Jewish identity.

Like you, I found myself living in a Jewish environment, which was totally different from the parochial *shtetl*-like ghetto that I lived in in Montreal. I had done everything I could to expunge that ghetto out of me. It was a long, slow process, and now here I am in Israel and it's not a ghetto and they're all Jews. I had no difficulty finding a relationship with them because, like you, I could choose the ones that I liked to be my friends and the others didn't bother me one way or another and I felt a wonderful sense of liberation. I had finally, for the first time in my life found a homeland. I didn't have to pretend I wasn't Jewish. Here I was in a place where I could take pride in the accomplishment of the citizens, the general air of liberalism that was the keynote of Ben-Gurion's first governments. Here was a new society, struggling to build itself up along quasi-Socialist lines which said, 'Yes, all men have the right to an equal chance.' They didn't talk about equality because that's not the issue – the issue is equality of opportunity and that was there in Israel. It was not a society of 'devil-take-the-hindmost', it was a society of 'let's catch up with the hindmost and take them along with us'. It was a marvellous society in those first years.

By the time you came to Israel in 1970 it had changed considerably. It was no longer that pioneer, progressive, vibrant society of social rights. What did I look for in Spain? A chance to create a modern, democratic, progressive society on the bones of hundreds of years of oppression by absentee landlords, by feudal barons, by a totally incapable monarchy, by a threatening Catholic church. I thought I could help them come to democracy. Historically, it turned out that we did. But here in Israel I had everything that I'd fought for in Spain, everything that I had yearned for when I was a young man working in the propaganda theatre of the Communist Party. When people ask me today, 'Who are you? What are you?' I say, 'I was born in Canada but my real home, my country of origin, my homeland is Israel.'

Book VI

Our Successful Years

Live
Television

THELMA

We've managed to catch up with each other chronologically.
The early fifties. You worked on TV in the early days of live
television and so did I. My very first television experience
was in a play called *Cranford,* dramatised from a classical
novel of Cheshire small-town life in the last century written by
Mrs Gaskell. We transmitted from Alexandra Palace, the first
BBC studios, to me a place of magic. We did two live
performances. As you said there were no recordings in those
days and the Sunday play of the week was always repeated on
Thursday.

There was a huge studio crammed with settings – a
parlour, a garden, a street – sets, furniture and props
everywhere. Frequently I had to exit from one scene and
race to a set at the other end of the studio to make an
entrance in the following scene trying to avoid all the cables,
cameras, props, sets, people on the way and to make the
entrance calmly, without panting! Sometimes I had to do a
costume change on the run. One of the most frightening
things was the camera, which was huge and lumbered
towards me for a close-up, ending up an inch away from my
face.

There was the floor manager, who was very important and
impressive in charge of everything that went on in the studio
and your only contact with the director was through him
and his headphones, and there was a stage manager who
held the script. She had a button, and if anybody dried, went

blank, forgot his lines, she pressed the button which turned off the sound, gave a prompt in a loud voice and pressed the button to turn the sound on again. The audience didn't notice because the sound was always breaking down. One actor is reputed to have dried and kept his mouth moving as if he was talking and everybody thought it was a breakdown of the sound. Frequently the microphone was in the shot. I found it hard to believe that while I was acting in a scene in Alexandra Palace, thousands, maybe hundreds of thousands, of people were watching me at that very moment all over the country. We are so used to it now we forget the wonder of those early days. I asked a technician to explain it to me: 'Your face gets broken up, shot through the airwaves in pieces and then put together in six hundred and twenty-five lines and if you're lucky the pieces are put back in the right order.' As television grew, I was a part of it. I did plays, variety shows, the very first colour studio transmission in a series of Intimate Revue programmes called *Before the Fringe* with the greats from the old revues – Beatrice Lillie, Hermiones Gingold and Baddeley, Douglas Byng.

I did a summer season, a televised concert party, weekly live shows in front of an audience called *Hi Summer*. Only five of us in the cast, singing, dancing, sketches. One of the five was an American comedian called Cliff Norton. One week we did a duet from *Kiss Me Kate* called 'Wunderbar'. The first verse starts, 'Gazing down on the Jungfrau...' so you can imagine how high we are supposed to be. We sang as we climbed the mountain and we had holes in the heels of our climbing boots which fitted around pegs on the platforms. This trick enables you to lean over much further than is normally possible. It is hard to do ... you can lean over nearly to the floor ... but it looks good. Especially going up the side of a mountain. At the end of the song it was arranged that I fall down the mountainside and reappear still in my climbing gear with wings and a halo – and flying!

On a wire. I am supposed to be landed on the top of the
mountain to say goodbye to Cliff and then flown away into
the roof of the studio. I have never flown before or since.

Each week we had only one day in the studio. We
rehearsed during the day and the show went out live at
seven that same evening. On the day of 'Wunderbar' it
was four o'clock before we started to dress rehearse that
number. Remember, this was our first time in costume,
the first time we had seen the set and Mr Kirby of the
famous Kirby Flying Ballets had come along to supervise
my flying to heaven. Under the costume I wore a harness
to which he would attach a wire. 'You don't have to do
anything,' he assured me. 'Just bend your knees a little
and the wire will take you away.' However, he had brought
the wrong equipment for the flying we had planned. Cliff
and I rehearsed the climbing, the swaying over to the
side, my falling off the mountain. Mr Kirby was there –
he had only a few bars of music to attach the wire, which
he did, and I did my little curtsey, the wire lifted me into
the air and instead of landing me on top of the mountain,
it crashed me into the side.

I was lowered to the floor. They took off my climbing
boots and my thick climbing socks and found my shin badly
injured with the blood pouring out. I was shocked and
shaking so they took me back to the dressing-room and
promised to rehearse again later on. But the crew always
insisted on an hour and a half break before the show – an
hour's break and a half-hour to what they call 'line up'. By
five-thirty they had not had time to rehearse the song again
so we started the transmission with me in a terrified state of
nerves and with a painful shin.

'Wunderbar'. We sang the song, we leaned over the side
of the mountain, I fell down the mountainside and Mr Kirby
attached the wire and he did it perfectly. He landed me on
the top of the mountain, as planned, to say goodbye to Cliff,
and then off into the heavens. And there I was left hanging

like a sack of potatoes – for some reason he couldn't get me down. That was what it meant to do live television.

It is unlucky that my best work on television was when only few people watched. I did nine months in a panel game called *Pick the Winner* with Ted Ray, Arthur Askey and Katie Boyle – an excellent and delightful show, but it was the first year of BBC2 and hardly anybody saw it. Granada had a top-rank variety show called *Chelsea at Nine*, on which I did part of my cabaret act – a burlesque on different sorts of sopranos. I was hailed in all the national newspapers as the natural successor to Hermione Gingold and Beatrice Lillie, the new top comedienne ... but it didn't happen. I never had my own programme – shame! The price of being a pioneer.

Playing Prince Charming in the pantomime *Cinderella* was my introduction to musicals. Then I did my first revue in Leatherhead. By chance I had met Peter Myers, Alec Grahame and Ronnie Cass, whose revue *High Spirits* was shortly to be put on in the West End. Peter Myers was to play a key role in my life. He was the leader of the group, the inspiration behind a string of successful revues. A large, overweight man with slack lips and a stammer caused by his brain racing along much faster than he could get the words out. Much of his humour was undergraduate, even school-boy. But, with enormous enthusiasm, he had a talent for tearing down pomposity, spotting the ridiculous. He was intensely loyal, which is why so many of us worked in his shows time and again and his early death from a heart attack was a shock and a loss.

The Leatherhead revue was a success, and the boys came to see it on the last night then came to my dressing-room full of praise and enthusiasm: 'We're putting on a revue in the West End and you would have been ideal for it but it is fully cast and already rehearsing. But things can happen – don't take another job without letting us know.' How they managed to dispose of a member of the cast I'll never know, but the call came and I was in a West End musical just months after my musical debut. *High Spirits* was at the Hippodrome, the coronation year revue, 1953. It was beautifully staged – the structure of the show, in honour of the Queen's coronation, was that the first half depicted skits and songs set in the period between Elizabeth I and Elizabeth II, and the second half was modern. In the company were Cyril Ritchard, Diana Churchill, Ian Carmichael, Patrick Cargill, Joan Sims, Dilys Laye, Leslie Crowther, Eleanor Fazan, Ronnie Stevens. A marvellous collection of artists and we were in Leicester Square, in the heart of London.

This was a new start for me – as a revue artist in the West End. The first time I'd worked with a proper orchestra. The first time I'd worked in a big musical show.

Hill 24 Doesn't Answer

PETER

In January 1953, when you were starting your musical career, I arrived in Israel and I got involved immediately with a production at the Cameri Theatre. *Desire under the Elms* by Eugene O'Neill. We had a dress rehearsal in Tel Aviv, and then we came to do our out-of-town opening in Netanya. The show ran along – technically it was good – and we get to the critical point where the young wife throttles her own baby who is two or three days old, and the audience laughed. This made me furious. It was bad direction or bad acting – or both. At the end of the show when I was called on to the stage, as is customary in Israel – the director of the play appears on the stage to receive the plaudits of the audience and the cast on the opening night – I get out on stage and shout at the audience in Yiddish, 'Stop your applause! You obviously didn't understand the play so there's no point applauding it. If you could laugh at that moment when she kills the baby something is terribly wrong. Either I directed it incorrectly, or you failed to understand what the play was about.'

A Peter Frye scandal! The papers were full of it the next day and what makes that evening especially memorable is that before I had stepped on the stage, I had received a phone call which told me that Batia had given birth to a baby girl.

Desire under the Elms was well received because the audience had great admiration for Hannah Marron, the leading actress. We overcame that business of the laughter, we rehearsed it and found what had been wrong and they stopped laughing. *Desire* was performed forty times, par for the course in Israel.

At this juncture Mr Zvi Kolitz turned up in Israel eager to make his film. He still had six sentences on an envelope and a title, HILL 24 DOESN'T ANSWER. He would try to raise the money for a production in Israel. He was a great talker. He talked people into investing, he talked people into working for him. He was a nice man. He was – like many conmen – utterly charming. I finished the script, the money is there, now – production. In the flat which I shared with Batia and our newborn baby – it wasn't yet properly furnished – we set up a big work table and there I interviewed every young film worker in Israel. I hired them: as production assistants, as assistant directors, a complete staff. Today they are the pillars of respectability in the Israel film business. I picked the best of the crop. This was the first major English-language film ever attempted in Israel. This was the beginning of the Israel film industry.

I saw all the locations. I was the producer in charge of production. I'd never done a film before, but I had done television, and I had done a small amount of filming as an actor, so that I had the feel of it. Everything was getting to be ready for D-Day, but meanwhile, other things had been going on behind my back. Margot Klausner who owned the studio had been visiting England, boasting about her studio in Israel, the first studio of its kind. She met Thorold Dickinson and she told him about this film which was in preparation in Israel and said, 'Why don't you come out and be the editor and maybe assist our young director? This is going to be his first film.' Or that's what she said she said. What happened in fact was that she got the rest of the consortium of backers to agree to add Thorold Dickinson to the staff. He came out and made every attempt to take over from me. His idea was, What is this young pipsqueak doing thinking he can direct a film when I am the man with all the experience.

I had my hands full because I had never had the experience of working in the set-up of large film production. Dickinson was a very impressive-looking man older than me, tall with long flowing white hair. We started to shoot the film with me directing and Thorold Dickinson directing behind my back. When I was on one location he was on another. It was Dickinson's idea and the producers agreed to it. Two directors working at cross purposes.

Thorold Dickinson started to go over schedule. I, as producer, had hired a group of some two hundred extras who had to be shipped in from Beersheba, which was quite a big distance from the location where we were shooting, at Avdat, a prehistoric Nabotean town. I had also arranged with the Israeli army to lend us a battalion of infantry with their equipment. The schedule called for four days of shooting. Thorold Dickinson kept doing take after take after take. He wound up shooting that segment of the film for twenty-four days. We'd hardly started and we are twenty days behind schedule. There isn't that much money. The army called back its troops, the extras had to be shipped back, but Thorold said, 'I've got to have them,' so they were brought back again. All of this cost money.

It came to a crisis and I said I couldn't continue this way. They held a meeting and they said, 'We think you should

continue as producer and let Thorold do the directing.'
'Impossible!' I replied. 'The man doesn't know the meaning
of a schedule, and the man doesn't know how to stage
things.'

In the end it came to a break up between me and the
consortium. I went to a lawyer with my contract and we took
the company to trial. My lawyer said that this was a struggle
between me, who was trying to do an honest film about the
War of Independence, and this Englishman who was trying
to make a film sympathetic to Britain. I won damages of
approximately 25,000 Israeli pounds, but I was no longer
the director *or* the producer of the film. I got screen credit
as the writer of the screenplay and co-producer of the film,
but I walked out. Dickinson spent one hundred and four
shooting days to make that film. It had been scheduled for
forty days. It was quite a good film, it was successful and is
still shown, but it should have been a much better film.

The Apollo Theatre

THELMA
At last I got a big part in a London musical. In 1955 there
was a new musical by Sandy Wilson, who wrote *The Boy
Friend*, called *The Buccaneer*. I played a very wealthy woman,
Mrs Winterton, who has a thirteen-year-old son, played by
Kenneth Williams, who was at the time twenty-nine. He
already had the nasal voice, uncompromising, crazy assur-
ance, the offbeat humour that was later to make him so well
known, but underneath I found a sweet-natured and vulnerable human being. He gave a wonderful, outrageous
performance in short trousers as a very precocious child, I
was his glamorous, scatterbrained, sexy mother. Good songs,
comedy scenes – it was a delicious opportunity. The
opening at the Lyric Theatre, Hammersmith, was well

received and I got good notices. We were doing good business and so the management, the famous H M Tennent, left us in Hammersmith instead of transferring us quickly into the West End. We ran there for a few months, then transferred to the Apollo Theatre in Shaftesbury Avenue but by that time it was too late, the momentum had gone and we ran in the West End for only a month. As *The Boy Friend* had been such a success this was a disappointment. But even if it was only for a month my childish fantasy had come true – I had been a leading lady in the West End, bowing to the applause of the multitude.

These were the halcyon days of my career. Straight from one job to another. Praise and encouragement, friends and fun and so much laughter. It was great to live through. After *The Buccaneer* back with Peter Myers and the boys of *High Spirits* again for the best two years of my professional life, *For Amusement Only*. People still remember it – strangers speak to me, reminding me of sketches I have long forgotten. I had the star dressing-room, and top billing. We went on a six-week tour before opening at the Apollo Theatre. The management was Linnit and Dunfee, headed by a very nice man called Bill Linnit. Top billing, star dressing-room! We opened in Southsea to a lukewarm reception. Next morning we all gathered in the stalls, Bill Linnit, the authors, the cast. The changes were announced: 'And this is out and that has changed and this is out and this is out.' Suddenly I realised that in the first half I was in the opening and the closing numbers and that's all, everything else had been cut. What was the point of the star dressing-room when I was barely in the show? I was sitting next to Jimmy Thompson and I took the handkerchief out of his breast pocket and I burst into tears! What an embarrassment – the 'leading lady' weeping and unable to talk to anybody.

During the six weeks of the tour we were changing and experimenting and I got back into the first act. How to describe to you what it's like to be in a revue? It isn't in the least like being in a play, where you have a written script. Revue can change completely from the first rehearsal to the first performance. It can change again completely from the first performance to the eighth performance. Constantly new numbers, songs, sketches, dances. Constantly changing the running order. You have to be so quick, because you are learning new things during the day, sometimes putting them in that night, sometimes rehearsing a new version of a number during the day and having to perform the old version at night until the new version is ready to 'put in'. Intimate Revue was a very special genre, I don't know if you had the equivalent in the States. No chorus line or orchestra, just one pianist in the orchestra pit. Ronnie Cass was sometimes distracting when he read the newspaper during the sketches and, standing and facing the audience, he would noisily turn the page. But he was a wonderful musician.

In *For Amusement Only*, nowhere on tour did we have a very enthusiastic reception. The last week before London was Brighton. There was a sketch in the show written by Alan Melville, a distinguished comedy writer, which portrayed a mix-up at the Old Vic – it was the beginning of the repertoire system at the Old Vic performing a different play each night of the week. I entered onto the balcony as Lady Macbeth, convinced that this was the night of *Macbeth*, and Hugh Paddick entered underneath the balcony as Romeo, convinced it was the night for *Romeo and Juliet*. Every word that I spoke was from *Macbeth*, every word he spoke was from *Romeo and Juliet* – brilliantly interwoven. Every time Romeo tried to climb the balcony I would lean over – I had a red wig with two enormous red plaits and a huge bosom – and growl in an evil voice, 'I have given suck!' and he would fall off the ladder with shock. Alan Melville lived in Brighton and came to see the show, after which he contacted Peter Myers and said, 'I think this show is going to be a disaster, I want my name taken off the programme.'

And so to London and once again to the Apollo Theatre. The morning of the opening night there was a scandal in the papers about Lady Docker. She was the wife of Sir Bernard Docker, who was the head of Daimler cars and he'd been given the sack that morning. In her own right Lady Docker was quite a character, always in the papers with her jewels, cars, yachts and other extravagances. When the news broke, Peter Myers phoned me and said, 'We've done a number about Lady Docker. Take down the words over the phone. You've got to learn it and perform it tonight.' I had to learn the number, get a wig to look like Lady Docker, get a dress and a fur. As the curtain went up I was dressed in a pink diamante evening dress, wearing jewels and furs, on the street selling matches with a sign hanging from my tray which read: 'Husband and four Daimlers to support.' It was so topical it brought the house down.

The Romeo and Macbeth sketch was a riot – Alan Melville never got the credit on the programme for writing it – and the final number, *The Vagabond Student* – a skit on amateur operatic productions – ran nine minutes at rehearsal but the laughter stretched it to twenty minutes in performance. Alan Melville wasn't the only one who got it wrong. When we got the script of *Vagabond Student* we *all* refused to do it. 'It's not funny,' we complained. Bill Linnit was called in and pleaded with us. 'Please try it. I give you my solemn word that if it doesn't work with an audience, we will cut it out immediately.' The result. I have never heard laughter like it in any theatre, either on the stage or sitting in the audience. Night after night I would look out and the audience had become a sea of white, because everybody was laughing so much they were crying into their handkerchiefs. We saw people falling out of their seats into the aisles – literally. All those who remember the show from thirty-five years ago remember that sketch in which we wore wild Ruritanian costumes and not being able to hear a single word of Ron Moody's dialogue – he was supposed to be the romantic leading man. *For Amusement Only* ran for two years, some people came to it again and again. Ron Moody and I were the only two who never missed any of the six hundred and ninety-eight performances.

I started at the beginning of the run to keep an autograph book of people who came to my dressing-room, which I treasure. People came round, many of whom I'd never met before, just to congratulate us, and mine was the dressing-room they came to. In my book are the autographs of Charles Laughton, Michael Redgrave, a Hollywood producer Pandro S Berman, a Broadway producer, Leonard Sillman, Jack Benny, Julie Andrews, Gracie Fields and many more. Ron Moody had a knack of recognising famous people in the audience during the opening number. One night he said, 'Princess Margaret' and we thought he was joking, but there she was, very short and surrounded by very tall escorts, somehow he had spotted her. It was the most successful show I was ever in. I don't know what killed Intimate Revue but it seems to have gone for ever.

Habimah Stars

PETER
I negotiated a contract with Habimah and told them I wanted to do *Medea*. But they told me, 'We have bought the rights to *The Caine Mutiny* by Herman Wouk (which was then a huge success in New York). If you do that for us we'll let you do *Medea* for your second show.' I came out of this nightmare of the whole quagmire of hatred I felt for the people involved in *Hill 24* and I'm preparing to direct two shows at Habimah. Habimah has a great name. There were two great personalities leading it. One was Aharon Meskin and the other was Hannah Rovina, the great Habimah star. She was now in her sixties – still beautiful, still magnificent,

still a wonderful personality – but she wasn't much of an actress in the professional meaning of the word. She knew how to behave on the stage. She had a series of clichés – clichéd vocal tricks, clichéd physical poses, which she used more or less logically according to the needs of the part, but they did not reveal the basic truth of a character.

The Caine Mutiny with Aharon Meskin was very well received. He had a magnificent bass voice and was wonderfully human, he was honest, he was sincere, he was *devoted* to the task in hand, which was to express the meaning of any particular part and any particular play in the way that he felt it in his guts.

He was a wonderful actor to work with. He was receptive, he was quiet, he didn't argue with you. He would say 'Good! Let's try it!' and he would do it. It was a great experience, and for me a great source of pride, that I worked with this actor a number of times. In *The Caine Mutiny* he played Captain Queeg. One day I said to him, 'The way you are using your voice is not bringing out the full value of the words you are saying in this scene. Let us say your voice is black, because it's so deep and it's so dark. I want you to think white when you say this speech. Don't think black. Black is there, you've got it. Think white.' I don't know how well he understood me, but he nodded and said, 'Think white! All right, let's do it!' He did it, and it worked. It was marvellous and suddenly, in addition to all this wonderful richness of voice, there was a richness of highlights which, by himself, he might not have found. These are the moments when a director experiences great joy.

Medea ... Rovina of course was going to play Medea. She had the stature – tall with a wonderful face and bearing. I got to know her as a human being and I loved her. My opinion about her as an actress changed from time to time but I was always in love with that woman.

The management look at my drawings for the set and

say: 'It's too big.' 'It isn't too big,' I replied, 'I have
calculated every step. Every centimetre of this set has
been measured according to the choreography which I
have developed for the play. Every centimetre of stage
will be used. There will be an actor standing on every
spot.' We wrangled but in the end I had no choice, I had
to give in. I cannot tell you what it meant for me, because
I was not lying when I said that every centimetre of the
stage had its uses according to my production plan. Instead
of twenty-four steps going up on stage right I had to cut
it down to eighteen. That meant I had to cut down the
cast. There would be fewer soldiers because there were
no steps for them to stand on. I made that compromise
but I said, 'That's all. I don't want to see any one of you
at rehearsals. When it's ready, I'll call you.'

As you know I had a great love of the use of music in
dramatic productions. In most of the shows that I did, if
it was possible to insert music as an organic part of the
storytelling, I would do it. I don't mean mere background
music. I mean music as transitions, music as a bridge,
music as a character in the play and this *Medea*, this
version which had been re-written by an American poet,
Robinson Jeffers, from the Euripides original, was a very
musical production. To do the music I chose Paul Ben
Chaim, the doyen of Israeli composers. He was a very
fine composer. He got very excited when I told him what
I had in mind – to invent a Grecian melodic pattern for a
play adapted by an American poet and played in the
Hebrew language. He was sweet and good and tender, so
concentrated, so creative and he wrote beautiful music
for me.

Let me tell you a little about how we arrived at a
conception of the kind of sound we wanted to hear. The
Greeks and the Hebrews were contemporaneous. The Jews
at that time already had a distinct Hebrew intonation
because they had something in the Bible which is called

taamay hamikra, the signs for reading, and every cantor who
sings the service in synagogue goes through a very rigid
course of studying *taamay hamikra*. We know that the Greeks
traded with the Hebrews so could it be that the Greeks came
to the shores of what is today Israel and traded with Jewish
traders and maybe went into synagogues to hear the singing
and maybe Greek music was somewhat affected? Paul Ben
Chaim said, 'We do know that in the Gregorian chant which
came many centuries later and which is the musical idiom
of the Catholic liturgy, it is very similar to *taamay hamikra*
... the same intervals, the same musical phrasing. If the
Romans picked it up, why can't we assume that the Greeks,
who came before the Romans, had also picked it up?' He
based his music on that supposition and added a Greek
flavour.

The rehearsals start and I begin to stage the play. It was
difficult – when you have a set which is full of stairways and
ramps and you're working on a flat rehearsal floor, it creates
problems. Rovina, after the first few days, gets into her
stride and starts giving me those tones which she had used
in *The Dybbuk*, and I don't want it. I want a realistic Medea,
who speaks a poetic text but speaks it realistically. I talk to
her, 'Rovina, when I started to work on this play I said to
myself – how do I conceive of the character of Medea, who
was Medea? Was she a real woman, was it a myth, was it a
fairy tale, was it a nightmare, what was it? I said, no she was a
woman. She was a woman two thousand five hundred years
ago.'

On what do we model her today? I stood in the street at
the corner of the Mograby Theatre and I watched the
people going by and, I thought, if I stand here long enough
a Medea will pass me. I stood there and all kinds of people
came by. Russian ladies, Polish ladies. German ladies,
Romanian ladies, Czech ladies. I stood there and there
were Yemenite women and Bukharan women and women in
Arabic clothes. Yes, yes such a woman could be driven out

of her mind by the fury of jealousy and she could kill her children. The minute I saw that, I knew how to direct the play. The play has to have the immediacy of a street scene in Tel Aviv although it's Grecian.

At rehearsals the next day I described this to Rovina and she told me that she agreed with me totally but the same phoney sound came out of her and the same phoney poses which she had used for the last thirty-five years. She had a wonderful voice, she had a good singing voice too, but she had developed a mode of speaking which was ... Rovina. I said to her, 'Rovina, could you possibly forget everything you've done before? This has to be realistic and when the people look at this woman's body and hear this woman's voice, they have to be reminded of all of those women that I saw in the street. They should say, "Yes, yes, this woman is of today, of now. She could do what she is going to do, because she's human".' 'Oh,' she said, 'that's very nice, very nice. We'll do it.' She wasn't capable. She had intelligence, she understood me but she was captured in the carapace of her previous mannerisms.

I didn't know what to do. She agreed with everything I said but she just couldn't do it. Then one day I finally lost my temper. I took my script and I closed it very fiercely, but I talked very quietly. 'Madam Rovina, you know how much I respect you and love you as a human being, but if you cannot do what I ask you to do then I cannot direct this play.' Very quietly. They could see that I was in a temper, but I didn't shout, I controlled myself. I put my script in my briefcase and I left the rehearsal hall.

I'm walking down the stairs and I hear a clattering on the stairs behind me. The whole cast is running down and they persuade me to return. I let myself be persuaded and I went back to rehearsal and sat down near her on the stage and said, 'Rovina, if you will let me I will show you every move,

give you the readings for every tone of voice that you'll
need. Just let me help you.'

'Yes,' she said, 'anything you want from me I'll give you.
Whatever you ask for I agree with you. I love you.'

OK. Peace at rehearsal. That was the moment when I
broke through. She found the real person at the heart
of the character and gradually shed the phoney mannerisms and the phoney tones. Then she was heartbreakingly
magnificent.

We open. The audience goes crazy. I never heard such
cheers in a theatre – I never heard them for me, anyhow. It
was tremendous. It was overwhelming. The press the following day was marvellous. The critics said, 'Not in years have
we seen Rovina so fresh, so magnificent, so compelling,' and
she was.

At that period, in the 1950s, every year in Paris they held
an international theatre festival at the Sarah Bernhardt
Theatre and, after about a hundred sold-out performances,
Habimah is invited to do *Medea* for the Festival des Nations.
I figure they'll take me to make sure that the play goes on
the stage in Paris the way it's supposed to – that the scenery
is in the right place, that the lighting is correct and so on.
But no! When I talked to the management committee I said,
'I'm going to Paris with you, of course.' They said, 'No, we
don't need you in Paris. The stage manager will make sure
that the show goes on the way it's supposed to. We can't
afford to take you.'

I make a scandal. By now I have reporters who write for
the press who are my allies, so I call up some of my friends in
the newspapers and I say, 'Isn't this a stinking situation that
the director of the show is not going to Paris?' Scandal in the
newspapers! They re-cast fifteen actors, who were totally
unsuitable, altered my set and my choreography and all my
staging. They went to Paris and they open the show there
and Rovina got rave reviews and Ossia Trilling, who was a
friend of mine, wrote about the magnificence and the

tremendous impact of Rovina in a rather mediocre production. And I tell you, my production was so beautiful, it was so beautifully orchestrated, so beautifully choreographed and all of that went by the board. That's Habimah!

Tyrone

THELMA

When I was in *For Amusement Only* I was asked to be in the star-studded midnight show called *Night of 100 Stars*. I was to be in a chorus line with well-known actresses, all of us wearing spangled leotards and feathers and showing our legs. The evening was organised by Laurence Olivier, and in my chorus line were Sheila Sim, Brenda Bruce, Jean Kent, Anna Massey, Peggy Cummins, Joan Sims, Dulcie Gray – and me. We started to rehearse a song and dance routine to the music of the well-known song 'Chicago'. One day we were told, in the middle of rehearsal, that after 'Chicago' we would sing 'Chattanooga Choo-Choo'. Singing in front of the chorus line would be Tyrone Power. As a body, we all swooned.

He arrived. Tall, handsome, healthy, beautiful voice. I was to discover later he was also beautiful inside. A gentleman and a gentle man. A sweetness about him. Added to that he was truly talented and serious about his work. We had fun at rehearsals. One day he was singing away until he came to the line, 'There's going to be a certain party at the station', instead of which he sang, 'There's going to be a certain party at the wedding'. The choreographer called out, 'That was fine, Tyrone, until you came to the wedding.' 'That's life!' Tyrone called back.

The last day of rehearsal, the day before the performance, he read to all of us a fan letter that he had received from a girl in Manchester. She poured out her heart about how she adored him and had every press cutting, every photo ever taken of him – she had loved him ever since she was a child:

'I'm overwhelmed that you are now in England and that you are coming to Manchester in *The Devil's Disciple*. The week you will be here I have made sure that my parents go to Blackpool so that you can come to me. I am only small, four feet eleven, but my heart is big. Signed, Rhoda Power. PS I have always thought it such a strange coincidence that your name is Power and my name is Power.'

That night, as a joke, I wrote him a letter and left it for him at the Palladium after the performance. It was a satire on Rhoda Power's letter and I signed it 'Ruby Station' with a PS 'I have always thought it such a strange coincidence that your name is Power and my name is Station.' No other indication as to who it was from.

The evening was a sensation. Just before we made our entrance, Bob Hope came up, leaned on my shoulder and called to the chorus line, 'Make sure you soften 'em up for me.' I looked around and saw who it was and said, 'Oh Mr Hope, I've always loved you' and on I danced. Next day the telephone rang. A deep, velvet, American voice said, 'Is that Miss Station?' Wow, did my heart beat? He invited me to dinner that evening at his house. Not alone – it was a dinner party. That is how I became friendly with Tyrone.

He came to see me in my show *For Amusement Only* and was mad about it. He came at least a dozen times, each time with different friends, and he brought them round to the dressing-room afterwards to introduce me. Jack Hawkins, Mai Zetterling, Van Johnson. He brought Richard Sale, who was the director of the film he was making in England, *Seven Waves Away*. Many other Hollywood folk. Van Johnson also became a friend, and he too came many times to the show. We always knew when he was in front because he had an enormously loud and distinctive laugh.

There followed a most glamorous period of my life. I

became Tyrone's girlfriend and he squired me all around London. Wherever we went all heads would turn and it was *I* who was on his arm. The friendship deepened and led to a glorious affair. I was crazy about him. But for all his courtesy, kindness and generosity, he was never serious about me. He was not married at the time but he said he would never marry an actress again. Jack and Doreen Hawkins had the ideal marriage, he said, with Doreen devoting her life to Jack's well-being. Little did he guess that, if asked, I'd have done the same. I didn't break my heart that there was never any question of marriage. Although I thought I was prepared for marriage to a non-Jew, I knew that for my parents any such marriage would have been devastating and heartbreaking, even to a Tyrone Power. Nearly forty years later I can see it would not have been a good idea ... I don't think it would have worked. I'd have felt I was not glamorous or self-assured enough for Hollywood highlife. I would never have been at ease in those surroundings. I imagine one requires a basic toughness to be the successful wife of a Hollywood film star. During the run of *For Amusement Only* one of the company, Jimmy Thompson, got married on a Saturday morning. I turned up at the wedding on the arm of Tyrone which delighted everybody. This certainly added a sparkle to the occasion. Tyrone was warm and friendly and had a delightful sense of humour.

He was in England for quite a long time with *Seven Waves Away* and *The Devil's Disciple*. One night when he took me out for dinner he was wearing an elegant, white satin, embroidered waistcoat which I admired. Right there, in the restaurant, he took it off and gave it to me! The sort of grand gesture that belongs to fiction. I still have it, and the Mexican bullfighters shirt and tie he sent me. When he left, weeks would pass. He always wrote to me (I still have his letters) and then suddenly he would appear in the dressing-room, that great tall god picking me up, sweeping me off my feet and up into the air. Then he went off to America for a longer period, and the next time he came back it was with a wife. Her name was Debbie. Unlike Anabella and Linda Christian, his two former wives, this one was totally unconnected with the theatre. He telephoned and invited me out for dinner. I met Debbie in their suite at the Connaught Hotel, and we went out for a meal. I was polite and friendly to Debbie, even though I was green with jealousy. What did she have that I hadn't? Apart from not being an actress. But I was glad that Tyrone and I were still to be friends.

Tyrone and Debbie were on their way to Spain – he was to make a film there. Debbie was already pregnant, though they had only recently been married. Tyrone had two adorable little daughters by Linda Christian, Taryn and Romina, and I had made a great fuss of them when they stayed with him in London, hoping to impress Tyrone with my motherly qualities. I took them to a Pantomime, I took them to the zoo. But he had always longed for a son to carry on the name of Tyrone Power. His father and grandfather had been well-known actors with the same name. Two weeks later I was stunned by the news that he had died on location in Spain, of a heart attack. Aged forty-five. It was all the more of a shock because he had looked so well and tanned – he used a sunlamp – and bounding with energy when I saw him. He loved to do his own stunts in films. He was athletic and strong. His manager, Bill Gallagher, told me that he had just completed a scene, and went back to his caravan. He clutched his heart and said to Bill, 'If this pain doesn't ease off soon, I'm finished.' The pain didn't go, and he died. In the full flush of his manhood. Baby Tyrone Power was born a few months later.

The fact that Tyrone liked me enough to be such a good friend, to spend time with me, did help to strengthen my self-esteem. When I floated around on his arm in public I felt I *must* have more quality than I'd thought, for him to choose me. It was a turning-point in my struggle to value myself.

PETER

What you have talked about right now you have not kept secret from me. It was perfectly clear to me that you were tremendously attracted to this individual and, had things worked out differently, you might have made him a very devoted wife.

Given my bias, my class bias, there are certain aspects of the affair that I'd like to discuss with you. You said he took you out and you floated into the restaurant on his arm. No doubt the restaurant was full of successful, wealthy people, so I assume you must have been dressed up to the nines for this occasion. That raises a question of your whole cultural direction. What was important to you in those days. Obviously it was important to have good clothes. You couldn't be seen with Tyrone Power looking like a *schlepper*.

THELMA

As an actress, I've always tried to dress nicely. I didn't buy special clothes for Tyrone – I had a good wardrobe. As a West End leading lady, I had to make a lot of appearances and meet lots of people, some of whom might help get me my next job. Most nights I was taken out somewhere. Of course I spent money on clothes.

PETER

At that time you must have been in your mid-twenties. When I was twenty-four I had come back from Spain with a paralysed right arm. At twenty-eight I was married to May. I was working in the publishing house and making a very minimal kind of living. Here are you buying proper gowns to be seen with in public with a Hollywood movie star. What am I trying to get at? That there is a difference between our lines of development is clear to us. It is interesting that in our years together, both of us have changed in adapting each to the other. But at this point in time, when you are gadding about with Van Johnson and Tyrone Power and Hollywood producers, I was still involved with my left-wing beliefs.

There's a song by Marc Blitzstein, a composer and lyricist, in his play *The Cradle Will Rock* in which the key line is, 'Oh there's something so damn low about the rich'. Marc believed that when he wrote it, and I firmly believed it when I heard it. In my life experience I have not met many wealthy people who are not low. This may have something to do with my cultural deprivation, with the fact that I didn't make it into the halls of the wealthy. But in contrast, here are you gadding about with Hollywood stars. What is it I'm trying to say? To me, your story of this period of your life is a perfect paradigm of upper-middle-class culture. From your parents, from your home background, you have inherited those feelings about 'making it', about 'getting up there', about being seen, about being known, about being properly dressed. This was your concern. I sound like I'm condemning it. I'm not. I'm simply trying to define it. Whereas I was still back in my working-class, hidebound, prejudicial outlook on life. 'Oh there's something so damn low about the rich.' I was still concerned with social problems, with labour problems, with trade unions.

THELMA
Was I hoping for a more comfortable life? Was I looking for money? You bet! Was it because of my upbringing? Yes. My father having grown up in deep poverty wanted me never to endure it on my skin. He brought me up in comfort. I insisted on earning my own living and refused an allowance from my father. But I hoped that from my earnings I could live in comfort and have nice clothes, good food. I loved going out to restaurants. The only thing I am ashamed of and the raw nerve which you have pressed upon is that, after

my left-wing, Labour party affiliations around the age of
twenty, my ambition to fight for a more just society ... by
the time we are talking about I was no longer actively
fighting. You are right there.

Trailblazing

PETER

In 1956, in the immediate aftermath of the Sinai campaign, I
got an idea that I should do a documentary radio show. I still
spoke very poor Hebrew, so how the hell was I going to
interview people in a language which I didn't speak very well
and edit the tapes after I recorded them? Nevertheless I
convinced the management of Kol Israel, the government
radio service, that I could do an unusual kind of documentary show. We called it *The Voice of Each and Everyone*. They
gave me an assistant, a young lad by the name of Yosef
Taragin whose job was to take care of me as I struggled with
my limited Hebrew, and to correct me when necessary and
to tell me what the people I was talking to were saying. We
worked out a very good, cooperative relationship.

At the end of the war we were still occupying the Sinai.
That's where the action is and that's where I'm going, I
decided. Because my Hebrew was so rudimentary, I didn't
get into any high-flown philosophical questions. I went to
Beersheba, which was the traffic hub for all of the men and
materiel going back and forth down to the Suez Canal. That
first programme was very successful because the whole
country wanted to know what the boys who were going in
and out of the Suez area were doing, thinking, feeling. They
hadn't had this type of documentary programme before. I
was blazing a trail.

I then did a series on preventive psychiatry. I went to
mental hospitals with a psychiatrist to arrive at some sort of

understanding of how mental disease, mental ill-health could be prevented, *if* it could be prevented. I did a series on minorities. Israel is a wonderful place in which to study minorities. How they behave, how they are treated and what is the meaning of Israeli democracy. I visited the Bahai in Haifa. I went to a Circassian village and learned the history of that village. These are Sunni Moslems from the north-western part of the Caucasus in the vicinity of the Black Sea – they were subjected by Russia in 1864 and a group came and settled in Palestine for religious reasons.

I also went to an Arab village and to some Bedouin encampments where I learned of the transformation from a nomad's life to life in the settled encampment which became a village, which became a town. I went to the Bedouin encampment of Sheik Audeh Abu Muammar. I sat under a goatskin tent in the desert in the Northern Negev – one of the most wonderful days I ever spent anywhere, sitting in that desert with that burning bracing air. They fed me, as is traditional, a cup of hot, very sweet tea, and there was a delicious flavour in it. I asked them what the flavour was in the tea. Sheik Audeh answered, somewhat grandiosely, rotundly, he said, 'It is the goodness which flows in my heart when a visitor sits in my encampment.'

'Yes, that's very lovely, Sheik Audeh, but what's in the tea?' I pursued the matter.

'It is the feeling of brotherhood which should unite all men under God's sky.' I sat with him for hours recording him and people around him. As I was about to leave, as it was growing darker, one of Sheik Audeh's sons came up to me, 'Open your hands,' he said and he allowed leaves to fall into them. He said, '*That* is what was in the tea!' And it was *nana*, a form of mint which the Arabs use.

I did a series on Matchmakers. With everybody's permission, I recorded the *shadchan*, the matchmaker, and the *shadchan*'s wife, the clients ... women, men ... the demands that people had! When people heard it they said, 'It's a fake. Those are not real people. Those are actors. He wrote it, it's like Shalom Aleichem.' There was one woman who said, 'I want he should play cards and that we should go to the movies at least once every week and I want he should have a lot of money and he should be a nice-looking man, but the most important is – he should play cards.' I hope she found him – it wasn't much to ask for.

Another series was about the ritual bath. Taragin and I went to the *mikva*, which is the traditional ritual bath. We sit in the bath and we get hit with birch twigs and I record all kinds of conversations that go on in the baths. I came to one guy who was having a massage. There was a big, heavy masseur and this man was lying on his stomach and the masseur was massaging his back and he was really whamming into him and the man was breathless.

'What do you think about when you're lying here and this guy is breaking your bones?' I asked him.

'Women!' he said, 'young, old, big, small, it makes no difference. I could fuck them all.'

When we put this on the air – scandal! The religious complained. Some instinct told me how to protect myself on this programme. There was a cantor from the synagogue who was in the bath and a group of men collected around him and sang *Yevanai hamikdash* ... It's one of the standard prayers. 'You shall build the temple, we shall rebuild the temple.' There were about thirty men collected – all naked – and we had a wonderful male chorus. The room had a high ceiling and marvellous echoes, so it sounded like a huge chorus. I enjoyed doing these programmes enormously and I was learning the Hebrew language by using it and listening to it.

The radio series of mine that is probably best remembered was called *Beit Avi – My Father's House*. I wanted to do autobiographies on the radio, delving into the lives of the best people in the country in every sphere. But I didn't want

to tackle the subject head-on, I wanted to encourage the
people to talk by asking about his or her father's house.
What we would get is a life story through the prism of the
relationship with the father, with the mother, with the
house, the relatives, the family. I interviewed writers, artists,
politicians, professors, the most famous people in the
country.

I sat with David Ben-Gurion for hours and hours to hear
his story. He was fascinating, so sharp and colourful. Yigal
Allon published his interview as his autobiography without
giving me a credit. David Hacohen gave an outstanding, rich
interview, what a juicy man. And Chaim Hertzog, our
president of the state of Israel, said to me: 'I went into public
office because of you. Before that interview nobody knew
about me, but when they heard it they said, "Aha, that
man speaks well" and they gave me jobs involving public
speaking.'

The programme used to go out on a Friday evening
between eight and nine – prime time. It became so popular
that one day a member of the Religious Party got up in the
Knesset, the Parliament, and complained, 'It is not fair to
put such an important programme on the Sabbath when we
cannot listen to it.' The complaint was handed over to Kol
Israel and they started to do a repeat of the programme on a
Wednesday. I can hardly bear to tell you this, it hurts so
much. Can you believe it? Kol Israel wiped out every one of
those tapes. They destroyed all my tapes. They never had
enough tapes, and so they recorded over mine and wiped
them all out. Irreplaceable archive material, so important
for future generations. All gone.

The Cameri asked me to direct *Look Homeward Angel*, an
American play by Ketty Frings, adapted from the novel by
Thomas Wolfe. I cast Batia in the lead. She was absolutely
marvellous, stunning. To play the young boy I chose Dedi.
Oded Teomi. At which there was an uproar in the theatre:
'Who is he?'

'He's a kid from the army,' I told them. 'He's been in an Army Troupe and he has been working in a Studio with me.'

'Yes, but who is he? He hasn't done anything in the theatre.'

'He just happens to be very good for this part.'

'No, we want Yossi Corman to play it,' they insisted.

Yossi Corman is a very good actor but he is of low stature. This play is about Thomas Wolfe and one of his problems in life was that he was so gigantically tall. Dedi was a very tall boy but I chose him because I thought he could do it. I had worked with him in classes and my classes – as you know, you have seen them – are tough. They demand a great deal from the actor and I got a great deal out of Dedi. I created this ruckus in the Cameri by bringing in an outsider – Dedi had never been to the Cameri school, he'd never done anything on a professional stage but I *insisted* that he was right for the part.

The machinations that were practised by the management! It's hard to believe. Yossi Corman was supposed to go abroad during the period of rehearsals. They said, 'Postpone it, go later! Don't take a haircut because the character in the play has long hair.' So Yossi Corman grew his hair long and he haunted the rehearsals. The idea was that I would see him and get used to him and realise that Oded Teomi couldn't possibly play the part and, as I had been known to do, I would switch in midstream and take their choice for the part.

I've got torrents raging all around me. There is the one current about Yossi Corman and Dedi. There's another current about Miriam Bernstein-Cohen, who they thought should play Batia's part. It was a very difficult show to do and I had started out my rehearsals by using some of my techniques. After we had read the play together I had a rehearsal of improvisation. I had the whole cast sit around in a big circle and I asked each person to get up and walk around the circle stopping to stand behind each chair and talking to the back of the head of each character, as his character in the play but not with the written lines ... his feelings about the other characters and working out his relationships with every member of the cast. A very difficult rehearsal and a very useful one because you are bringing the entire cast into the whole play. This was something I had learned from Michael Chekhov, this was something I had learned from Piscator, this ideal of a theatre in which there is a profound unity of all of the forces who together are going to make the play and together means *together*.

The managers of the theatre brought in an expert, a young professor of literature. He watched the first dress rehearsal and, when I was giving notes to the cast, he said, 'You need to make some cuts.'

'I don't think this is the moment to discuss that,' I told him. 'I'm giving notes to the actors right now, I'll be glad to discuss any suggestions with you as soon as I'm through here.'

'No, you're just wasting time,' he persisted. This gives you an idea of the unremitting pressure that was on me all through the time. We got through the dress rehearsals and we opened the show and it was a *sensational* success! Dedi became a star overnight. People still talk about this production.

In 1958 I was invited by Professor Israel Ephrat, the rector of Tel Aviv University which was a year old, to prepare a programme for the creation of a Department of Theatre Arts, the first University Theatre Arts department in Israel. I put a strong emphasis on a number of Piscatorian ideas like the sociology of theatre – why we have theatre at all? What is the role of theatre in the development of civilisation? I started to teach at the end of 1958. We started out with fourteen students and seven teachers. The subjects were History of Drama and Playwriting, Theatre Literature, Speech, Music, Art History and Acting.

One of the first productions we did at the school during

our first year was a translation of Bertolt Brecht's play, *Fear and Misery of the Third Reich*. My student Tom Lewy did the translation, adaptation and he directed it. There was a building which was a combination botanical, zoological, chemistry and physics laboratory. That was our theatre. There was no auditorium and we adapted. It was a peculiar room with two steps all round. We pushed the equipment to one end of the room, and performed in the sunken area with the audience sitting on the stairway. We did a very interesting production in the round – it was wonderful.

It didn't go easily because, to my sorrow, I had enemies at the university. A lot of the professors were irritated that a *schmendrick* like me, who hadn't gone to university, was head of a department. I was invited to a committee of the senate to talk about what I planned to do. There was one professor who asked, 'What are you going to do, are you going to organise a branch of the Li La Lo in our university?' The Li La Lo was a revue theatre which had been very popular.

'Tell me,' I answer them, 'which is preferable? That students at your university should study the Greek Theatre in the writings of Aristotle, writing *about* Aeschelus and Sophocles and Euripides, or that we should study the text and *produce* the plays of Aeschelus, Sophocles and Euripides?'

I heard a whisper in the room ... 'Oh, he knows Aristotle, he knows Sophocles, he must know something!' I think that's what swung them in my direction because they said, 'OK, go ahead, try.'

I wanted to have a real Theatre Department and I wanted to have a Theatre Department that was firmly rooted in production techniques. Despite the problem of no production budget, the department grew and prospered and I am very proud of it today – a huge Faculty of the Arts. We started at Abu Kabir which was a small Arab village on the outskirts of Jaffa from which all the Arabs ran away during the War of Independence and it was deserted. Jewish new immigrants lived there for a while in the broken-down houses and then it was taken over by the newly created University of Tel Aviv. For the first year we had a wooden shed. No office. The daughter of the rector, Ghila Scharfstein, was the first secretary of the department and she spent all of her time sitting in our classes with the whole of the office in a bag on her lap. Frequently a goat wandered into the classroom until the owner would come rushing in to *schlep* the goat away. In the winter our unheated shed was freezing cold and in the summer it was a furnace. Fortunately, the university closed down for four months in summer.

I never got a budget. I was never the official head of the department. They said, 'You are the acting chairman of the department,' the department which I had founded. I asked them why I was only the acting chairman?

'You don't have a degree and according to our constitution the head of the department has to be a professor,' they told me.

'So make me a professor!' was my response.

They said, 'No, we can't make you a professor because you don't have any degrees.'

This contest went on for a number of years until at last I got my professorship but it was a long-running battle.

Orson Welles

THELMA
In 1960 I auditioned for Orson Welles and when I confessed that I had never appeared in a Shakespeare play, not even at drama school, he was delighted. Orson had adapted the two parts of Shakespeare's *Henry IV* to make one play, concentrating on the story of Falstaff, a part which he would play, and he called it *Chimes at Midnight*. When two old men, Shallow and Silence, are reminiscing with Falstaff about the

old days, remembering brave and romantic exploits, remembering those now dead, Falstaff says: 'We have heard the chimes at midnight, Master Shallow.'

Hilton Edwards and Micheál MacLiammóir – of Gate Theatre, Dublin, fame – were the producers of *Chimes at Midnight*. They had given Orson his very first acting job when he was travelling around Ireland with a donkey as a boy of sixteen. From time to time Orson showed his gratitude by returning to Dublin to appear in one of their productions. I was cast as the Hostess of the Boars Head Inn, Mistress Quickly. I was involved in the raucous, boisterous shenanigans of Falstaff, Prince Hal and their gang. Orson thought that my background as a comedienne and revue actress, without Shakespearean preconceptions and mannerisms, would bring a fresh approach to the part. Orson Welles was the star and Hilton Edwards was the director.

Summer time. First day of rehearsals in London. Sunshine streaming in through the windows, the air thick with the smoke from the huge cigars of Orson and Hilton. It is customary for the director to make a little speech on the first day of rehearsal before the reading starts. Hilton, a few wisps of white hair around his bald head, a round man with a gentle, sweet smile and still very English despite having lived for many years in Ireland, told us that he had spent many, many weeks preparing this production. He took a wadge of papers out from his briefcase, each one a detailed sketch. These illustrated where everybody would be sitting or standing for each scene. 'This is my way of working,' he said, 'and I hope you will all cooperate.' Before anybody else could speak, Orson said, 'If I can work like that without complaint, I'm sure everybody else can.' We read through the play, had a coffee and went home and that was the last we saw of Orson Welles for three weeks. We were told he was ill, and that we must carry on without him. Without our Falstaff, around whom the whole play was built, there was a great hole. We worked conscientiously, as actors do, following Hilton's preordained scheme meticulously.

Hilton was a dear man, pedantic and precise. There was no discussion of characterisation ... I suppose he was marking time, waiting for Orson to turn up. When there was less than a week of rehearsal to go, Orson appeared. And turned everything upside down. None of Hilton's careful blocking suited what he wanted to do.

'I can't play an intimate scene with Hal when he is at the other side of the stage. He has to be near, I have to grab him, to touch him.' So all of the staging was changed. This, as professional actors, we could have coped with. What we couldn't cope with was that Orson hadn't learned any of the lines and was still reading from the script. Hilton was very much in awe of Orson and Orson was an overpowering man. Not only impressive because of his past achievements, but also because of a coruscating personality which, combined with that voice and that bulk, made it very hard to criticise or disagree with him. Hilton and Orson represent the extremes of theatre tradition on both sides of the Atlantic. Hilton strong on beautiful stage pictures, clear verse-speaking, good costumes, sets, lighting. Whereas Orson is of the American school, unafraid to show emotion, concentrating on the script, the meaning, the character, the acting. We loved the injection of life Orson brought to the show when he came back to the rehearsals. So, off we went to Belfast by train and boat on the Friday, for an opening night at the Opera House the following Monday. Orson had a compartment to himself – just him and his tape recorder, trying to learn his lines.

Our first call in Belfast on Saturday evening turned out to be a costume parade. Then we were sent home – no rehearsal, no run-through, no Orson without a book. They spent all night organising the sets and lights. Technical rehearsal was called for Sunday afternoon. It was a bitterly cold February and the heating had broken down in the theatre. Micheál MacLiammóir arrived and never moved from his seat in the circle. The technical rehearsal went on all night until eight o'clock on Monday morning. We were in costume, Orson wasn't – he shared all the technical decisions with Hilton – he would go down from the stage to the auditorium to check every light change. He tried to act without holding the script, but he needed a prompt for nearly every line. Several times throughout the night he lost his temper uncontrollably and his was the worst explosion I have ever come across ... his voice became thunderous and the whole theatre shook. Generally the victim of the explosion was an electrician, the stage manager, some poor bugger who had fallen down on the job. Once it was an actress called Anne Cunningham who was a commère, reading from *Holinshed's Chronicles* at the side of the stage. For those few moments he became totally crazed. I thank heaven that I was never at the other end of such an outburst.

When the rehearsal was over, exhausted and frozen as we were, we all expected to be given a few hours to rest, and then back in the early afternoon for a run-through. We had never had a run-through, not even with Orson holding his script. But we were told, 'Opening night tonight at seven. Those in the Boars Head scenes, go to Orson's hotel at three this afternoon to work on them.' At the hotel we struggled through the scenes, and at a quarter to five a car came; we had quite forgotten that Orson and I were due to do a TV interview live at five. Orson said he couldn't go, so I went off with Micheál MacLiammóir, and got back to the theatre just in time to get dressed and made up for the opening night, a gala night with the governor-general of Ulster in the audience.

We stood at the side of the stage waiting for the performance to start, with more than the usual dose of first-night nerves. Suddenly there was a complete stranger standing next to me – it was Orson dressed as Falstaff. Enormous as he was, he had padded himself to twice the size, a wig with a

mass of white hair with white sideburns falling down his
cheeks, black eyebrows, a false nose fashioned out of wax
and I suspect there were sponges in his cheeks to make his
face look fatter. Totally unrecognisable! We were all in
shock. He sailed onto the stage and gave a brilliant, word-
perfect performance. I am a great admirer of his, but what
he put us through at that first performance was very unfair.
Just to have seen him in costume, just to have had one run-
through – surely not too much to ask.

There was an old actor called Terence Greenidge playing
the Lord Chief Justice. He became totally befuddled and did
not know what was going on. A very short actor called
Henry Woolf played Nym, Falstaff's servant, and at one
point he goes to the side of the stage announcing, 'Here
comes the Lord Chief Justice'. Being my first experience of
Shakespeare, I had wondered all through rehearsal what
would happen if anything went wrong. How does one
improvise Shakespeare? On the first night, Henry Woolf
said, 'Here comes the Lord Chief Justice,' but Terence
Greenidge was upstairs in his dressing-room wondering
which theatre we were at and what was the play. Once again,
'Here comes the Lord Chief Justice,' ... the sound of
running feet to pull Terence Greenidge down the stairs and
onto the stage. Henry Woolf walked slowly back to Orson,
they both sat on steps, and Henry said, 'I said he cometh,
but he cometh not'!

The notices were ecstatic: 'Welles's Falstaff is a gigantic
figure' one headline, and they didn't just mean his size. I am
rather pleased to see that I got good notices, maybe that first
performance wasn't as devastating as I remember. But it was
after the first night that the real work on the play began. We
ran for a week in Belfast and then six weeks at the Gaiety
Theatre in Dublin, and we rehearsed every single day,
including the day of our closing night. Orson took over the
direction completely. He knew that he was going to make a
film of it and he was experimenting and improving. I was

disappointed, of course, when he cast Margaret Rutherford
for the film instead of me.

As Orson was trying to work out the film script, he kept
changing the order of the scenes. I had the beautiful speech
of the death of Falstaff from *Henry V* and he found it hard to
decide whether to have it as the prologue or the epilogue. It
was a surprise that, in Shakespeare as in revue, you kept
changing the running order! He replaced Anne Cunningham
as the commère and cut Hotspur's wife from the show
altogether. He took a special liking to Keith Baxter and
myself, and every night we were invited to his suite at the
Hibernian Hotel to sit with him and his beautiful Italian wife
Paule, to talk until the dawn. He was very knowledgeable, his
inquiring mind ranged over every subject, he was eloquent
and fascinating. I would have felt inadequate – so many
subjects he tackled I knew nothing about – but it was
necessary only to murmur, 'How fascinating', 'Oh, yes' now
and again, because he talked non-stop. We had very good
notices in Dublin too, but the houses, surprisingly, were
thin. I don't know why we didn't attract big crowds – it was
an outstanding theatrical experience and a rare treat.

To try to add to the excitement and boost the takings,
Orson announced to us that we could have two nights off, as
he was going to do a one-man show. The first half he did
readings – favourite poems and extracts from books – and
for the second half he had arranged for BBC television
to come over and film him answering questions from the
audience. He was great. Orson announced that the television programme was to be part of a series called *Orson
Welles Meets* ... on this occasion it was to be the Irish, and
future programmes would be the Germans, the French, the
Dutch etc. It was a sell-out. The stage manager went around
the audience with a microphone to catch everybody's voice
and the evening was a huge success. Recently I heard a post-
script to the story. Nobody, including myself, noticed that
there were no television cameras and the microphone was

not plugged in. The programme did not exist. They never came over from the BBC. They had those brilliantly bright lights, as they do for television, which is why nobody suspected. The whole thing was a confidence trick. Orson got fed up with the feeling that people weren't coming!

In my forty-five years as an actress, only three inspirational directors spring to my mind: You, Peter, Jonathan Miller who directed me in my only other Shakespeare performance – Goneril in *King Lear* – and Orson. Orson gave you the feeling that you were creating a performance together, his language was colourful, and despite what I have told you about his temper, as a director of actors he was patient, encouraging when you did something he liked, not destructive. He was deep in his soul an actor himself, and he had a tremendous sense of what provokes acting in people – a love of it and a total excitement when it was happening, rather than just having theories about it. He was so physically and vocally huge it was sometimes a bit daunting, but luckily I have a strong voice too. I think he enjoyed that. Orson never lost touch with the truth. I found him very moving and still remember the heartbreak of the scene when the newly crowned Hal says to Falstaff, 'I know thee not, old man' – in this huge frame, in this face, was a crumbling spirit. There was something in Falstaff that touched him very deeply.

He was seventy when he died. He became so overweight that for the last four years of his life he couldn't move his own limbs – he used to have a truck to move him around. We 'shall not look upon his like again'.

Scandals

PETER

For some years I had my own company, the Peter Frye

group, which travelled all over Israel. We decided to give a performance in Tel Aviv in the Cameri Theatre in Mograby Circle on a Friday night. In my naivety I had forgotten that the religious were constantly agitating not to allow any performances on Friday evenings after the start of the Sabbath. There was a status quo agreement between the various religious parties and the municipal government of Tel Aviv that certain things were permitted and certain things were not permitted. Restaurants were permitted to open and some restaurants were turned into private night-clubs and in that way the bloody stupid hypocritical laws were overcome. They put on striptease and shit like that – *that* was allowed – but a performance in the theatre was *not* allowed.

We set up a little box office – a table with a money box – across the road from the theatre, outside the Café Noga. When I arrived, to my amazement the whole square, Mograby Square, was flooded with people, most of whom wanted to come to the theatre and see the show. They bought tickets and went into the theatre. Then, at a certain point according to a given signal, a large group of people in the square turned out to be religious fanatics who were there making a demonstration, trying to prevent the performance. The first thing they did was to upset the table which was our box office and to steal the money box. Then they stood at the doors and shouted and screamed, 'You are defiling the Sabbath,' and they tried to prevent people from going in, but the audience had bought their tickets and fought their way inside.

It was a full house. Sitting in that crowded auditorium was Moshe Dayan. Before the performance I stepped up on the stage and made a brief speech: 'I'm sorry that you had some difficulty getting into this theatre. I want to say that what we are doing here tonight is *my* form of worship. If I can help it, so long as I live, I will try to practise my form of worship wherever and whenever I can. Thank you very much for

being here.' There was great applause and the show was
tremendously successful. Nevertheless, later that week I was
arrested. The police came to me with a warrant saying that I
had been unruly and caused a disturbance on the Sabbath.

I went to a lawyer and then started a hilarious foldarol of
going to court and trying to prove that not *I* had caused the
disturbance but the *religious* had caused the disturbance.
'Nevertheless,' said the prosecution, 'if you hadn't put on a
show the religious wouldn't have demonstrated so you are
the cause of the disturbance.' I had a very clever lawyer and
he called the mayor of Tel Aviv Mordechai Namir, as a
witness for our side. On what grounds? On the grounds that
the mayor used to speak at political meetings on Friday
nights and was accompanied by entertainment. There were
posters to that effect, saying 'Tonight the mayor will appear
accompanied by entertainment', either musical concerts or
entertainers, singers, comedians. We assiduously collected
the posters and brought them to court.

I get a telephone call from the mayor, he was a charming,
delightful man: 'Frye, stop it.'

'Stop what, sir?' I replied ingenuously.

'What is this nonsense, you calling me as a witness?'

'Your honour, I have to protect myself and since you and I
are in the same boat I thought it would be very nice if you
would help me out.'

'Frye stop it!' he repeated.

'I didn't start this trial. I was arrested. I was charged, I'm
only defending myself.'

'What can I do?' he asked.

'Stop the trial. You must have some influence in the
courts, on the judges, tell them that the whole thing is a
mistake, and that will stop it.'

It didn't help. We didn't bring him as a witness, we never
expected him to appear. Nevertheless, the mayor must have
called up the judge and the next time I came to court – I
must have had ten court appearances with this thing ... it

dragged on for ever – the judge said to me, '*Adon* Frye (Mr Frye), why don't we stop this nonsense? Plead guilty.'

'To what?' I said.

'To causing a disturbance.'

'But I didn't cause the disturbance.'

'Let's agree that you did cause the disturbance, I'll fine you five pounds and let's forget it.'

So my lawyer said, 'Pay the fine.'

My career in Israel was beset with scandals. I seem to have a great talent for getting myself into trouble with the establishment. I once booed a play at the Cameri when I was the artistic director of another theatre. It was the way I felt at the time, but maybe it wasn't wise. It made all the newspapers.

As you know, in Israel I was involved in left-wing politics and became a candidate in the elections for the Histadrut, which is the all-powerful trade union organisation in Israel. I was elected and I am invited to a gala celebration, the fiftieth anniversary of the founding of the Histadrut. The celebration took place in the auditorium of the Cinerama building which was originally built for the circus – a circular building which seated more than three thousand people. The stage was very, very wide, easily eighty feet. The huge stage is in front of the Cinerama screen and seated on this stage are all the top officials of the Histadrut and of the government. There was Golda Meir, at that time prime minister, and on her right sat the president of the state, Zalman Shazar. They are chatting and as I sit and study this array of the top politicians, the top leaders of Israeli society, I become curious to see whether there is an Arab amongst them. I was certain there would be at least one token Arab out of the population of half a million Arabs who are citizens of Israel, to represent the Arab workers who do a great deal of the work in the country.

There must have been sixty people sitting there in a row – and I do not see a single Arab. When the chairman started the meeting – a gala performance, everything very carefully worked out – I stand up in the geographical centre of the hall and in that same stentorian voice I shout out, 'Point of order! Where on the platform is the Arab delegate to sit with us on the occasion of this great celebration of fifty years of Labour in Israel?' Silence. The chairman is stopped cold in his tracks, looks around for help but nobody is helping him. I see Golda Meir staring out to see who has raised this question. I repeat, 'Point of order, Mr Chairman. I would like an answer. Where is the Arab delegate to represent the hundreds of thousands of Arab workers who have lived and worked in Israel since the establishment of the state? Are they not members of the Histadrut?' No reply, the chairman is baffled. He was a delightful man and it was very cruel to do this to him.

I see the president of the state turn to Golda – he must have said, 'Who is this *schmuck* that is interfering and spoiling this wonderful celebration?' Golda must have replied, 'That *schmuck* is the well-known *schmuck* Peter Frye who is always making scandals,' or words to that effect. I don't know what she said. There's a hubbub of whispering in the audience, everybody is looking at me. I'm still standing there waiting for a reply, the centre of attention of this whole goddamn celebration, when out of the corner of both eyes simultaneously I saw some goons advancing towards me. Big fellows. Chuckers out. Bouncers. It seemed to me, as far as I could discern from the corners of both eyes, that they were heading towards me, so I thought to myself, 'Wouldn't this be a good time to sit down and to hell with the answer, I've had my answer.' So I sat down. The big men came to the area where I sat, looked around – they didn't see anybody. I had sat down and I was lost in the anonymity of the crowd. So they moved back to their positions and the steamroller got started again and rolled on and they completed the celebration of the fiftieth anniversary without further interference.

Some time shortly after this, I directed at Habimah Elie Wiesel's play *The Jews of Silence*. On the opening night Golda Meir was present. After the performance she came backstage and the whole company of actors – there were at least twenty-four actors in that large cast – trooped by to shake her hand and to receive her plaudits. I very diffidently stood at the tail end of the queue and after everybody had gone I stepped up to her, she gave me her hand but turned her head away from me and didn't say a word. I'm sure it was because she remembered me from that Histadrut meeting.

THELMA

There is another PS to this story. In 1978, when I had married you and moved to Israel, I was chosen to go to South Africa to play the part of Golda Meir in a play about her life. Before leaving I was taken to her house in the Ramat Aviv district of Tel Aviv, very near to our apartment.

I told her that not only was I Thelma Ruby the actress, but I was also Mrs Peter Frye. As she said goodbye to me at the end of the visit I said, 'Peter would very much like to see you and talk to you. He feels he has all sorts of things that he'd like to discuss with you.' By this time she was eighty and retired from all public activity. She had been gracious and most friendly during the meeting, and at this she smiled and said, 'Certainly my dear. When you come back from South Africa you must both come over and visit me.' Unfortunately, when we came back three months later, she was already in hospital and soon after she died. But I have a feeling that you were on the edge of a *rapprochement* with Golda Meir.

Jay

THELMA

After *Chimes at Midnight* I came back from Dublin to

London. March 1960. I went for an interview for a film called *Invasion Quartet*, starring Spike Milligan. Talking to the director, who was charming, softly spoken and kind, I thought, 'What a lovely man!' To my delight he cast me in the film. His name was Jay Lewis and he had directed/ produced several successful films, including *Morning Departure* and *The Baby and the Battleship*. The more I worked, the more I found myself being very, very attracted to this man and I was thrilled to bits if he invited me to watch the rushes with him or chatted with me on the set. It was just a business-like, professional friendship though I'd hoped for more.

My last day on the film, I said goodbye to him and thought that was probably the last I'd ever see of him, which made me sad, but that's the way life goes. Then I was invited to an end-of-shooting party, a 'wrap' party as it is called, when you wrap up the production. I had another date that night which I broke and went all the way to Elstree. That's where I first *really* talked to Jay as a person instead of in a director/actor relationship. To my delight he invited me out. He was relieved that the film was over.

It had been made under tremendous difficulties. They had seriously underestimated the budget. In order to speed things up the producer took it into his head that they should use two stages and Jay would be directing a scene in one, and the producer would be directing another scene in the other. (Where have you heard that story before? Thorold Dickinson, rest in peace!) Jay had to go through hell in order to complete that film.

On our first date a few days later Jay took me to a beautiful restaurant in the country, overlooking an old water-mill wheel. That started my romance with Jay that went on for nine wonderful years. I had always dreamed that the man I fell in love with would be Jewish. On that first night, with my fingers crossed, I said, 'Lewis is a Jewish name. Are you Jewish?' 'Alas no,' he said. 'There are Welsh

Lewis's and there are Jewish Lewis's and I'm a Welsh Lewis. My grandfather was called Lewis Lewis.'

Jay came from Birmingham. He was born into a middle-class family. His father, a dealer in antique furniture, had died long before I knew him. Jay was sent to Eastbourne College and had a thoroughly British upbringing. He had all the best qualities of that British upbringing, courtesy and gentleness, kindness. Beautiful manners. His family had nothing to do with films or theatre at all, but he was always mad about films and always wanted to be a film director.

He was married, but separated from his wife. Although we were together, it wasn't the same as being married and in my heart of hearts I would have loved to marry Jay. I loved him very, very much indeed. He would say, 'We've got so much. What more would we have with a piece of paper and a ring. We live together, we go out together, you're known as Mrs Lewis. We are completely happy together. We're not missing anything by not being married.' I never said anything, but in my heart I thought, 'Oh I would love that piece of paper, that ring. I would love it to be official.' Oh Peter, you can't know what it meant to me when I was literally and legally married to you. No more of the embarrassment of not being married to Jay, even though we were living together. At last, a hundred per cent married and Kosher. I knew that it never would happen with Jay. One of the worst aspects of the situation was that I had to hide him from my parents. I hated it when they came down to stay with me from Leeds and I had to hide all of Jay's belongings while he got out of here and went back to his own flat. I eventually told Mom about Jay, but, although I lived with him for nine years, Dad never knew.

I won the part of Fraulein Schneider in the Kander and Ebb musical *Cabaret* in 1968. I auditioned for Hal Prince before it opened and later discovered that it was a toss-up between me and Lila Kedrova for the part. She was a much more famous actress and everybody remembered her from her superb performance in *Zorba the Greek*, so she was chosen. She was unhappy in the part and three months later I was asked to take over from her.

Fraulein Schneider is a wonderful part, the part I had been longing for and dreaming of all my life. It is touchingly dramatic, funny, singing, dancing. Four terrific songs and a big dance routine. To cap my rapture in playing this part, I was co-starring with Judi Dench. She is a superb actress and a marvellous partner on the stage. In one scene I tell of my life and my decision to break the engagement, followed by a haunting song, 'What would you do?' Judi's sympathy, warmth, tears, utter stillness while facing upstage and looking at me were an inspiration. The art of listening is the mark of a great performer. Offstage her warmth, her sweetness, her gaiety, her fun, her generosity were quite overwhelming.

One day at the Palace I walked in and saw a priest sitting on the stairs outside my dressing-room chatting to a group of chorus girls. He was the theatre chaplain, John Hester. He knocked on my door and asked if he could come in for a chat. I said I would be delighted if he didn't object to the fact that I was Jewish. After that he came frequently and I looked forward to his visits, a man of sympathy, understanding, humour, a love of the theatre and a love of people. It was soon to be a very important and valuable friendship.

One evening, not long after the show closed, Jay collapsed. He lost consciousness, but came round quite quickly and we took him to St George's Hospital. They couldn't find out what was wrong with him but they suspected heart trouble and he went through a careful six-week recovery period. A few weeks later it happened again, this time Jay's son Jeremy was having dinner with us. This time he did not regain consciousness until he was in the hospital.

They kept him in hospital for quite a while and did exhaustive tests. They were baffled – no sign of anything on the ECG. After some neurological tests, they thought they had the answer. 'You have maturity onset epilepsy,' they said. They gave him pills to keep it under control. I said to Jay, 'Now we know the cause, so if you should become unconscious again at least you won't wake up in hospital. You'll be here in your own bed.'

We went to our little house in Ibiza and had a happy holiday. Jay bought the boat he had wanted all his life. When we came back he was preparing to direct a film with John Cleese. On Monday, 2nd June we went on Wimbledon Common with our much-loved dogs, Candy and Gigi, and Jay walked well and came with me to Safeways. We bought melon, French yoghourt, fish, and he chose the bacon. I cooked it for him for Wednesday lunch and he said, 'Just as I like it – it's crispy because it's cut so thin.' It had been a cause of laughter between us through the years – because of my Kosher upbringing I would not cook bacon for him in the early days and he used to wail that he was suffering from 'bacon starvation'.

On the Tuesday he drove to the Common by himself to take the dogs for a walk. He had not been well but he started to look better and hope grew inside me that he would be well enough to do the films that were being planned. Friends were due to come for dinner on the Thursday, so on Wednesday morning 4th June 1969 – Derby Day – I was out shopping when Jay took a call from the Nottingham Play-house offering me a job in a new musical. After our bacon lunch, as we sat down to coffee, he went to get his heart pills because he had a pain. The pain grew worse and he asked me to take the cover off the bed so he could lie down. I sat on the bed stroking his hand and his forehead because the pain was so acute. He said, 'What'll happen if I get one of these attacks while I'm directing?' I reassured him, 'We'll get some strong pain-killers and you'll have to say you've got a bad headache and need to lie down for an hour.' From Mona I got a very strong pain-relieving tablet and gave it to him and by 3.30 the pain had eased off enough for him to come into the sitting-room to watch the Derby. Mona was with us.

We all went through the list of horses running in the Derby and phoned through our bets to a bookie. Jay chose two horses – Agriculture because the jockey was called Lewis and the trainer was Featherstonhaugh, the name of a boy he had known at school and which we had used in a script because it made us laugh, and Diendonne because the commentator said it didn't have a ghost of a chance and that 'it's never won a race'! During the race I sat holding his hand until at one point I slid onto the floor with excitement. Nearing the finish the commentator was heard to say, 'The back-marker is Diendonne...' Jay said it wasn't fair, there should be a special prize for coming in last. None of us won.

I made tea, Jay smoked a cigarette and said the pain had eased. I poured a second cup for him and I had just bitten into a biscuit when it happened. Once again Jay had collapsed. I called the doctor who lived next door and, while waiting for him, tried with trembling hands to re-assemble the oxygen tank which had saved him before and which the chemist had sent back refilled but not assembled. Michael arrived, examined Jay and said, 'I can't hear his heart.' I cried, 'Maybe he can be resuscitated, what about a pace-maker...' It was too late, but I wouldn't accept it. Michael called an ambulance and we took him to St George's. They rushed out to try to resuscitate him in the ambulance – gently they told me that he was gone.

He had died after having watched the Derby, having his tea, in his own chair in his own room, relaxed and happy, expecting to direct two more films, having had a happy holiday in Ibiza aged fifty-seven.

Now that I am so wonderfully, completely happy with you and you have given me more than Jay – that ring I longed for, more admiration and appreciation, more constant openly expressed love – I sometimes forget how very happy I was with Jay. He was cremated on a fine sunny day. The service was conducted beautifully by my friend John Hester. Friends were there, flowers were there, and Jeremy, Jay's elder son, looked after me and Jay's mother Mildred. I did not know until later but Jay's younger son, Kit, sat at the back with Jay's real wife, also called Mildred. She had travelled up from her home in the Cotswolds and, with great sensitivity, had slipped in and slipped out quietly at the end. I never met her.

Between the death of Jay and the meeting with you was the worst period of my entire life. My life stopped. Happiness stopped. The desire to carry on stopped. I wanted only to join Jay in the grave because there didn't seem any point in going on living – life without him was too bleak and too difficult. In my desperation, I wanted to believe that Jay was continuing somewhere, and that there was an after-life. I even went to the Spiritualists Association in Belgrave Square to try and see if I could get a message. A lady pointed to me and said, 'There's a message for you!' I thought, 'The test is that this must be a message that says something that only Jay and I would understand. It was, "You'll move to another town and travel abroad within the next year."' I realised that there wasn't much comfort in following that path.

I am Jewish, Jay was not, and the Christian religion, it seemed to me, had a clearer vision of an after-life. I felt that I'd meet him in an after-life if I veered over – I don't say that I would ever have converted – but if I veered over to Christianity. Still splashing around searching for comfort, I went to see John Hester and I told him some of my feelings. It's a measure of his outstanding qualities as a priest and as a human being that he said to me, 'You're going through this period of grief and mourning. You don't believe me now but you will come through it and what is more, you will be enriched by it. You will be the stronger for it. As for your interest in Christianity, the best thing you could do for Jay is to find out more about your Jewish roots, because that's where you come from, that's where your heart is and that's where you belong. Before you leave that, try and find out more about what you're leaving behind rather than what you're going to.' John remains to this day a valued friend. He was always a friend of Israel and he leads a pilgrimage there every year. John is now the precentor at Chichester Cathedral. Christianity is a proselytising religion, so it showed enormous understanding, sympathy and kindness for him to talk to me as he did.

Films

PETER
I had worked on my first film in 1953. It took me seven years and a lot of money invested in buying scripts and in researching scripts, until I made my second film *I Like Mike* and four years more until I got to make *The Hero's Wife* and that was the last film that I made. The doctor said that, after I had a heart attack, another film would kill me. I figured it was wiser not to try any more because it was too heartbreaking, in every sense of the word.

To sum up this period of my film career which wasn't so brief – chronologically speaking from 1953 to 1964 – I made only three films with so many difficulties and problems. You had been going through exactly the same thing with Jay, and almost in the same period. Are the experiences that I am recounting similar to the agonies that Jay went through?

THELMA
It delights me that there are many parallels between you and Jay, as people and in your careers. But the great difference in your careers was that Jay was *totally* a film man, unlike you. He didn't round his life off with the university, the theatre, the lectures. His whole life was film and it was very distressing to me that in the nine years I lived with him he

made so few films. In his whole lifetime he directed only five
major films.

PETER
That's two more than I did.

THELMA
When my romance started with you I thought you were well-
heeled ... you took me to good restaurants and stayed in
good hotels. When I first met Jay he was directing a film, he
gave me a job, he was friendly with top stars so I assumed he
was a busy, well-paid, successful director. I guess I was wrong
both times.

PETER
Give me some of the names of the people he was involved
with.

THELMA
Richard Attenborough and John Mills. I've kept some of
their letters to Jay. Bryan Forbes' letters always started, 'My
dearest chum'. In one letter he wrote: 'Whether you know it
or not you really started me on the right path, because it was
with *The Baby and the Battleship* that I first became aware of
taste, that elusive quality which can't be bought over the
counter. You have it, mate – and you're one of the few. Let's
work together again one of these days – we weren't a bad
team all things considered were we?' Richard Attenborough,
replying to congratulations: '...Your approval means a lot
to both Bryan and me. Here's to the next time *together* – I'd
adore it.' John Mills: '...I would so much like to find myself
working with you on another film – there has been far too
long a gap as far as I am concerned.' Doesn't sound as if they
are written to a man who made only five major films in a
lifetime, does it?
    In the early days with Jay I knew absolutely nothing about

what was involved in getting a film off the ground. But I
soon learned of the years of dedication, energy, hard work,
concentration and talent that were necessary to get one film
in front of the cameras. Years – not only with no money
coming in, but investing all the money you possessed on
buying 'properties' and developing them. Despite Jay's
earlier successes he hardly ever had the price of a cup of
coffee during the years we were together. Everything he had
went towards trying to get the next film made.

One of Jay's sparkling scripts was called *Hearts and
Flowers*. It is about a couple who get married – they have
both murdered six previous husbands or wives and now are
trying to murder each other. Similar stories were made later,
Jay's was the first and it was witty and elegant. Excitement
was great when Rex Harrison agreed to do it, if the lady was
a comparable star. Sophia Loren said yes, then dropped out.
Shirley MacLaine was mad about it – I still have the cables
she sent to Jay – but she dropped out ... and the whole
project collapsed.

Puncher's Private Navy was a sequel to the successful *The
Baby and the Battleship*. It was about Puncher, an able
seaman, the lowest rank of sailor, who comes into a fortune.
Everybody expects him to leave the navy but he loves the
navy and doesn't want to leave. They sail past a great
battleship that's on its way to be broken up and Puncher
says, 'I'll buy it!' He buys up old vessels until he has his own
private navy.

Everybody was mad about the script of *Puncher's Private
Navy* and they promised Jay the finance. He needed to shoot
a week of naval exercises off the coast of Plymouth and if he
missed it he would have to wait another year to catch a
similar exercise. The backers said, 'Go ahead and shoot',
which Jay did. Then the finance collapsed and Jay had to
pay for the whole of this expensive week of shooting from
his own pocket. He had to get a loan which took him
years to repay. In my cupboard I still have huge reels of

35mm film – a week's shooting of naval exercises off the coast of Plymouth.

Following the success of a short, silent film called *A Home of Your Own*, he wrote a full-length script without dialogue, *Shorty and Goliath*, which was brilliant. Once again, the finance seemed secure and Michael Crawford was signed to play the lead and shooting was ready to begin. Michael Crawford was offered a part in the Hollywood film with Barbra Streisand, *Hello Dolly* and disappeared – again the whole thing collapsed. Each one of these represents years of work. And Jay had the added disappointment and hurt that, after he had conceived, written and directed *A Home of Your Own* and it had been such a success, the producers decided to make another short silent film as a follow-up, *San Ferry Ann*, and they did not ask Jay to do it.

My theory is that it was the frustrations and disappointments of film-making that killed him so young. You talk often of the cruelty of wasted potential and here is a clear example. A man of skill, of imagination, of humour, of creativity spending most of his life suffering the humiliation of his unfulfilled dreams.

PETER
Listening to you talk about Jay I am turning the pages of my own experiences in the world of film and I am checking and I am saying, 'Yes, Jay and I made the same stupid mistakes. We invested our own money, we weren't able to get anybody to commit himself, we expected people to fulfil their promises.' My story is so like Jay's. The money that I made from *I Like Mike* I invested in scripts on which I lost the option, and in writing scripts and in secretarial expenses and travelling expenses. Why, in the face of all this, do I walk around with the feeling that I have missed the greatest opportunity in my life?

On *I Like Mike* I really was the boss of that film and I say without any modesty whatsoever, I made that film in every sense of the word. It was a tremendous success. It opened a pathway for others to follow in my wake. Why didn't *I* follow in my wake? There is one thing left to say, and this is difficult to express. The profound disappointment which one feels in one's life when one has had a taste of film work and then for whatever reasons – in Jay's case, in my case, in the case of thousands of others who have tried in the same way that we did and don't make it – the sense of disappointment that you are not working in film which is the combination of all the arts, is devastating. I don't want to say it is the greatest of all the arts because what does it matter what is great and what is greater and what is greatest. What matters is that film is a great art. In my case I had started acting when I was very young. I had the soul of an actor and the ability to make that actor's soul flourish. I loved the human voice and what it could do. I had the drawing experience which I picked up from my wonderful friend Mr Jackalin, the Swedish drawing master, and that highly developed visual sense is terribly important in film making. As I told you, from the time I was a little boy, I had wanted to work in films. I *loved* films and all my life, whenever I could, I went to the films. As a child I went to the cinema at least once a week and as I grew up and started to earn money, which I did at a very early age, I would go to the cinema more often – twice a week. I knew everything that was going on and, to this day, as you can well attest, when we watch old movies – silent or talkies – I know the names of all the actors.

To me the greatest ambition that anyone could have was the dream to be a film director. It seemed to me that there was nothing that could possibly match the excitement of putting something together which would be recorded on film. I thought I was the ideal person to become a film director. I thought, I have all the training – this will sound immodest – I have all the talent and that's what I am going to be. As you know I almost got to Hollywood but McCarthy changed my entire life because I believe I was destined to be a film director. Sometimes I wonder whether I would have been tough enough to handle myself in Hollywood because I was pretty naive and even stupid about contracts. But I might have learned, and I would have had an agent and I would have rolled with it and learned the game, so there's no saying now what might have happened. That was my dream and it was shattered.

Oh, to work in this great art and to feel the enormous satisfaction of a day's work well done! You've shot a difficult scene, you've faced problems and worked them out – shot it once or twice or three times or four times, and by God the fifth time it works. Everybody knows that it works. The tremendous satisfaction that everyone feels. The actors and the crew and the director and the producer, if he's hanging around, that you have finally made that good take and you know if you continue making them at this pace, by the end of a certain number of days, whenever the film was scheduled for, forty days or fifty days or sixty days, that you are going to assemble all these good takes and you're going to have a film.

Yes, a great, great art, a compendium of all human abilities and all human possibilities. Anything that you can dream about you can make a film about, and that's a lot. Thus in a similar magnitude is the disappointment you feel when you cannot continue working in it.

The Silence of Elie Wiesel

PETER
Elie Wiesel wrote a play which more or less followed the structure of his book called *The Jews of Silence*. I had read that book and thought it a good book. *The Jews of Silence* was not a novel, it was a documentary about the conditions of Jewry in the Soviet Union. About Jews not being allowed to

practise their religion. As a former Communist this was something that I didn't really want to believe. I would have preferred to hear that in the Soviet Union they were making every effort to root anti-semitism out of the Russian psyche. It's been there for a long time.

After I read that book I agreed with Elie Wiesel that there was a great deal to tell about the condition of the Jew in Soviet society. In 1970 the Habimah National Theatre of Israel bought the rights to the play and asked Yosef Millo to direct. He went to work on it – the designs had been prepared and some of the scenery had already been built – but for some reason it was decided that he would not continue with the direction of the play.

I get a call from my friend Shimon Finkel, who was at that time artistic director of Habimah, who asked me to take over the direction. I hadn't read the play but Finkel said, 'You've got to decide tonight. I have faith in you. I know that you can do this.' 'OK, Shimon,' I said, 'if you believe that I can do it then I take your word for it and I will try to do it. I'll see you at rehearsals on Monday.' It was not a simple process for me to direct this play, particularly as, when I read it, I discovered that it had an unfortunate way of going off into many unnecessary directions and was very hard to pull together so that it made sense as a play.

I thought I could do it. I went to work with one of the actors in the company – a wonderful human being and a quite marvellous actor, Avraham Halfi. He helped me cut the play into small pieces and reassemble it like a jigsaw puzzle. The material was there, the material from the book was excellent, and with Halfi's help suddenly things fell into place and scenes became scenes. They had a beginning, they had a development, they had an end. At which point I discovered that the scenery which had been designed and built was totally unsuitable to my conception of how the play should be staged. I had the terrible task of going to the management and saying, 'I am not looking for additional problems in my life but that scenery is totally unsuitable for me.' When they asked me what I wanted to do, I replied, 'I want to throw it out!' To their credit they said, 'All right, we throw it out.'

The question was, what was I going to put in its place? The work that I should have done months ago before I undertook to direct the play, I was doing now when I was in the midst of directing it and there, looming ahead of me, was the deadline of an opening night. I came up with something which was not very expensive. It called for technical expertise and for some new lighting equipment. I asked for and got a new backcloth onto which I was going to project pages from the prayers of the Yom Kippur service, because one of the central scenes of the play is where the chief rabbi of Moscow who, all these years, has remained quiet and did not protest to the authorities, finally breaks out and says what he thinks about the way the Communist Party deals with Jews in the Soviet Union. In front of these projections I had boat trucks which rolled onto and off the stage. On these boat trucks were different constructions for different scenes. By moving these boat trucks skilfully from one side to the other according to necessity, I created a certain amount of variety. It worked extremely well. It didn't cost anything – the cost of the projections is negligible. We were home and dry.

Towards the last days of rehearsal I came to the conclusion that the play was too long and that it required cuts. Here I was with a cast very well rehearsed and everything more or less in place but suddenly you need cuts. That is always a very difficult situation. Actors don't like to have their lines cut, particularly two or three days before the dress rehearsal or before the opening. I knew it would be difficult. I went through the script with my dear friend Halfi and together we found very clever cuts, clever blending of lines from one situation into another which improved the play immeasurably because suddenly the play became taut, the scenes were more crystallised, sharper, quicker. I came to rehearsal and said to the actors, 'Today we're going to spend a couple of hours cutting the play.'

I started to read out the cuts. It went along swimmingly in twenty-three of the twenty-four speaking parts until I came to an actor whose name is anathema, but who is also known as Yisrael Becker. (I found out later that he thought that he should have been asked to direct the play.) I come to Becker and tell him what I want to cut. He let go in an explosion of vituperation such as I have rarely heard in my life and added, 'I do not accept any of your suggestions for cuts. My part remains as it is. *Schluss!*' Which means, closed. The End.

You know me, my temper is on a very short fuse. You have heard me explode, you have seen me explode and you have always suggested to me that it might have been better if I had not exploded. Most of the time I think you were right. However, this time I said to him, as quietly as I could, and in as controlled a fashion as I was able to muster, 'Despite what you say, you are wrong. I don't want to linger on the point now. I will talk to you later and I will show you that your part will be improved by the cuts that I am suggesting. Now may we please go on.' But Becker wasn't quite through with me. He said, 'Before I'm through with you, you'll have a heart attack. That's what I'm waiting for.'

No one had ever said anything remotely like it to me in my entire life. I had dealt with quite a number of villains up to this point but this was the most villainous yet. Again, fortunately, I reacted calmly. After a long, long pause I said, 'Becker, only God can forgive you for what you said just now. I am going to continue the rehearsal.' That finally shut him up. The rest of the cast sat there aghast. Becker did not take the cuts, he never took the cuts.

Thelma darling, you had just arrived in Israel as we approached the dress rehearsal. I discussed with you my feeling that the ending of the play was a little flat and it needed something to lift the spirit. I said, 'In the book, Elie

Wiesel describes a huge demonstration that took place outside the great synagogue of Moscow, where there is a big public square, on the holiday Simchat Torah, the Joy of the Torah. Despite all the repression and anti-semitism, crowds of Jews had danced with the Torah in the streets of that great square. If we could somehow find a way of putting this symbolically on the stage it would give the play the kind of lift that I feel it needs.'

In the play there is a boy whose parents are members of the Communist Party and therefore atheist – the father insists that the boy will not be made barmitzvah. But the boy's grandfather is the chief rabbi and he says, 'The boy *will* be barmitzvah.' The last scene is where the rabbi is rehearsing the child in the portion of the law that he has to read in the synagogue on the day of his barmitzvah. The play ends with the fact that the boy *will* be barmitzvah, despite the whole goddamn Soviet revolution. That's the end of the play. Not very original, not a new idea but one that has worked very well since the destruction of the Temple.

You and I, Thelma, sat down and contrived an ending which didn't call for any great changes, it just called for a little epilogue to the play in which the rabbi and the boy come outside and in the street around them there takes place the stage representation of that famous demonstration in the streets of Moscow when Jews with the Torah came out and danced. The whole play ended in a blaze of light, red lights and gold lights, yellow lights and green lights came down in the upstage area. The foreground became black. The rabbi and the child were silhouetted against that golden sky. They step down from the platform which was the rabbi's home into the scene of celebration and the curtain came down on the dancing. We rehearsed this and the actors were very excited and everybody participated.

Now I have to go backwards again. All through the period of rehearsal where I was re-writing and re-shaping the play and changing the scenery, the manager of Habimah, Gaby

Zifrony, had been talking on the long-distance telephone to Elie Wiesel, saying, 'We'd like you to come to see what is happening. There have been changes made in the play and we want you to come to approve of them.' Five thousand dollars in long-distance phone calls to Elie Wiesel who always said, 'No ... no, I can't come ... no, I'm not coming ... No.' But towards the end of rehearsals he said, 'I will send someone with my power of attorney to look at it and he will either give you the OK or he won't.' The man he chose to send was a man by the name of Dr Moshe Lazar. He watches the first preview with an audience and he watches their reaction. The audience jumped to its feet when that ending came, they rushed down to the front of the stage, the way they sometimes do at a concert or in the opera, and tried to shake the hands of the actors. Great excitement in the theatre because this ending really reached them. It was the right ending.

Then there was a meeting with Lazar. He said, 'That ending was not in the script so we can't have it.' Here I stand guilty of having lost my temper. I cocked up my case simply because I lost my temper. I should have said, 'Phone Elie Wiesel or telegraph him or write to him or whatever you like. Tell him that we have put an ending on the play which came out of his book *The Jews of Silence*. Tell him the reaction of the audience. Tell him I need that ending in order to deliver to Habimah what I have promised to deliver, which is a potent production of his play.' Unfortunately I didn't do that.

When the play opened to the critics and to the audience and to Golda Meir that scene did not end the play and it was sorely missing. The play started to run. It was very well accepted. Everyone had great respect for any writings of Elie Wiesel. My production was praised. Of course they didn't know that I had remoulded the entire play and that I'd made a play out of what had been a very messy collection of bits and pieces of scenes, so Elie Wiesel got all the credit. He didn't come to the opening night, although he was invited. He didn't come to any later performances.

One day, some two weeks after the opening, when it was running well and drawing its audiences, Gaby Zifrony called me and said, 'We have something of a problem. Elie Wiesel flew into Israel yesterday. He bought a ticket and came to see the play incognito. Didn't speak to a soul in the theatre. Then he went straight to Jerusalem to Israel Television and gave a scathing review of what he had seen and denied all connection with it. He said he hadn't been here during rehearsals, he hadn't approved of the changes in the script and it had nothing to do with him.' Israel Television had phoned Gaby and said to him, 'We think, in all fairness, there should be a reply to this.' Gaby said, 'We have to go to Israel Television and we have to reply.'

We went to Jerusalem at once and saw the video tape of what Elie Wiesel had said. He'd flown out of the country right after giving the interview. It wasn't very long but it was scathing and it was denunciatory. Full of his Wailing Wall repertoire. I said, 'Can I have a couple of hours to think over what I've seen here and to frame my reply?' 'You can't have a couple of hours but you can have one hour,' they replied. Gaby and I worked out a satisfactory reply, pointing out that we had invited him over and over again but he didn't come and that his power of attorney had approved the production. When we went on the air, I said my piece and Gaby defended everything I had done. Wiesel's sneaking into the theatre and then going on television with a vicious diatribe was unconscionable but we had the last word.

Habimah was invited to send my production of *The Jews of Silence* in the Hebrew language to Brussels as the highlight of a conference in support of Soviet Jewry. They went without me – that's typical for Habimah. That was the second time they shipped a production of mine abroad without sending me. I didn't even know about it or I might have bought my own ticket and gone along. But they sent the whole company of twenty-four actors, the scenery and the lighting effects that I'd designed, everything to Brussels. They performed in a vast hall with thousands of people in the audience.

At the end of the performance on the first night there was loud applause and, to everybody's astonishment, who should appear on the stage, who should come out to take a bow, but Elie Wiesel. There was great excitement in the audience – cheering, applauding, standing. The Wailing Wall had arrived. He kissed the actors and the actors kissed him. They all embraced each other. He was at the centre of attention that night and he was the hero of the whole production!

Book VII

Love Story

THELMA
Now we have reached the moment in our lives when our paths met. Let's recall how our lives intertwined – it will be fun to see who remembers what.

PETER
May 1959. I worked with your brother Geoffrey in 1958 on a radio programme and I liked him immediately – a very charming man with a penchant for making puns all the time – if you like Geoffrey you get used to the puns. One day in 1959 a telephone call comes from Geoffrey, 'My sister is here in Israel. She is an actress. This is her first time in Israel and she knows nothing about the Israeli theatres. Would you be good enough to take her around and show her what goes on in our theatres?' I said that I'd be delighted. You arrived at the flat that I shared with Batia and our little six-year-old daughter, and you came and had tea with us and both Batia and I were very taken with you. We thought you were charming, we thought you were very vivacious, we thought you had a wonderful sense of humour. You had a sexy figure. You were young and energetic and enthusiastic and Batia knew who you were from having studied theatre magazines.

   That same evening I said, 'I'll take you out on a theatre crawl.' I took you to the Cameri, Habimah, the Ohel. To see Batia acting, and to see a piece of a play that I had directed called *Cactus Flower*. Then you left to go back to England and we exchanged addresses and telephone numbers. I said, 'When I come to London may I get in touch with you?' You said, 'I'd be delighted to have you get in touch with me.'

That was the beginning of a very special relationship that developed between us for the next eleven years.

THELMA
Whenever you came to London you would phone me up and whenever I went to Israel I would phone you up. This wasn't more than five or six times at the most over the period of eleven years. It was no close friendship – we didn't write to each other . . . just one of these theatrical colleagueal friendships. And yet . . . there is more here than we knew at the time. Was it already written that eleven years after we first met we would marry and embark on the dangerous seas which carry a man and a woman to the Paradise Isles, to the Discovery of Love? Were we – to coin a cliché – destined for each other? Did we both, at our first meeting, make unconscious decisions that would guide us to each other?

PETER
We have had twenty marvellous years of marriage and we have learned a great deal one from the other. The more we love, the deeper grows our love for each other. Our learned forefathers wrote that the Creator of the universe made man and woman in one body, sharing one soul. Then he separated them and sent them from the Garden of Eden to fulfil their tasks on earth – two separate bodies still sharing one soul. Sometimes they find each other and the soul is reunited. That's why we are together writing our joint autobiographies – we've grown back into one soul and cannot bear to be separated again.

1966–67 I went on a sabbatical to Canada, stopping off first at Ethiopia to try to set up a co-production to film the story of Solomon and Sheba. Very simply, the idea was that we would film King Solomon with his entourage coming down from Jerusalem to the Dead Sea and the Queen of Sheba coming down from the Ethiopian plateau to the port on the Red Sea, and then her journey up the Red Sea to meet King Solomon at the place where, according to legend, they met and had congress.

The Ethiopian producer said, 'What we have to do is get the Emperor Haile Selassie to OK this deal and it will get done. In Ethiopia the Emperor has to be in on everything.' The Israel Ambassador, Chaim Ben-David, took it upon himself to arrange the meeting. That took three days – we were in, we were out, we were on, we were not on, we were up, we were down! Suddenly they demand we have to take a photographer – the photographer can come, he can't come, he will be there, he won't be there, when does he have to be there? We haven't had the word yet from the Court as to when the Emperor would receive me.

The meeting with the Emperor finally did take place. We arrived at the Palace. First we went through a set of doors which were guarded by two large Ethiopians in very fanciful uniforms, then through a large ante-room and we come to another set of doors and here the two guards are even larger and their spears are even longer and they've got feathers and they've got ribbons and they've got medals and they've got gold braid – I don't remember how many sets of doors we went through.

Finally we were introduced to the Emperor, a very short man, and I had been told to speak French to him because he preferred French to English. I was nervous. I spluttered and I muttered and I said 'Votre Majesté', no that's not enough, he's an Emperor, he's not just a King. 'Votre Altesse' – Your Highness, no that isn't enough, what do I call him. 'Vive L'Empereur!' No I can't say that. We struggled through a bit of conversation. The Emperor had read our very complete synopsis and had had it checked by some historical commission and finally he said, 'Yes. I approve. Now you must talk avec mon Ministre de Finance.' Aha, we're getting hot. We're going to the Finance Minister.

When he dismissed us, I remembered they'd said to me, 'When you leave the Emperor you have to bow yourself out'. I started to leave and I was bowing. I suddenly remembered they told me I mustn't turn my back on him. I turned around and bowed to him and then turned around again and remembered for the second time that I mustn't turn my back on him. I turned around again and the fact is I was doing figure eights. If I'd had ice skates on it would have been a wonderful trick the way I let myself out of the Emperor's august presence – I kept doing pirouettes and figure eights. I finally got out!

We visited the Finance Minister but I was simply too naive and too inexperienced to understand that in a country like Ethiopia you can never get a deal like this off the ground until you grease some palms and so nothing came of the whole project.

Autumn 1967. When I came back from my sabbatical at the end of the Six Day War, Batia was not at home in Israel. She had purposely gone off to Paris to study with Gurjieff, her latest guru, three days before my arrival so as to avoid meeting me and it was clear we had come to the end of the road. The financial part of it had been settled a year earlier, before I'd set off on the sabbatical: practically everything I thought I owned had been signed over to her or to her father. Now she made it clear what the situation was by her absence.

There was no flat because in my absence it had been sold. Here I was left with nothing and I had to go look for an apartment which I could rent. Finally I found something and fortunately had enough money to put down for a guarantee. My daughter Jackie had been living with her grandparents and when I established my apartment I asked Jackie to come and live with me. Which she did. I picked up my life and tried to make a new home for my teenager.

1968–70. I came to the decision that I had to divorce Batia, this was no way to live. I discussed it with her parents. They tried to be helpful. Batia's mother, may she rest in peace, was a very sweet woman, a good-natured woman, angelic, and she agreed that it was best that I should apply for a divorce. Batia had left a power of attorney with her father. So it turned out that when I went to the Rabbinical divorce court I had to go with her father, because he was the power of attorney. I explained my case to the dayan, a Rabbinical judge of the highest order. He asked the necessary questions but it was a prima facie case. The woman wasn't there. I now had an apartment, the child was with me. He asked who will be responsible for the care of the child. I said, 'I will.' When he asked me, 'how long?' I said, 'For ever, as long as is necessary.' My father-in-law stood there beside me in front of the young judge with the long black beard staring at us down from his elevated platform. Herman Zvi Lancet had nothing to say in defence of his daughter. He just said yes or no to the questions that were put to him. The divorce rabbi said, 'Yes, all right, fine, you're divorced.' So I divorced my father-in-law! Who vigorously shook my hand on the deal and said, 'I'll find somebody for you. I know exactly what you need. What you need is a woman with a Volvo and a villa and reparations from Germany.'

My ex-father-in-law went to work to find me a proper wife with the necessary – as he saw it – qualifications. With his wide acquaintanceship he was very active in finding me a new wife – this is my ex-father-in-law! He went so far as this – on one occasion he put an ad in the newspapers, listing my desirable qualities. I couldn't get the old man to stop. He insisted that he would solve the problem for me because he cared for me. Through a member of his family, he found a recently widowed lady in a wealthy New York suburb in the United States, and he insisted I go and see her.

July 1970. This lady met me at the airport with an air-conditioned Cadillac and drove me to her house outside New York. As we approached the house she pressed a button and the garage door went up and we drove into an air-conditioned garage. This I had never known in all my life. We got out of the air-conditioned car into the air-conditioned garage and we walked into the air-conditioned house.

It was a nice house in a wealthy suburb with many rooms, several bathrooms, only it was very crowded. In what way crowded? It was *full* of furniture. There were big tables and there were sets of chairs around them and there were coffee tables, chiffonieres, sideboards, sofas. It turned out that her husband had been in the furniture business. Imitations of Italian provincial, imitations of Spanish provincial, imitations of French provincial.

The lady was pleasant, but it was clear from the outset that it wasn't going to work, so after three days we left the air-conditioned house, went into the air-conditioned garage, we got into the Cadillac with the air-conditioning which she immediately turned on. She pressed the button and the garage door opened, we backed out and she took me to New York. I wrote you a letter and said that I was in New York. That I would be going up to Canada to visit my sister and would be going home to Israel via London and could I meet you.

*   *   *

THELMA

February 1970. I had been asked several times to play the part of Golde, Tevye's wife and the mother of five daughters, in *Fiddler on the Roof* in the West End, and always I was busy doing something else. Now I was asked again, but this time it was not in the West End but for a national tour, which means that the show was still running in London but an entire new production was mounted – new cast, sets, costumes, orchestra – to tour the provinces.

My leading man was a Dutch actor, Lex Goudsmit, who had been playing the part of Tevye for six months in London and before that in Holland. A wide man with a huge beard, twinkling eyes and a wonderful singing voice – he was terrific. At first I wasn't enamoured of the part because I knew it was Tevye's show. When I'd seen *Fiddler* the first week it opened with Topol, he had been so magnetic I remembered nobody else. Golde kept running on and off the stage saying, 'So! You've finally come home!' and 'So! You did me a favour and came in?' But as I started to work on it I realised that Golde is a delightful character – the heart of the family, the essence of Jewish wife-and-mother-hood – bossy, strong in adversity, capable, intuitive, fierce in the defence of her family with a loving, Yiddish heart. Tevye, who is somewhat afraid of her, is busy with his dreams, his religion, his visits to the Inn and *she* is the one that keeps the family together. I enjoyed rehearsing – I always enjoy rehearsing – and we had a splendid cast.

To Manchester for a three-month season with two dogs. Four weeks into the Manchester season Candy came into heat. If a dog is going to have puppies, the first litter should happen before her third birthday. This would be Candy's last chance. A lovely tall, slim Lithuanian-Canadian girl called Rita Merkelis was playing Tzeitl, my eldest daughter. Rita loves dogs and she adored Candy. One day I said to her, 'Isn't it a shame Candy won't have puppies.' She asked me why not and I said, 'Don't be silly, how can you have puppies on tour?' She said, 'Why not? Please go ahead and do it – we'll all help you. It'll be great!' So I did.

I found a man who bred wire-haired miniature dachs-hunds in the countryside outside Manchester, and he had a champion available whose name was Guy. I tried to teach Candy to sing 'I'm in love with a wonderful Guy'. The romantic rendezvous was arranged. Appropriately enough, Candy and I were accompanied by the girl playing the matchmaker in *Fiddler* with whom I was friendly, a large, exuberant lady with the voice of a young girl – Miriam Margolyes. Candy and her young husband were put in a field together to play and get to know each other. Miriam and I were standing at the edge of the field with the breeder. We were riveted – we'd never watched a dog-mating before – and after a while the natural coupling occurred and they locked together for about half an hour. Miriam was concerned, 'Is she enjoying it? It's probably the only time she's going to have it. Is she enjoying it?' she urged the breeder. We were assured that she was! When we arrived back at the theatre a friend had sent a huge bouquet of white flowers for Candy as a bridal bouquet.

After another six weeks in Manchester we moved on to Bristol. I lived in a charming cottage in Bath. Bath is only a twenty-minute drive from Bristol. The lady who owned the cottage was a secretary to a headmaster and a maiden lady. I had confessed to having two dogs before I arrived. As soon as I met her I told her about the puppies due in three weeks and promised her faithfully that there would be no mess or damage. At first she gasped and my heart sank but by then Candy had charmed her and when I asked, 'Will it be all right with you?' she replied, 'Could I please be allowed to come over and see them? I've never seen new-born puppies.'

From then on I concentrated on research – what does it mean to give birth to puppies? I knew nothing. I bought a couple of books and studied them thoroughly. 'The birth can take place anywhere in the house. Create warm, dark, cosy places for her to choose from, place boxes piled up with newspaper. When the time comes she will choose her box, tear the paper and make a nest. She will go off her food for a day – or even two – and when the scratching and tearing start you will know the labour is about to begin...' Actors would come into the dressing-room and see me with a long roll of cotton wool, turning it round and counting, 'One, two, three. One, two, three. It says in the book that if a puppy is not breathing when it is born, this is the best way to bring it back to life.'

The two dogs used to come to the theatre with me every

night. What would I do, I thought, if Candy had her puppies here in the dressing-room? In the middle of the show? I phoned Mona who agreed to come to Bath to 'puppy-sit' for me. The breeder had told me that the usual gestation time for miniature wire-haired dachshunds was nine weeks plus one day. 'That would be marvellous,' I said, 'because it will be a Sunday.'

Sunday, the appointed day, Candy still gave no signs of the impending birth. The two dogs used to sleep on my bed, under the quilt, and they were quietly sleeping there while I had my Sunday morning lie-in, breakfast in bed and the Sunday papers. Ten o'clock Rita phoned, 'Any news yet?' 'No, no, not yet. I'll phone you the minute something happens. She hasn't gone off her food, she hasn't started to tear the paper.' 'Phone me the minute it starts. I want to be there.'

I put the phone down and I felt underneath the quilt and it felt damp. I threw back the counterpane and there was a puppy! Candy was looking as astonished as I was. Gigi asleep next to her and there was a puppy, on the bed. I leapt out. I ran into Mona's room. 'Mona, Mona, quick, quick, there's a puppy on the bed. Quick!' I took Gigi away and phoned Rita who came shooting round to be with us. I'd never seen birth before, never having had a child, never even seen an animal being born. Can you picture we three women who had never given birth standing around gasping, 'It's a miracle!'

For a dog of Candy's size four puppies would be a good litter. More than four, I read in my books, we might have to hand-feed them with an eye-dropper, if they survived. I watched as the puppy slid out quite easily in its bag. Candy cut the cord with her teeth, broke the bag, cleaned up all the afterbirth, licked the puppy clean and made it possible for it to have its first drink. I moved the puppy out of the way while she circled around until the next puppy popped out. After the fourth one, everything was quiet.

All on the bed. Candy had ignored the cardboard boxes in

cosy dark corners, the piles of newspaper – she decided to have her family on my bed. The books told me to keep the puppies warm with a hot water bottle wrapped in a towel. We went down to the kitchen, and when I came back a few minutes later with the hot water bottle, Candy was just dropping number five. I settled Candy and the five puppies and the hot water bottle comfortably and went down to make a cup of coffee. Twenty minutes later I went up to check on them and Candy was just dropping number six!

Suddenly, instead of having two dogs on tour I had eight dogs on tour. The day after the puppies were born I received a letter from you – that you would be coming through England and it would be very nice if we could meet. I had always liked you and so I was sorry that I would miss you as I was not in London. The thought of a romance never occurred to me, I was still grieving for Jay ... and I had just given birth to six puppies.

PETER
After writing to you, I went up to Canada and when I arrived, on the second day of my stay there, there was a letter from you. The letter was cheerful, as your letters always are, and you wrote about the puppies and that you didn't know how it would work out, whether you could meet me, because you were in a show that was on the road touring, and what followed then was a very precise and efficient list of all the places you were going to be at within the coming weeks. The theatres, the telephone numbers backstage, the digs or hotels where you were staying with the proper telephone numbers and at the very bottom of the letter you added a paragraph, 'Did you know that my dearest Jay died just over a year ago. It was the first time I have witnessed death, just as yesterday was the first time I have witnessed birth. Yours affectionately, Thelma.'

It was as though the finger of God touched me on the centre of my forehead and I knew precisely what to do.

Without an instant's hesitation I picked up the telephone, looked at the newspaper to see the date, looked at your list of theatres etc., found out where you were on this date at this time, telephoned you long distance, the phone rang and you said,' Helloooo – oh!' the way you always do and I said, 'Thelma, this is Peter Frye. I just had your letter. I will be coming to London immediately and I will call you when I arrive.'

'You are as clear as if you were in London, where are you calling from?' you replied. When I told you where I was, you exclaimed:

'Montreal! How are you going to...'

'Don't worry, I'll be there later tonight or tomorrow.' You were somewhat flabbergasted. I put down the phone. I picked up the letter and made my way upstairs, calling airily to my sister, 'Sylvia I just made a call to England. I have to go.' I told her I was going to London. She said, 'When?' And I said, 'Now.'

Packed, called for a taxi and went to the airport. I shopped around at the airport to see who had a plane going to London. I had to waste a few hours waiting at the airport thinking, daydreaming, speculating about love and marriage ... I managed to get on a plane and arrived in London the following morning. I got on a train to Bath. You were very glad to see me. You were forty-five, I was fifty-six. You didn't look well. You were very thin and you were still deep in grief over Jay, you were not the Thelma I had known before.

To my dismay you told me that the show you were in was *Fiddler on the Roof.* You asked, 'Will you come and see the show tonight?' and I said, 'Yes of course,' not telling you that I had already seen the show eight times. I said to myself, 'This time you're not going to cry. You've cried enough for this show.' The show started and the minute you came on the stage I started to weep because, by then, I knew that you were going to be my wife. I knew that you had passed through a terrible experience. I knew that you were not at your best but you were so beautiful on that stage – tall and slender and you gave an excellent performance. Although *Fiddler* is a show that always made me cry, this time I cried for a different reason.

When the show ended I came backstage to pick you up and we went to have dinner at a restaurant run by Harveys, the world-name sherry company which had their head-quarters in Bristol. The following day after lunch, when you went off to the theatre, I said, 'If you don't mind, Thelma, I'll go off and look around. I'll go into Bristol with you. You go off to the theatre and I'll walk around so I get the feel of this town.' Somehow or other I wound up under the famous suspension bridge which goes over a deep canyon near Bristol. All of a sudden I knew I wanted to see Thelma on the stage again. How do I get there? It's clear that where I am right now there's no main road, there's no tramline, there's no bus line. I don't know how I can get to the theatre but I think if I climb up the side of this canyon and get onto the bridge, surely someone there will be able to tell me how to get to the theatre, which is right in the centre of Bristol.

I enjoy telling about this because God knows, I certainly couldn't do it today. I was then fifty-six years old. I climbed up the canyon. I wanted to see Thelma and I wanted to get there in a hurry so I climbed the canyon which goes up to a height of about eight hundred feet. I got to the top and made my way to the bridge and yes, sure enough, there was a bus there which would take me right into the centre of the town. I got to the theatre in time for the end of the intermission and I saw the whole second act. This time, I said to myself, for sure you won't weep. Really you've wept enough. You've seen Thelma, she's lovely, she looks beauti-ful on the stage and you don't have to weep any more. But the minute you came on I started to weep and I wept all through that second act and I wept for the tragedies of the Jews, for my mother and my father and for the glory of the future that we were going to have together.

At the end of the show I came backstage, 'Let's go and have some dinner. Where's the best restaurant?' You lead me to this place which was called Le Gourmet and we sat down and I looked at the wine list as though I knew what I was looking at and ordered a bottle of very expensive wine. I figured if it's more expensive it's probably better, which isn't necessarily true but at the time I didn't know that. I ordered a bottle of white wine because you were having fish. You had ordered some Dover sole. I looked at the price of Dover sole and it was also eight pounds, the bottle of wine was eight pounds and I started to calculate what this dinner was going to cost me and I said, 'Boy, I really can't afford this, but never mind, it's just the one night.'

Then we started to open our hearts to each other. I said, as gently as I could, that I thought it was time that you stopped living in the grave with Jay and came back to the land of the living. That started you weeping and you wept all over your Dover sole and I sat there looking at the tears falling onto this expensive fish and I thought, 'Boy this is an expensive psychotherapy session. She's spoiling the sole. She won't enjoy the wine!' Aloud I said, 'Thelma, you're a wonderful woman and a lot of people love you. You've lost Jay but you don't have to spend all your time with him. You can live with us here in your own home and garden, and, whenever you need to, go off and spend a day with Jay.' That made you weep all the more but it seemed to do the trick, you came out of it, pulled yourself together and then the conversation went on in the normal way with a certain amount of laughter.

THELMA
When you talked of Jay, begging me to leave him in the grave and come back to the land of the living, you touched the tenderest corner of my soul. You have a great talent for helping people with emotional or physical problems. You don't shy away, as I do (though I have learned from you and

am now more open and daring), you shoot darts at the heart
of the problem and by airing it you start the healing process.
That is what you did to me.

PETER
You finished the Dover sole which pleased me immensely. I
figured after all it was just some salty tears – that couldn't
hurt. Was it clear to you at this point that I was courting you,
that I was offering marriage?

THELMA
The fact that you'd come all the way from Montreal in such a
hurry gave me a clue that maybe you were serious ... but
marriage? I don't know.

PETER
Then I took you home. I stayed with you in your cottage and
we stood there in the kitchen and there was a tension
between us. I'm standing close to you and looking into your
changeable blue eyes. It seems to me, those eyes are blue
when you want them to be and when you're busy with
something else they change colour. It was clear that I wanted
to embrace you and you whispered to me that deathless line,
'Will you kiss me just once and nothing more?' I have had
more encouraging invitations but I took into account that
you were a woman with a problem at this moment. You were
not quite through with your widow's weeds, so I kissed you
very delicately, very gently. It wasn't a sexy kiss.

THELMA
It was.

PETER
I didn't think it was. Just once and I made no more
movements towards you and we went to bed, you to your
room with eight doggies and I to mine, alone.

THELMA

The following day I took you to the station and you said, 'I think you're going to miss me!' And when you'd gone I *did* begin to miss you. I found myself thinking about you all the time and very excited by that thought.

PETER

He's handsome, he's rich.

THELMA

Yes! You took me out beautifully and you were dressed beautifully and you behaved beautifully – senior lecturer at the university, an eminent director in Israel. More than that – for the first time since Jay died you woke up my heart. I wanted you more and more as each day passed and I thought, I can't let this man go back to Israel and not see him again. I had helped to find you a hotel in London so I knew where you were staying. You left Bath on the Wednesday morning, and three days later, on the Saturday, I phoned you and said, 'You're right. I do miss you!'

I remember your beautiful voice – I love to hear your velvet voice on the phone, 'Ah,' you said, 'that's more like it. That's different. If that's the case I'm going to get back to you as soon as possible.'

PETER

Back in London, I went out and bought theatre tickets for every night of my stay. The Saturday night I was going to see John Gielgud and Ralph Richardson in *Home*. Wednesday, Thursday, Friday I waited for a call from you and it didn't come. It didn't come until Saturday morning. When you said, 'You were right. I miss you,' I said, 'I'll be there tonight. I've got some theatre tickets, but I'll get to you just as soon as I can. You do your show and then come and pick me up at the station.'

Before I decided to go by train I went downstairs and

talked to the concierge and asked, 'What is the fastest way I could get to Bath? Is there a plane?' When he said no, I asked him, 'Do you think I could rent a small private plane to take me there?' 'It's not likely, it would only take half an hour but I don't know how, I've never had a request like this,' he replied.

What about if I rented a car? If I rented a limousine with a chauffeur, could he get me to Bath in a reasonable amount of time? I examined all the possibilities and in the end I decided to go by train and the train was scheduled to leave at ten o'clock in the evening.

THELMA
How could you have paid for a private plane if you were worried about £8 for the Dover sole?

PETER
Don't spoil my story! I saw the first act of *Home* and remembered nothing about it, nothing, because I was looking at my watch and at the intermission I decided to go to the railway station. The train I got was what we call in America a 'milk train'. It stopped everywhere. It dragged on, and I didn't arrive in Bath until about two o'clock in the morning but you were there to meet me. You were really glad to see me and I was oh, in *ha-rakia ha-shviyi*, Hebrew for 'seventh heaven'. You drove me back to the house and we didn't waste much time talking, we made love for the first time. At a certain point I said to myself, 'This is going to be fine.'

THELMA
You arrived after three in the morning and when you got off that train, you came and sat in my car and kissed me … fireworks started to go off. I had wanted you so much. We got back to the cottage and frankly I was ready to rush straight up to the bedroom.

PETER
And I said I was hungry!

THELMA
You said, 'Have you got anything to eat, I'm hungry.'
Poor man, you'd been on this long train journey where
there had been no food and you were hungry for food
and I was hungry for something else. I couldn't wait to
get to bed with you. We went into the kitchen and had –
what did I give you? It couldn't have been much, because
it was my last night in Bath and I'd packed up all the
food.

Next morning you were booked to fly to Israel and I was
off to Nottingham. I said that I would drive you to the
airport and poor you, poor Peter, because there was my
luggage and the eight dogs in the back of the car including
six two-week-old puppies. I had to keep my eye on them and
make sure they weren't going to crash to the floor and you
were trying to talk romance and about our future. You said
that the next time that you had a break from the university
we could meet in Rhodes or Cyprus – in some lovely place
on neutral ground. Maybe we could meet in December.
Distractedly I was saying, 'Er, well, yes. Yes. Maybe.' The
dogs and I took you to the airport and I really was in a whirl
because I was attracted to you but convinced there couldn't
be a second Jay and frightened that my hunger might be
clouding my judgement. We waved you off, back to Israel.

PETER
I had come to two conclusions on the basis of our first
explosion of love. One, it was obvious that you were not a
smoker and that made me feel very ashamed that I was. I
promised myself that the minute you would come to me, if
you were going to come to me, I would stop smoking. The
other decision is more complex and is rather interesting. I
decided to stop dating any other ladies. I had determined

that because I wanted you so much and because I wanted you to accept me as a lover and then as a husband that I was going to go through a period of sexual abstinence in order to purify myself. I had not discussed this with you, this was something that I promised to myself.

THELMA
When you got on that plane and flew back to Israel my next stop was Nottingham to stay again in the flat of Jon Whatson, who had been so kind to me the year before just after Jay died and I had been in *King Lear*. The day after I arrived there was a telegram from you. The telegram read, 'For a thousand summers I would wait for you', quoting the lovely song from *A Man and a Woman*. Then the letters started to arrive, first of all every few days and then every day. I fell in love with you by correspondence. I got to know the real you through the letters. You wrote me wonderful letters in which you exposed all your deepest feelings and it gave me the opportunity to write everything I was thinking and feeling in my letters to you – a most glorious experience. I catch my breath when I think of some of the letters I wrote to you which were full of doubts. I might have lost you. But I wasn't sure. I was far from sure. I was still coming round back to life – you brought me back to life.

PETER
Then I started telephoning and the telephone calls became more and more frequent and lasted longer and longer.

THELMA
It was because of you that I decided to leave the show. The tour was for a year but I took up my option to leave after six months because I felt that here was something far more important. I decided to travel to Israel as quickly as possible to see if you were as wonderful in the flesh as in your letters. My problem was that I didn't want to tell anybody. Having

once broken off an engagement I did not want it to be said,
'She always gets cold feet at the last minute.'

But I phoned my parents. They had moved to Ashkelon in
Israel in 1967 and always met me at the airport on my trips
there. I told them on the phone that I was coming to
Israel ... 'but I don't want you to meet me. Do you
remember Peter Frye who came down to visit you?' You
went to visit them when you returned from England. 'Yes,'
they said, 'a very nice man.' 'He's going to meet me and we
want to be with each other for a while,' I told them, 'to get to
know each other better because we think that there might be
a future for us together. I'll phone you when I get to Israel.'
Mother said she even slept with her fingers crossed from
then onwards.

PETER

And you came in October. I had bought myself some new
clothes – a yellow outfit. Yellow linen trousers, because you
came in the early fall which is still very hot in Israel, and a
yellow shirt. I had said that the day you arrived I would stop
smoking and the day arrived. I looked around my apartment
and there were packs of cigarettes all over the place. I always
kept a reserve so there must have been oh, twenty-five packs
of cigarettes in various drawers. There was a tin of pipe
tobacco because I used to smoke a pipe. I had a collection of
some thirty pipes – very lovely pipes, very interesting original
ones. I had boxes of cigars because what I enjoyed most was
smoking a good cigar.

I decided I would leave the packs of cigarettes and the
pipe tobacco and the cigars in the apartment. I wouldn't
throw them into a wastepaper basket, I would leave them
there as a constant temptation but I was not going to give in.
I was not going to smoke any more once you had arrived. I
went to the airport feeling terribly virtuous and rather
stylish in my yellow outfit. I looked at the board to see when
your plane was scheduled to arrive and there was a two-hour

delay. So what did I do? Without thinking I went to the cigar store and bought myself a big long cigar, very expensive, started to smoke the cigar and walked up and down in the corridors of the airport, figuring out, 'How do I waste two hours until she comes?'

Suddenly I caught myself with the cigar in my hand. I said, 'What are you doing, you idiot. You stopped smoking this morning!' I threw away the better part of this very expensive cigar and filled myself with coffee and mints to take away the smell. It was getting close to the time of the scheduled arrival of the plane and I went into the baggage-collection area. I picked up a couple of trolleys. I had no idea how much luggage you would bring. I had arranged, through influence, to meet you before you went through customs. You appeared. You were still picking up your luggage and you wore a very cute hat that you had bought. It was a sort of a playboy bunny hat. White fur with a big pom pom on top. 'Of course,' I said to myself, 'of course, that's the girl for me...'

THELMA

You gave me a lovely smokeless kiss. We went back to your apartment and we made glorious love. And you have never smoked since that day.

That same afternoon you took me to see your daughter Jackie, by now seventeen. She had moved out of your apartment and into her mother's house to make way for me. A very tall and lovely girl, very like you, soft-spoken, sweet-natured – I liked her instantly. Batia, your ex-wife, was not in the house for this meeting. Then you took me back to the apartment, showed me that it was filled with thousands of books (this was before the days of television), you told me to make myself comfortable and settle down to a good read, that you had cancelled the day's rehearsals, but you had to rehearse that evening, apologised and went off to rehearsal, saying you would be rehearsing until quite late. After you left, a phone call came from Batia, 'I know you are on your own, why don't you come and spend the evening with us?' Which I did ... and enjoyed very much. Batia was an actress, very intelligent and knowledgeable about the theatre and spoke excellent English. I shall always be grateful to her. I had rushed over to Israel to get to know you better with a view to our sharing the rest of our lives together and the first evening I spent with your charming ex-wife!

It was bliss, both of us in paradise and terribly excited. After two weeks you started to talk about marriage, and I said, 'You haven't proposed to me.'

'Do you want a formal proposal?' you asked me.

'I certainly do!'

'Will you marry me?'

'Yes!' The following day we went down to Ashkelon. When we got there Mother and Dad were in the sitting room and you got down on one knee in front of Daddy and said, 'I've come to ask you for your daughter's hand in marriage.' You fifty-six and me forty-five! What an explosion of joy and excitement ... this was what my parents had hoped and dreamed and prayed for for forty-five years. Geoffrey and his wife Devorah were there as well. We were all over the moon.

We chose 23rd December for our wedding – just two months after my arrival. During those two months we lived together in your flat on Shalom Aleichem street. My mother was a little shocked because she was still very Victorian but Mom and Dad both fell for you the moment they met you. You were everything they had been dreaming of: Jewish, handsome, talented, amusing, artistic, famous in Israel, a theatre man which meant we would have so much in common, a university senior lecturer, and a great cook. We kept it from them that you were not exactly rich.

The two months of living together gave us a chance to get

to know each other because, despite our daily letters and
our phone calls, we'd had very few meetings and we had
spent very little time with each other. My parents had waited
so long for the great day they wanted it to be a 'real
wedding'. You and I, because of our advanced years, didn't
want any fuss or one of those huge Israeli weddings with five
hundred guests. In the end we were all content – just forty
people invited but all the panoply and trimmings of a 'real
wedding'. We were fortunate that a couple whom we both
knew and liked, Jaapi and Molly Bar David, invited us to
have the wedding in their house in Savyon, a wealthy suburb
of Tel Aviv. I was very moved when one day your ex-wife Batia
telephoned telling me that she had your mother's wedding
ring and would I like it. Your mother had given it to her. I
accepted gratefully and have never taken it off since we were
wed.

PETER
The first thing we did was to go along and get a marriage
licence. We repaired to the building which was inhabited
by the Chief Rabbinate of Tel Aviv. We were ushered in
to see a man who was sitting there in that peculiar *capote*
– capote is the Russian name for a Lord Chesterfield coat
which goes to the knees or below. Double breasted. He
was wearing a Lord Chesterfield *capote* and a big black
yarmelke – and he had a good-sized wart on the right side
of his face, right beside the nostril. If we hadn't seen that
wart at first we certainly would have noticed it because he
kept fingering it all the time – there was no way of
avoiding that wart. There it was. He kept pointing to it,
we kept staring at it.

All of this was going on while he explained the rules. The
rules were that I had to state what the 'bride-price' was.

'What do you want to pay for her?' he said.

'What's the usual?' I said.

He says, 'It varies with individuals.'

'Fifty pounds?'

He laughed and fingered the wart.

'That's silly, she's worth much more than that to you.'

I said. 'A hundred pounds?'

'No, no the very minimum, the very least that you should put down is five hundred.'

'I don't want to put down five hundred pounds,' I remonstrated. 'No, fifty pounds, that's what I'm willing to give!'

THELMA

You always got your brides at a cut price, didn't you? Remember your wedding to Batia when you refused to give the Justice of the Peace what he asked for? Only later did we find out that if ever we got divorced fifty pounds would be all that I would be entitled to. Happily, we've never divorced. Here we are, still in legal harness twenty years later – good and married. Otherwise I'd really be in the soup. My parents asked me to spend the night before the great day with them in Ashkelon, 'It isn't very proper that you get up from the bed of your future bridegroom to go to your wedding.' I had to refuse.

Rabbi Yedidya Frankel, later Chief Rabbi of Tel Aviv, agreed to marry us. He said, 'I will bring along my own cantor, my own *chasan*.'

'What about meeting you beforehand?' we asked.

'No that's not necessary, I'll be there and I'll bring the *chuppah*, the wedding canopy.'

23rd December. A beautifully sunny, warm day. You took me to a *mikva*, the ritual bath, in old Tel Aviv. A lady in a woolly hat and snakeskin high-heeled shoes stood at the side of the pool and told me: 'Immerse yourself completely three times,' which I did. 'Now say this blessing after me', which I did. A curious outdated custom but it was rather pleasant. I had a glass of lemon tea outside in the tiny courtyard in the warm sun, then out into the street with my hair flying in all directions. To the hairdresser. Collected my Finy Leitersdorf wedding-dress (white Bethlehem lace and a magenta sash because I hadn't the courage to wear pure white), which wasn't quite ready. Finy and her girls finished making it on my body and improvised a head-dress – and off we went to our wedding.

Six-thirty at the Bar-Davids. It was the appointed hour for the ceremony but there were no guests, no rabbi, just my parents, our hosts, Mona, who had come specially from England, and the caterer. Waiters were wandering round with drinks and cocktail snacks looking for customers. At six-thirty-five the guests started to arrive and I went up to the mezzanine where I would not be seen by the incoming guests. It soon turned into a cocktail party. Mona brought me up the occasional brandy, other friends came up to say hello and, unlike the solemnity that precedes a ceremony in England, the air was filled with gaiety, greatly enhanced by my two tall, handsome teenage Jerusalemite nephews, Shimshon and Meir. Meir was dressed in a long, embroidered Arab cloak, a djellaba, festooned with beads around his neck – Israeli-hippie style.

At seven I peeked over the railing of the mezzanine and there, arriving, were two short men with big black hats and huge beards – evidently Rabbi Frankel and his *chasan* had arrived. Immediately there was a maelstrom of action. You, accompanied by the two black hats, Daddy and Geoffrey disappeared into another room to sign the Ketubah, the marriage contract, signed before the ceremony and I had no part in the negotiation. At last. The ceremony. All was confusion. Rabbi Frankel had forgotten to bring the *chuppah*. Jaapi, our host, pulled out a huge *tallit*, a prayer shawl, yellowed with age and bordered with the requisite broad black bands and fringes. It was large enough for two *chuppahs* and was held up in front by Shimshon and Meir – Shimshon is six foot two and Meir is six foot four. In the rear were Geoffrey and our mutual friend Rabbi Moshe Davis –

it made a very impressive canopy. In the confusion instead of being on a platform as planned, the improvised *chuppah* was right in among the dining tables. Too late to change it, the *chasan* had started to sing and I was beckoned forward. But nobody had told us whether I went in on Daddy's arm to be given away as in an English ceremony, or Mother was to take me in and lead me round the bridegroom seven times, as we did in *Fiddler on the Roof*. There wouldn't have been room for that even if we'd wanted to – I just found myself standing totally bemused next to you.

The guests stood around, each holding a candle, and the rabbi, eyes flashing and beard aquiver, launched into a spontaneous, unscheduled dissertation. Everybody roared with laughter but I didn't understand a word. The entire proceedings were in Hebrew and I said nothing and understood nothing. Mother and I stole a glance and a private giggle – we'd never seen a wedding like *this*. I drank the wine and you put the ring on my finger. The poor *tallit*-holders were exhausted and from time to time the canopy collapsed onto our heads and around our ears ... but Rabbi Frankel was magnificent, sweeping through with style and panache. I'd forgotten to take the glass for you to smash underfoot at the end of the ceremony. Once again our hosts to the rescue, this time with a cocktail glass which was firmly crushed underfoot and we were married. I hadn't said anything, I hadn't understood anything, I hadn't signed anything but we were married. Rabbi Frankel stayed for the party afterwards. He was a ball of Chassidic fire, telling at one point a story of how he had performed a wedding in the Tel Aviv zoo for one of the keepers when the only guests were the animals. 'I felt it was like the wedding of Adam and Eve must have been in the Garden of Eden.'

The rest of the evening had an air of intimacy and informality. Our dinner was delicious, everybody made a speech and somewhere along the way we found ourselves singing the duet from *Fiddler* – 'Golde, do you love me?' At

that point we knew we were married. Even our wedding
night was unconventional – my parents and Mona were in
adjoining rooms in the hotel and we all ate smoked salmon
and drank champagne, laughing and talking most of the
night...

Postscript

THELMA

As in all good love stories, we lived happily every after ...
truly. We continued to be active, but now shored up by the
ideal partner-friend-beloved. Peter had his stroke in 1987, a
heart bypass in 1989. He came to me in Bath in July 1970,
and died in 1991, so we had nearly twenty-one years
together. Here is an extract from the letter I wrote to our
friends after he died:

June 1991

Dear Friends,

I suppose this is the saddest letter I've ever written or
ever will write. It's purpose is two-fold. First to tell all of
you who do not already know that my dearest, most
beloved, wonderful Peter died on 2nd June. And to all of
you who have showered me with an outpouring of
sympathy, love and concern, this is a thank you. For the
past two weeks I have been held together only by the
concern and kindness of our friends. As if it needed proof,
it shows the quality of my Peter that he drew unto him such
rare and outstanding friends.

Peter did not go out much this winter – the cold
weather did not agree with him. The happiest day was
23rd December our twentieth wedding anniversary. Mona
offered to make a party for us. It had been a standing
joke between Peter and me that because at our wedding
I hadn't understood a word, hadn't said anything, hadn't
signed anything, we were not really married and he always

responded, 'Any time I'll marry you again, any place –
temple, church, mosque...' So when the twentieth anniversary party was being planned I said, 'This is it – I want to
get married again.' We contacted our cousin, Gerry Wise,
who is active at the West London Reform synagogue, and
said, 'You don't need a qualified rabbi to perform a
wedding, would *you* marry us?' There were sixteen of us in
our living room. What we had said to Gerry was light-
hearted, but Gerry had taken his role as rabbi very
seriously. He brought along prayer-books and skullcaps
and a *chuppah* – a prayer shawl but unlike at our wedding,
this one was held up by four bamboo poles. Even the
required marriage certificate on which instead of my
promising to be a good wife it said that after twenty years
I promise to *continue* to be a good wife. Four friends held
a bamboo pole each and Peter and I sat underneath –
Peter was too disabled to stand. Gerry performed the
genuine marriage ceremony ... translating into English,
asking me to make my pledges as I had not done twenty
years ago, Peter put the ring on my finger once more, and
what started as a joke became profoundly moving and
meaningful for us all – a couple of elderly folk after
twenty years of marriage, renewing our vows in front of
dear friends. It was to be our last anniversary.

The spring brought a lift to Peter's spirits and when our
close friends and travelling companions, Ted and Pat
Apstein, suggested we join them for a holiday in Belgium
in July, Peter became enthusiastic, and suggested that
after Belgium we should all go to Scotland, which he
loved. We planned to spend October in Israel. Peter
thought it would be wise to do a short trip in England to
test if he was well enough to undertake such an active
itinerary, so on 15th May we went to a lovely area of the
south of England – Dorset and Hampshire. We were both
delighted that not only was he well enough, but he loved
every minute. We stayed in a delightful hotel deep in the

countryside near Wimborne Minster, a hotel which had a special room adapted for disabled people. On the way down we visited Romsey Abbey and Peter was full of his typical enthusiasm, calling it one of the most magnificent churches of its kind he had ever seen.

On the top of the page in my diary for Thursday, 16th May I wrote: 'What a glorious, wonderful day we had...' We saw Wimborne Minster, Bournemouth, a lovely south coast resort, Poole, with its enormous harbour beside which we had lunch in a pub, the picture postcard village of Cerne Abbas in Dorset – touring around looking, chatting, laughing in the way we always loved. Still consciously breathless at the miracle that we should still enjoy each other's company so much after twenty years of marriage.

The following day we came home, via the New Forest and Jane Austen's village of Chawton. Peter was so encouraged by the fact that for three days he had toured in the car from eleven in the morning until six at night, we immediately sat down with the maps and guidebooks to plan our holiday in Belgium. On Tuesday, 21st May the weather was hot and glorious – very unusual in London this year – and we went to the Royal Horticultural Society gardens in Wisley, a visit I have always wanted to make but this is the first time either of us had been there. Beautiful gardens, ablaze with azaleas, rhododendrons and camellias and we had lunch in the restaurant sitting on the terrace in the hot sunshine.

On Thursday, 23rd May Peter had an operation on his toe. As usual he flirted with the nurses and made everybody laugh during the operation (under local anaesthetic, of course). The whole operation was over in about four minutes. 'Hell,' said Peter to the surgeon, 'that's an easy way to earn a living,' at which one of the nurses said, 'We've been dying to say that to him for years but we've never had the courage.'

On Tuesday, 28th May, a boy in his twenties, David
Lyndon, came to Peter for help with his doctorate – he is
writing a thesis and wanted Peter to tell him of the place
and importance of improvisation. Of course, Peter told
not only of its importance in the theatre, but in the history
of civilisation and in everyday life. He talked brilliantly,
and David was very grateful. That evening we went to see
the surgeon to check up on his toe. Peter walked into the
hospital, and then walked into the doctor's surgery without the help of the wheelchair. He was really amazed and
said several times afterwards, 'I didn't know I could walk
as well as that, maybe I am getting stronger.'

In April both Peter and I had acted in a video made by a
charity called Holiday Care Service. It was made to
illustrate how they help people who have problems having
a holiday – wheelchair disabled, blind, deaf, elderly, single
parents. On Wednesday, 29th May, Peter was invited to do
another job for Holiday Care Service. A paid job. It was a
training day for tour operators, demonstrating all the
things that must be checked for the disabled when
booking hotels. Peter was there to demonstrate the difficulties of staying in a hotel for those tied to a wheelchair.
We were at a hotel called the Stirling right in the middle
of Gatwick airport.

The lady in charge was splendid. She started off in the
car park: 'All right,' she said, 'we've arrived, this is the only
car park available, how on earth do we get into the hotel
through barriers, up and down pavements. And we arrive
in the hotel what do we see? Just an escalator going up
saying "Reception". No signs pointing to the lifts. And
what if we want a toilet? Hidden away with no indication
at all...' We find the toilets. 'And once we do find them,
the normal toilets are facing us and have easy access, and
the disabled toilet is around two corners with an impossible door and far too small to get into...' And so it went
on. We had a coffee break. I said to Peter in Hebrew, 'Are

you finding it boring?' 'Not at all,' he said, 'and I think what they are doing is very important.'

After the break we went up to what is supposed to be the disabled bedroom. Totally unsuitable and inadequate ... Peter said he wanted to show them what it was like to sit on the bed – when he tried to get up his legs wouldn't hold him. Also his speech had become slightly slurred. Nevertheless, he finished his job and we drove home. On the journey he said, 'Maybe I've had another little stroke,' and I agreed that the thought had occurred to me also. The doctor came around at once and confirmed that she thought he had had a small stroke, but she hoped it was the sort that cured itself in a matter of days. Peter refused to go into hospital. He said he had been in so often in the last few years and he didn't want to go again.

Peter's wonderful physiotherapist, Vicky Roberts, came, as always on a Wednesday, in the early evening and our young and attractive doctor, Gill Provost, came again at the same time, and Peter flirted with them both. As the evening progressed, he became more and more distressed. I got a nurse in to help me, but then he had trouble breathing and I contacted his cardiologist who arranged to send an ambulance and get him into hospital. The ambulance came at 11.30 at night. Peter was in heart failure and having serious trouble breathing. He became unconscious as they carried him down the stairs and he never regained consciousness. He died at 10.20 on the morning of 2nd June, less than four days later, of a massive stroke.

Forty minutes before he died, Peter's sister Sylvia and her husband Stip arrived at the hospital from Montreal. The three of us were quietly talking and a lovely Irish nurse called Kate was tending to Peter. At 10.20 Kate beckoned me over urgently. I took Peter's hand and called to him, 'I love you so much, my darling.' Then an extraordinary thing happened. He made a big movement from the waist until his face was looking into mine, for an instant his eyes opened, he gave a big sigh, and died. Stip and Sylvia were watching Peter transfixed. I gave a great howl of grief and despair and it was Kate who put her arms around me and hugged me. It was so terrible – and so beautiful...

Peter wanted no funeral but he had often said that what he would really like after he died would be for his friends to have a party – a kind of Irish wake – with good food and drink, at which he would be remembered kindly. Whenever he said that, I would reply, 'Peter, how could I ... how could I have a party just after you died?' But I did it. Four days after his death, on Thursday evening, the night before Sylvia and Stip returned to Canada, twenty-six of our nearest and dearest came to our home, including Jeremy Lewis who had helped me through this agony once before after the death of his father, dearest Jay. Jen Gosney, my very old and good friend who is a caterer, brought the most marvellous food, there was sparkling wine. And exactly in the nature of Peter's parties, where everybody gets a chance to talk and there is one general conversation on an interesting topic rather than many noisy meaningless conversations – exactly like that we had an incredible evening. Everybody spoke eloquently and brilliantly – there was so much laughter, so much love, concern, appreciation, insight ... Peter was so much with us. Our friends Anna Tzelniker and her husband Phil Bernstein, who have just celebrated their Golden Wedding and his eightieth birthday, came all the way on the tube from the East End, Phil carrying his violin case. Anna is a fine Yiddish actress and Peter had great rapport with her, and loved to talk Yiddish with her. She ended the evening, as I had asked her to, by singing Yiddish songs with Phil accompanying her on the violin. It was a rare warm fine evening. After the songs, people had more to eat and drink, sat on the balcony, talked, felt uplifted. Not one person who was there has failed to phone me since to tell me it was the most wonderful evening which they will remember always.

I want you to know that each phone call, each letter has been of terrific help to me – it is less than two weeks since Peter died – to my surprise I am still here, and that is thanks to all of you. I'd like to end with the words written to me from New York by Charlie Nusser, Peter's commanding officer when he fought in Spain in 1937: 'You know for certain, Thelma, that you were with a man who tried to make this planet a little better place for all. If there were more Peter Fryes in this world, it would be a world with far less misery and much more happiness.'

Peter had the greatest capacity I have ever seen for loving and reaching out to and understanding and caring for people. He loved you all. I love you too.

Epilogue

Peter often said, 'I hope I live to see our book completed.' Alas, he didn't. I shunned the task of completing it alone. As with everything in our marriage, it had been such a close joint venture. Four months after he died I got increasingly stronger visions of the hundreds of pages we had worked on yellowing with age and the great stories he had told me of his life crumbling away into nothingness. Once I found the courage to start I wanted the task to continue for ever – I had to listen to the recordings we had made and once again he was chatting to me, even making me laugh. Once again we were working together and my efforts would help to give him the touch of immortality he yearned for. I apologise to his spirit, which is surely watching over me, for every word I have cut that he would have left in.

My career had been in doldrums since marrying Peter. You have to be around, to follow through, and being in Israel for eleven years took me out of the stream of working actors. There were jobs, and I enjoyed them, but I didn't have a career and I didn't mind. Peter had become my whole life. From ten days after he died, my career returned. Just when I most needed it. Could Peter have been organising it? I like to call him my agent in the sky.

Jay died on 4th June, Peter died on 2nd June. When Jay died, the following week I went to stay with Norman and Erle Krasna in Vevey, Switzerland. When Peter died, the following week I went to stay with Samy and Josée Bak in Vevey, Switzerland. The first job I got after Jay died started rehearsing at the beginning of August and opened at the

Edinburgh Festival ... yes, the first job I got after Peter died started rehearsing at the beginning of August and opened at the Edinburgh Festival.

For the past four weeks I have been appearing in a concert performance of a musical by Moss Hart and Cole Porter called *Jubilee* at the Barbican – a delightful show and a big hit. *Jubilee* was written and produced on Broadway in 1935, it is a funny satire on the British royal family. I played the Queen and Willie Rushton played the King. Moss Hart's widow, Kitty Carlisle, came over specially from the US to see it, and told me afterwards of her great enjoyment, saying she hadn't seen it since its first production fifty-seven years ago, as it was never revived.

Yesterday I finished the final edit of this book, *our* book, after three and a half years' work. The word processor sits on Peter's desk and I decided to tidy some papers. Underneath, in a box, were three programmes which have been sitting there for at least eight years. I'd never seen them before. When I saw they were from the 1945 season Peter did at the St Louis Municipal Opera, I was curious to read them. I must add that *all* Peter's papers connected with his professional career – programmes, production-scripts, photos, everything – have shipped to Israel and form the Peter Frye Archive in the Tel Aviv Theatre Archives. Only these programmes were overlooked.

When I got into bed at 1.15 this morning I opened the first programme. The title page read, '*Jubilee* by Moss Hart and Cole Porter. Staged by Peter Frye.' It might have been the only production between the original in 1935 and the one in which I appeared last week. I had nobody to tell. Who can you phone at 1.15 in the morning to tell of such a coincidence. I would so like to believe that it was Peter's way of telling me he knew I had completed this enormous job ... and he was pleased with me.

23rd December 1970 to 2nd June 1991 were the best years of our lives – for both of us. To the end of his life Peter evinced terrific intellectual curiosity. He was a sucker for mail-order shopping and quite a bit of my time was taken sending off for books on science, geography, anything that would enlarge his knowledge and keep his brain alert. His great appetite for life made every day an adventure. If we got lost in the car he wasn't upset, he was delighted saying we were seeing new places we would never otherwise have seen. He had *chutzpah*, cheek. In a lift, in the departure lounge of an airport, in a hospital waiting-room, wherever we were, within minutes Peter started everybody talking and laughing. Wherever he was, light shone more brightly. One morning during the trip to Dorset two weeks before he died, I went into a shop, leaving him sitting outside in the car. A lady was selling flags and collecting money for charity. Peter called her over and asked what was the charity. She told him it was Christian Aid. He asked what they did, and she said they tried to help people in need all over the world. 'Good,' said Peter. 'My wife has all the money, but when she comes back I'll ask her to put something into your box but you must understand that this is *Jewish* aid!' She laughed delightedly and for an instant Peter lit up her morning.

When we married he promised to surprise me every day – and he did. Creating a new dish, a gift hidden under the pillow, plans for a new project. He surprised me with his insights, his acute memory, the passion he brought to everything he did – not just wild energy but an intelligent, focused concentration. He could see around and under things. He said he would take me for a honeymoon every month – we would go off to a kibbutz guesthouse overnight or for a drive through the hills of Judea. He relished responsibility. He was wise and he was funny.

Many people who wrote to me described him as 'larger than life' and he was. When he walked into a room, the entire room was filled with his personality. His voice was loud, his body was big, his enthusiasms and appetites great. He shared in everything – the running of the house and garden, the planning of trips, designing and choosing my clothes. I didn't face any decision alone. And he loved to make love. Disabled and ill as he was, aged seventy-seven we still cavorted at least a couple of times a week – the last time just three days before his last conscious day on this earth.

He supported me, folded me around and enveloped me with his love, talked about it, 'Have I told you today how much I love you?' Three weeks before he died, during a sleepless night he had scribbled a note to me, now I have it framed and hanging beside my bed. It says, 'For Thelma. I just want you to know that every night before I go to sleep I say to myself, "I hope she knows how much I love her and cherish her, my beautiful, talented, generous *bubaleh viebeleh* my angel ... *dein Mann, Pinye.*"'

Dead is dead. I look for him everywhere, but he isn't there – to discuss with, learn from, laugh with, consult, share, plan, admire and adore. I dread that a day may come when friends will get tired of my talking about him, quoting him, conjuring him up. Maybe he *will* exist for just a little while longer – for as long as I live, Peter lives.

Index